THE SEVEN
STAGES
OF
MONEY
MATURITY

THE SEVEN

STAGES

OF

MONEY

MATURITY

Understanding the Spirit and Value
of Money in Your Life

GEORGE KINDER

Delacorte Press

Published by
Delacorte Press
Random House, Inc.
1540 Broadway
New York, New York 10036

Library of Congress Cataloging in Publication Data
Kinder, George.
    The seven stages of money maturity : understanding the spirit and value of
money in your life / George Kinder
        p.   cm.
    ISBN 0-385-32404-9
    1. Finance, Public.   2. Money.   I. Title.
HG179.K554   1999
332.024—dc21   99-17085
                                                                          CIP

Charts on pages 143, 144, 183, 330, 331, 335, 337, 343, 346, 347, 348, 349 by Hadel Studio.

Manufactured in the United States of America
Published simultaneously in Canada

May 1999

10 9 8 7 6 5 4 3 2 1

AUTHOR'S NOTE

The three characters—Mahealani Sapolu, Derrick King, and Susanna Swartz—whose financial lives are followed in this book are composites built from various people I have worked with over the years. Likewise, the names and other personal details of clients and friends cited as examples in the text have been changed to protect their privacy.

To my father, Gordon T. Kinder, and my mother, Cary Stuckey Kinder, whose teachings continue to instruct me

And to the members of the Nazrudin Project

ACKNOWLEDGMENTS

The byline on the cover carries only my name, but a great many people had a hand in shaping this work. I wish to thank them all.

My many wonderful friends provided abundant insights and exceptional patience as I learned how much time and effort it takes to write a book.

My clients too have taught me a great many important lessons, not only about money but also about the intricacies of the human soul.

The community of students I work with in Massachusetts and Hawaii has been a source of conversations that have deepened my ideas time and again through the years. My thanks to every one of you. Joan Luzier and Jean McManus, in particular, showed exceptional dedication in transcribing the tapes that kept me connected to the spiritual side of money. Paul Murray, Albert Zeman, and Todd Thuro grasped the Seven Stages early on and shared many personal stories. Natalie Pace sharpened my thinking with penetrating questions as to the nature of suffering.

Jean Piuck gave me the push I needed to speak at a national conference—thanks, I needed that—where I met Dick Wagner, then chairman of the Institute of Certified Financial Planners. Of all the many CFPs I know, I owe the most to Dick, for immediately grasping the power of the Seven Stages, even in rudimentary form, and for endlessly encouraging and supporting me in the development of my ideas over the years. He helped too in cofounding the Nazrudin Project, a think tank of CFPs dedicated to the exploration of issues of heart and spirit around money. Gratitude to all the members of the Nazrudin Project.

Bob Veres and Tahira Hira gave me support and encouragement early on as well as a creative framing of money issues that helped me think and rethink my ideas.

Jeannie Pechin and the people of Hana showed me what it means to live Aloha. John Levy and Kenny Brown challenged and taught me most deeply about the nature of money by raising profound questions, by reflecting on culture, history, and spirit, and by sharing their own Aloha.

My brothers—Peter, Dan, and Tom Kinder—and my father, Gordon T. Kinder, provided stories, thoughts, memories, and loving support. My stepmother and favorite medieval scholar, Suzanne Wemple-Kinder, shared many marvelous ideas as we explored our mutual love for *The Divine Comedy.*

My staff—Lynne Reem, Jonathan Wolfarth, Sanda Ljubovic, Adam Strauss, Caitlin Warde, and Joanne Rogers—were all extraordinary in their dedication. They thought deeply and professionally about both technical and general issues in the book, and they read and discussed the manuscript thoughtfully. Whatever was necessary in the moment they did, whether typing, copying, researching, printing, collating, or running to the post office. Most of all I owe them for their patience and forbearance during the final year of writing.

Kathy Lubar didn't just read the whole manuscript through. She grasped the book at every level, showed me where to make it better, and stood by me down to the wire. Greatest gratitude to you.

Colleen Mohyde of The Doe Coover Agency was everything a literary agent should be, and more. Among other feats, she found Tom Spain of Delacorte, who convinced me he was the right editor for *The Seven Stages of Money Maturity* when he said this was the book he had been looking for all his life. Thanks for saying so.

Robert Aquinas McNally, poet and writer, brought to bear on this book his considerable professional skills. He helped turn my abundant and sometimes anarchic volumes of notes into something we both knew was a real book. *The Seven Stages of Money Maturity* would not have come into being without him, his Macintosh, and his love of sentence and story.

Someone I'm sure I've overlooked. I thank you all, the missing and the mentioned, for the blessing of your being and your many gifts. Aloha.

George Kinder
Cambridge, Massachusetts, and Hana, Hawaii
October 1998

CONTENTS

THE SEVEN
STAGES
OF
MONEY
MATURITY

chapter 1

MEETING MONEY MATURITY

Midway in our life's journey, I went astray
from the straight road and woke to find myself
alone in a dark wood.

Dante Alighieri

The mass of men lead lives of quiet desperation. What is called
resignation is confirmed desperation.

Henry David Thoreau

"I understand what you're saying," he said, "even though I hate admitting it to myself. "

The statement took me by surprise. I had known this man in a passing way for years, and I both admired and disliked him. My admiration came from his success as a financial planner, the same profession I practice. He was known far and wide for creating one of the largest, most multifaceted planning firms in America. But I disliked him because he stood publicly for a point of view I reject—that making money, lots of money, is an end in itself. So I was taken aback when he came up after my presentation on Money Maturity to a national meeting of financial planners and asked me if I wanted to have coffee. I could tell there was something on his mind.

He came right to the point. "I know how to make money," he said. "I've poured all my savings into the stock market for years. Now I've got more than enough to live on for the rest of my life. My problem isn't making more money."

"Then what is it?" I asked.

"The money's not enough," he answered. His tone shifted from confident to plaintive. "I have wealth, but something is missing. I don't know what it is. All I know is I'm not happy. That's why I wanted to talk to you. After hearing what you had to say, I think you may be able to tell me what to do next."

I may be a financial advisor by profession, but I often find myself working more like a priest in the confessional than a money manager. His was an admission I had heard many times before.

During the morning I had spoken on integrating money goals with personal objectives, a topic I have been presenting to my colleagues for years now. Financial professionals have discovered that if they don't understand what their clients are truly seeking, all their good advice goes for nought. In my presentation that afternoon, I had gone back to basics. Money, I explained, can be seen as the place where our internal selves engage the external world. If either side—internal or external, self or money—is slighted, the whole of life suffers.

Now, talking to my colleague over the coffee cups, I picked up on that theme in his life. "That distress you feel inside, that pain—it's there to wake you up," I said.

His face screwed up quizzically. "What do you mean?" he asked.

"It's a signal, an alarm. It's telling you, in no uncertain terms, that it's time to find out who you really are in relation to money."

"But what's that got to do with anything?" he snapped. His expression changed from quizzical to protective, as if I were getting altogether too close for comfort.

"Look at it this way. You could put all your financial statements from the past few years in front of me, and I still wouldn't know what I really need to understand in order to even begin to help you decide what to do next," I answered. "How can I work with you if I don't know who you are? Think about it. It's your own discomfort with yourself that is keeping you from seeing your way ahead."

His defensiveness gave way to curiosity.

"You've been thinking all along there's only one question about money—'How much?'" I continued. "But the truly important question is 'What does money have to do with who I am?' You think you're a success, but your feelings tell you otherwise. They're telling you 'When it comes to money, you're a mess.' Finding Money Maturity means resolving your inner conflicts around money. It really comes down to discovering a sense of ease around money. Without ease, where's the success?"

For a second or two, he was silent, thinking. Then he said, "Tell me. How do I find that ease?"

THE PROMISE OF MONEY MATURITY

My colleague's search for ease in his relationship to money—even his difficulty in understanding that ease and freedom were what he was really seeking—is hardly unusual. The same drive for a deep-seated sense of peace on the financial side of life occupies center stage in the concerns of client after client I've worked with. And it's not just an issue for the well heeled, like my successful financial-planning colleague. The desire to achieve ease and freedom around money is as true for those who come from impoverished backgrounds and the middle class as it is for those who inherit wealth or make it big in the business world. Experiencing ease around dollars and cents is what I call Money Maturity.

When clients come to me to handle their money, or when I talk to participants in my seminars, I hear the desire for Money Maturity implicit in every statement they make about what they want their relationship to money to be. No doubt you yourself have said similar things. For example:

- "I want to be wealthy in life, not necessarily in money, but I know the two are related."
- "I want to be able to do whatever I want to do without thinking about the money."
- "I don't want to always be afraid around money."
- "I want to be free."
- "I want to feel balance between life and money. Too often money wins and life loses."
- "I don't want to worry about money."
- "I want to get what I need without feeling guilty about it."
- "I want to work and contribute in ways that are meaningful to me without having to worry about how much money I'll get from it."
- "I want to feel I can be myself without money tripping me up."
- "I want to know money won't get in the way of my doing what needs to be done."
- "I want to be able to focus on finding value in what I do rather than finding money in what I do."
- "I want to feel that I don't have to give up who I am or violate my deepest values just to get money."

Each of these statements is a cry for freedom—a desire to build the life you want from the deepest part of yourself. Just like my financial-planning colleague, you are seeking what is missing inside. You want to discover who you are in relation to money and, on the basis of that knowledge, experience freedom in the financial part of your life. That's exactly what Money Maturity offers.

Most financial advisors and books about money approach finance as if it were simply a skill to learn, the same sort of thing as hitting a fastball or speaking French like a diplomat. Money Maturity does include skills, such as understanding investment options and using a budget effectively, but it goes much deeper—to the feelings, the heart, and, yes, the soul.

Money Maturity helps resolve the troubling emotional conflicts around money that never seem to go away. For many of us money represents anything but peace. If you answer yes to any of these of these questions, you know what I mean:

- Do you sabotage yourself around money—by, say, saving toward a goal only to fritter your money away in a shopping spree, charging less for your work than you need to make a living, or refusing to save for the future?
- Do you feel chained to a job that limits your ability to express yourself and hampers your freedom, just because you need the money?
- Are you so caught up in the rat race, and so fearful that somebody else will take your place if you stop for a breather, that you can't relax, not even for the weekend?
- Does the pursuit of money leave you so drained that at the end of the day you don't have the energy for what you truly love to do—play tennis, music, write, sculpt or paint, listen to J. S. Bach or Bob Marley, spend time with your spouse, partner, children, or family?
- Do you want to give more to your community yet also feel you can't because your financial situation blocks you?
- Are you always in debt, ever struggling just to make the next payment—and still spending too much, digging an even deeper pit of indebtedness?
- Do conversations about money with your spouse or partner have this way of erupting into fights?
- Does staying home with the kids day after day leave you feeling

powerless around money issues—resentful of and excluded from the marketplace, as if you don't have a voice?

- Are stock market losses devastating experiences? Or do you feel the agony of self-reproach when the market goes up and you're not in it?
- Do you feel stupid around money decisions, not knowing how to make them on your own or how to select a trustworthy advisor to help you?
- Would you just as soon avoid checkbooks, account statements, investment decisions, and insurance policies for the rest of your life?

If you find yourself saying yes to any of these questions, Money Maturity is the answer you've been seeking.

THE BENEFITS OF MONEY MATURITY

Money Maturity provides seven remarkable, insightful ways of understanding your own conflicts, dilemmas, difficulties, and pain around money and taking positive steps to resolve them. Money Maturity holds the promise of a new way of living financially, one that acknowledges the whole depth and breadth of human nature, not just the greed of Wall Street or the green eyeshades of Main Street. Most important, Money Maturity offers the ease and success that come from letting go of old, painful patterns around money and learning how to create your own life based on a deepened understanding of your power and purpose.

In the years I have been developing and teaching Money Maturity in my financial-planning practice and in seminars, I have seen one person after another transform his or her life. Not that the task was easy; often the road to understanding the source of emotional conflict was rocky. Still, the power of the transformation was undeniable, sometimes even miraculous. As my clients and students came to terms with lifelong messages about money—and let go of them—they discovered the clarity to take practical steps like building a budget, creating an investment plan, or redirecting their careers toward work they truly wanted. Once they had seen deeply into their emotional pattern concering money, they found themselves capable of creating a new kind of life, one that beamed with the very freedom and ease they were seeking.

⟦⟧

Cheryl and Bob wanted to live as writers, but they felt a conflict between what their families told them hard work was all about and the purportedly effete artistic life. The conflict was so intense that they couldn't do either well. If they dedicated themselves to writing, they felt guilty about betraying their families; if they dedicated themselves to making money, they felt guilty about betraying themselves. So Bob drove a taxi and Cheryl waitressed—tough, demanding jobs that paid relatively little and left them both too drained to do more than dabble at writing. In addition, they were terrified of the stock market, and had put all of their small inheritance and work savings into low-yielding certificates of deposit and money market accounts. I suggested that, if they really wanted to live as writers, they could do it—first by facing their guilt and fear, then by investing the majority of their assets in the stock market, cutting their employment to half time, and living very simply. That was ten years ago. Now, every time I bump into either of them, they thank me. Doing what they always wanted, they are earning as much from their writing as they used to from taxis and restaurants, and they feel satisfaction and fullness across the whole spectrum of their lives.

⟦⟧

Tanya came from one of the toughest neighborhoods on Chicago's South Side, where she learned to get away with everything and anything she could. A smart, ambitious woman, she had won a major scholarship to college and graduated with a business major. She was studying for her CPA exam and seemed poised on the edge of a brilliant career, but somehow her heart wasn't in it. Something was holding her back.

She had begun to doubt what she was doing. All along she had worked hard to prove something to herself and her family, but at this juncture of her life she was beginning to question the integrity of her life. Was it fair for her to make money when someone else couldn't? Was the system itself fair? The audit rules, the tax regulations, the whole legal network of governments and corporations—did they have a basis in integrity? Or did they simply serve to exacerbate the differences between rich and poor?

Taking the bus home after the first day of my money maturity seminar, right at the end of the section on integrity, she noticed that nobody was paying full fare and the driver wasn't making a fuss. At first she said to herself, "Cool, I'll get a cheap ride too." Then she thought about it for a moment. "If I pay less than what I should, what's that say about the kind of person I am?" She reached into her purse, found a grand total of 87 cents, counted out the 75 cent fare, and took her seat.

Next day, in the seminar, she crowed about the incident all day. In paying full fare she had discovered a personal quality of virtue around money she had never known before.

Later she told me that the choice she made on the bus, small though it might have appeared, was a turning point in her life. It changed her attitude toward herself and helped build the emotional base to pursue the career she was capable of.

"In a moment I realized that all my doubts concerned my own integrity and voice. I was feeling powerless," she said. "Suddenly it was clear to me. If I have integrity around money personally, then I have both the ease and strength inside myself to speak out on issues that are important to me, and I also have the confidence to pursue my own goals. I knew then I have everything I needed to build the career and life I want."

Carlos had a job he disliked but couldn't leave. Beset by severe diabetes, he knew that if he changed jobs, no health insurer would accept him. So he stayed where he was. Yet rather than give in to despair over a job he would have otherwise gladly left, he took charge of his work environment. He brought in flowers to mark birthdays and anniversaries for his coworkers, picked up doughnuts and muffins for coffee break, and arranged going-away parties for departing colleagues and moms-to-be taking maternity leave. Under his kind tutelage, born of insight and necessity, the corporate work group he was part of changed from hard-edged and competitive to a true community.

A financial-planning client, Dorothy, announced that after working through the seven stages, she could—for the first time in her life—walk through a mall and not spend a penny. "I've learned where my impulses come from. I recognize what they mean for me," she said. "I understand now that by avoiding spending for frivolous things I'm not depriving myself, only making a choice for what really matters to me—the freedom I'm saving for. You'd be amazed how free that makes me feel!"

When yet another client, Richard, originally came to me, he was filled with despair, stuck in a dead-end job with no hope of professional development. Gradually, as we worked together over a period of years, he moved toward meaningful work. Recently he said to me, "As long as I assumed the world was all darkness, particularly the world of money, I couldn't begin to learn how money works. Now I see how the deepest darkness comes from inside myself. In coming to terms with that darkness, I was finally able to start a new career. But what's most amazing to me is the feeling of ease and security that's come along with the job. I'd never known before what success meant."

THE ROAD WE WILL FOLLOW

Like these examples, people who have worked through the process of Money Maturity feel connected with each of the Seven Stages as if they existed within their bodies. They feel too as if they have access to the stages—perhaps one, perhaps two, perhaps all seven—needed to resolve a particular money issue. Instead of feeling bad around money, people who have mastered the Seven Stages feel happy. Instead of feeling shattered, afraid, or confused, they feel whole and at peace around money. In this process of understanding money, they have reframed what success means to them. It is no longer some far-distant promise but a palpable experience they can sense in their bodies and souls right now. For the first time they have both hope and confidence in their future, because they have begun to feel a new integrity in their relationship to money that includes the darkest aspects of themselves as well as their deepest aspirations and most profound ideals.

As we move through this book, we will work through each of the Seven Stages of Money Maturity in turn. We will experience a process of development, much like a child learning to crawl, stand up, and finally walk. This route is something like waking up, sometimes slowly, sometimes with the suddenness of profound insight. By exploring your personal and family history and by examining the roots of your current experiences, you will learn how to identify the messages that entrap you. You will learn too how to identify the feelings that continue to block your ease of action. And then you will learn how to act with energy, understanding, and accomplishment in the world of money. You will pick up countless practical skills to approach your own financial plan, and you will be taught meditative and psychological techniques to put an end to the stresses, anxieties, and suffering you feel around money. You will learn ways to approach money tasks with greater vigor, access and accomplish your most idealistic visions around money, and bring a touch of kindness and generosity to each of your money relationships.

Each chapter will have exercises to complete and questions to answer that will give you the skills you need to:

- Discover the sense of purpose within yourself that is essential to accomplishing your goals.
- Determine what freedom means for you.
- Invest with simplicity, profitability, and peace of mind in order to build for freedom—not merely a doddering retirement.
- Find the practical resources, including the capacity to save, you need to accomplish your financial goals.
- Find ease within every money encounter.
- Live from a spirit of everyday generosity and kindness.

MY OWN PATH TOWARD THE SEVEN STAGES

Even ten years ago, had anyone suggested that I would become an expert in healing the wounds money causes spirit, I would have broken out laughing. In fact, Money Maturity developed slowly within me as a result of my struggle to come to terms with the facts of financial life while exploring a deeper interest in literature, psychology, and the spirit. In the process I discovered a way of joining the two seemingly disparate areas of money and soul that has brought greater depth to the whole of my life.

Early on in my career, I assumed—as most of us do—that a sharp divide separates money and soul. In my own professional life that split yawned wide. Yet as vast as the chasm between the hard necessities of economic life and the profound spaces of emotional and meditative life seemed, I was determined to come to terms with both and to ignore neither. Little did I realize then that I would come to see the two worlds as joining together in the same path toward freedom. Never did I expect to find a way of development around money that, as the seven stages do, promises the rewards of spiritual and emotional transformation.

Always good at math, I started out as an economics major when I entered college at Harvard. Curiously, however, a professor in one of my sophomore classes laughed at a paper I wrote—arguing, correctly it turned out, that the 1970s would see a massive worldwide inflation. In flight from the ridicule I took refuge in my other love: literature. I majored in English, and to this day I take much of my guidance from William Blake, William Shakespeare, and Dante Alighieri.

Following college, I was accepted into Harvard's Ph.D. program in English, but rather than pursue an academic career, I moved to the country determined to live a life of spiritual practice and writing. My parents, however, were horrified at the lifestyle I was choosing, and my father provided me with work for a few hours a day, analyzing technical patterns in the stock market. Although I didn't do well at picking individual stocks, I learned a great deal about the movement of the stock market as a whole.

After two years in the country, inflation and higher gas prices swept through the nation, and it became clear that I needed to find gainful employment. Still, I was in conflict. To me freedom meant meditation and writing. I wasn't about to give them up. I remember traveling home despondent one holiday, wrestling with the question. I'd thought of farming as a possible part-time career because I didn't want to leave the fields and forests that surrounded me. When I mentioned the idea to my parents they just laughed. They understood that the hard life and long hours of their farmer friends were not for me.

My mother suggested accounting. Doing tax returns meant I could work part time, an arrangement that appealed to me. The next fall I entered graduate school in accounting at Northeastern University. Yet

I remained in conflict. So intense was my desire to return to writing and spiritual studies that I quit school a few months short of completing my master's. I took the CPA exam that same year and scored third highest in the state, winning the bronze medal.

For the next thirteen years I made my living as a tax accountant. At first I worked part time, an arrangement that let me pursue my other interests in writing, painting, and meditation. The business, though, grew, by leaps and bounds, as I discovered my own capacity for entrepreneurship. When tax season neared, I was up at four on frosty winter mornings putting advertising leaflets on cars all over Cambridge. Before I knew it, I had more clients than I could handle. Pretty soon I had taken on employees, business partners, and seventy-hour workweeks.

The tax practice grew naturally into a financial-planning business. Many of my clients were making bonehead investments, ones that served their interests poorly. Often they made these investments on the recommendation of supposedly professional financial advisors, many of whom were raking in big commissions for bad advice. Angered by this combination of ineptitude and greed, I figured I owed my clients a chance at something better. In time, I moved away from tax preparation to focus on comprehensive financial planning, which includes tax planning, investments, retirement and estate planning, and insurance, with a particular expertise in money management. Having done tens of thousands of tax returns and hundreds of financial plans, I eventually narrowed my professional focus to the financial care of ninety individuals and families with a combined net worth of $100 million.

In the mid-1980s, as part of the effort to develop my business, I began teaching my first money seminar, called "How You Might Retire in Twelve Years by Saving 12 Percent Per Year," at the Cambridge Center for Adult Education. The course was extremely popular, and I eventually began offering it in Hawaii, where I started living part time, and California. Then, at the urging of a close friend, I took my developing message about Money Maturity to a national conference on financial illiteracy sponsored by the Institute of Certified Financial Planners (ICFP). Even though I was a complete unknown at the time, my speech was extremely well received. That success led to other speaking invitations with national financial planning organizations and major brokerage houses, plus a long, continuing string of interviews with *The New York Times, Newsweek, Fortune, The Wall Street Journal*, and other prominent publications. Through my seminar business and public appearances, I have spoken to tens of thousands of people over the years.

At that ICFP meeting I also met Dick Wagner, then ICFP president and, it turned out, a kindred spirit. Together he and I founded a gathering of financial planners interested in understanding and resolving dysfunctionality around money. We called ourselves the Nazrudin Project. The group has grown into an influential behind-the-scenes think tank of some of the most powerful and visionary financial professionals in the country.

There was good reason why we chose the name Nazrudin for the group. In the teaching stories of the Sufis, the mystic branch of Islam, Mullah Nazrudin figures as the holy trickster, much like Coyote in the Native American tradition, the wild man who upends people's blinkered, conventional ways of thinking and forces them to look at themselves anew. One of the many stories about the Mullah tells of the day Nazrudin went to the bank to cash a check. The teller examined the draft, looked at the Mullah, and said, "Can you identify yourself, sir?"

"Certainly," said the Mullah, without a moment's hesitation. He rummaged in his satchel and pulled out a small hand mirror, in which he admired his own face. Then the Mullah announced proudly, "That's me all right!"

The whole thrust of the Nazrudin Project is seeking out ways to help people discover their own identities and to bring that discovery to bear on their presence in the world of money. I was doing the same in my own life. Even while I was building up my business and my reputation as a financial planner, I followed the Mullah's lead in discovering who I was. In addition to psychological workshops and ongoing studies of Blake, Dante, and Shakespeare, I took up a Buddhist way of living and in time became a Buddhist teacher. In addition to instructing many individual students every week, I lead five silent weeklong retreats each year in New England and Hawaii.

My involvement with literature and Buddhism has contributed a great deal to the Seven Stages. Dante, Blake, and Shakespeare share similar views of the process by which humans progress toward awakening and freedom, and I have borrowed from their writings to develop the Seven Stages, as you'll see throughout this book. The Asian concept of chakras, physical energy centers used in acupuncture and meditation as well as Buddhism, has also played a role, since each of the Seven Stages corresponds to a chakra. And Buddhism introduced me to the *Bodhicaryavatara*, a long poem that was the first Buddhist book I ever read cover to cover, one that continues to influence me every day of my life.

Written by the eighth-century sage Shantideva, the *Bodhicaryavatara* is said to be the root text of Tibetan Buddhism, something like the first five books of the Old Testament in Judaism. Indeed, Shantideva's poem has been the subject of several books of commentary by the current Dalai Lama. Other than its pedigree, however, the *Bodhicaryavatara* most impressed me for its clear rendition of the world's suffering darkness. We all feel some of that suffering in the realm of money—humiliation and shame when work feels desperate, terror when investments go sour, anger when lawsuits over money explode, anxiety when a job disappears, outrage when inheritances are divided unequally, and diminished self-worth when hard work devolves into cheating and pettiness, debts mount, or savings evaporate. Shantideva described the suffering of the world, but he emphasized most his own personal involvement in that suffering. That is, rather than blame his feelings on some impersonal outside force, be it government or multinational corporations or some ethnic group, he looked inside himself to find the source of suffering within. And, most wonderfully, he found there not only the seeds of his suffering but also everything he needed to become free.

THE SEVEN STAGES OF MONEY MATURITY: A PATH TO FREEDOM

In the Buddhist view, the world of suffering—which Shantideva and the Buddha called *samsara*—constitutes the First Noble Truth. Samsara is noble because of what it inspires us to do. Seeing suffering in ourselves and in others, we resolve to comprehend it, meet it, and bring it to an end. The bearing of suffering becomes noble when it prompts us to pursue freedom.

The pursuit of freedom was what I found so inspiring about Shantideva. Shantideva wanted freedom not only for himself but also for everyone. I see this same drive in my financial-planning clients. When I ask them what they want, most say freedom for themselves, then they name freedom for their families, friends, and communities. Shantideva perceived that freedom is possible, and he devoted himself to it, by developing the Buddhist pursuits called the Six Perfections, or the Six Paramitas. The Seven Stages of Money Maturity apply the insights of this ancient wisdom to the world of money.

THE TWO STAGES OF CHILDHOOD: INNOCENCE AND PAIN

The world we enter as children and continue to live in as adults is the world of suffering. The tangled web of beliefs we cling to and painful feelings we strive to avoid make up the samsara Shantideva devoted his life to understanding. Convinced that his false beliefs and treacherous feelings mired him in a world of dreams, Shantideva dedicated himself to a "mind of awakening" in regard to them.

INNOCENCE. Innocence represents the beliefs, thoughts, stories, attitudes, and assumptions about money we hold on to for dear life no matter how fiercely the world works to remind us of their untruth. The process of entrapment in beliefs begins early in childhood, when parents pass on their own often-unstated attitudes about money. We seize upon these beliefs, sometimes burying them so deeply within our beings that we don't even know they're there—yet they still influence every money decision we make.

Innocence is related to the first chakra, at the base of the spine, the physical realm that governs basic survival activities like eating, drinking, and defecating. As the former chair of the ICFP Dick Wagner puts it, "Money skills are the survival skills of the twenty-first century." The desperate, often unconscious way we cling to our beliefs around money reflects the urgency of our basic needs.

Jake and Mary, two clients of mine, show how Innocence works. Throughout his career, Jake had always had good jobs. Meanwhile,

Mary raised the children and never thought about working. Her father had always told her, "You'll never have to worry about money," and she never did, because Jake was a good provider. So it came as quite a shock when they came into my office—he was sixty, she fifty-seven—and I let them know the six-figure retirement savings they thought they had was probably worthless.

The message Jake had heard from his father throughout childhood was "Work hard and swing for the fences. Go for broke." And that's what he did. He worked hard, was a good father, and paid all the bills. When it came to his savings, he always swung for the fences. Sometimes he hit home runs, sometimes he struck out. The good news was that all of his retirement had been invested in cellular phone rights when cellular phones were young and prices were low. The bad news was his rights were subject to a lottery, and he'd lost.

Jake and Mary are much better off now than when I first met them. Mary works part time. And whenever the next roll of the dice tempts him, Jake calls me for a reality check before acting. Confronting their childhood messages wasn't easy, but now their assets are steadily growing.

Innocence works upon our lives even when we are long past early childhood. Somewhere, far back in the unremembered past, Jake and Mary had taken their childhood money message so deeply to heart that they never thought to question them, even around an issue as critical as retirement savings. For all of us, bringing beliefs like these into consciousness, long before tragedy strikes, is the first step toward the freedom of Money Maturity.

PAIN. The suffering of samsara comprises feelings as well as beliefs, the difficult emotions inextricably tied in with deeply held assumptions and stories. These feelings are connected with the second chakra, the center of sexuality, a zone that comes alive in adolescence and is often the seat of conflict, guilt, and shame. Appropriately, I call this stage Pain. I remember well the first time I encountered its power around money.

When I returned to school after Christmas vacation in the sixth grade, I made a point of listing all my gifts to one of my best friends. His dad was a miner who worked in one of the many coal pits in the corner of Appalachia where we lived. My dad was a country lawyer. I didn't yet understand the financial difference between our fathers' worlds. Starting with my stocking gifts, I told my friend about the tangerine, the Scotch tape, the two ballpoint pens, the Silly Putty, and the deck of cards. I still had more to go when he stopped me.

"I don't believe you," he said. "I don't believe you got all that."

"What did you get?" I said.

"A deck of cards. That was it."

Instantly the eyes of this rough tough kid clouded with tears, and he ran to the teacher for consolation. All that week I felt terrible and confused. I had just stumbled into the difficult, emotional revelation that some of us have more money than others.

We make two fundamentally painful discoveries about money. The first, the reality that hit me smack in the face after my sixth-grade Christmas, is that each of us is richer than some people yet poorer than others. The second discovery is that we will have to work to get money for the things we want, a lesson that shatters the comfortable dependency of childhood. As we move into adulthood, we relearn and relive these painful lessons again and again.

Most of us recycle between Pain and Innocence in a way that prevents us from moving forward toward Money Maturity. Say, for example, that your basic Innocent belief was "Live for today. Who knows what tomorrow will bring?" Acting on that naive belief, you've spent everything you've ever earned—plus quite a bit more, thanks to the miracle of credit cards. Now you're approaching fifty, your children are talking about going to college, and you don't have the savings to afford their tuition. You also find out that the occasional pain in your chest is an early symptom of heart disease—and you without a cent put away for retirement. Suddenly you feel like a complete idiot. Panic sets in as Pain displaces Innocence.

At this point, many people substitute a new Innocent belief for the one that is causing their suffering. Facing the despair of your own lack of resources, you may remember the family story about Uncle Ernie, who went into debt to buy a drought-ridden corner of Oklahoma. Everybody thought he was a complete fool for the six years before oil was discovered on his land and he traded in his dented pickup for a long white limousine. "If Uncle Ernie could do it, so can I," you say to yourself, and plunk down every penny you're able to beg, borrow, and steal on some trendy investment scheme. You'll probably lose it all and set the scene for yet another round of Innocence becoming Pain becoming Innocence yet again.

There is another way. We can use Pain to wake ourselves up. We can let its discomfort propel us toward the depth and wisdom that blossom from Money Maturity. Pain can serve as the warning signal to the deep self that moves us toward Money Maturity.

THE THREE STAGES OF ADULTHOOD: KNOWLEDGE, UNDERSTANDING, AND VIGOR

Shantideva called freedom *bodhicitta*, a word of complex meaning that refers to the awakening of the heart or soul to a dedication to freedom. *Bodhicitta* inspires us to develop the internal skills we need to move beyond our cycles of suffering around money.

KNOWLEDGE. First Shantideva realized that in order not to fall again into the pit of suffering he would have to perfect and guard his moral conduct, or virtue. The Money Maturity stage of Knowledge, while filled with practical things like budgets and taxes and investments, is actually rooted in virtue and integrity. Without integrity economic systems and relationships fall apart. Shantideva's determination to act always with integrity in the day-to-day world forms the only healthy basis from which we can approach the universe of information and Knowledge about money.

The practical part of Knowledge is the financial-planning process. It begins at the point where we translate our desire for freedom into concrete goals and commit ourselves to achieving them. Financial planning comprises three steps: identifying your goals, assessing the resources you have to accomplish your goals, and selecting a path from your resources to your goals.

This path is a path of power. Knowledge resides in the third chakra, which is centered in the solar plexus, the place where power resides. The third chakra, however, is primarily about digestion and Knowledge is the most difficult area for people to assimilate or digest. It can require, among other things, an assessment of your assets, liabilities, and capacity to save. It involves an understanding of investments, insurance, taxes, retirement planning, and general economic theory as well. In the chapter on Knowledge, I will provide charts of high-return asset categories that have provided investors with short-cuts to economic freedom for decades.

UNDERSTANDING. Next Shantideva realized that regardless of his determination to act virtuously, the world throws endless curveballs. In fact, to avoid stumbling into the world of suffering's many pitfalls, Shantideva knew he had to cultivate enormous Patience, the second perfection. What Shantideva called patience I call Understanding, which springs from the heart, the fourth chakra. Understanding teaches us how to achieve peace in the midst of the anxiety, stress, and suffering that arise from money issues.

Alice, a former client of mine, provided for a sister suffering from a disease that was sucking her life away, but only very slowly. Like Sisyphus endlessly pushing his big rock up the hill, Alice felt tied to a demanding high-paying job. Although her work exhausted and depleted her, she said she needed the money to pay for some expensive technological miracle that might one day come along to spare her sister's life. Yet Alice never saved a penny. To assuage her misery in her work and her despair and helplessness over her sister's slow decline, she bought herself costly trinkets and took expensive vacations. Enslaved by the desire to attend to her sister, distracted by false hopes for a technological breakthrough that would end the need for round-the-clock care, racing day after day from job to sister's bedside and back again, Alice used frenetic activity to block the grief she felt over knowing she could never alter her sister's fate.

When I first helped her tap into these feelings, pent-up tears overwhelmed her. Over the next year, as she admitted her feelings to consciousness and allowed them to live within her, she dropped the false desires that caused her suffering, shifted the focus of her life to deepening herself, and moved into a career she had always wanted yet never thought she could afford. And, remarkably, she started saving.

Beneath many similarly difficult financial situations lie unbearable feelings about money such as envy, miserliness, greed, jealousy, shame, humiliation, and guilt. Resolving these emotions, which is the benefit of Understanding, makes it possible for us to act effectively in ways that earlier appeared incomprehensible.

VIGOR. Once Shantideva had the perfections of moral conduct and patience under his belt, he was freed from many of the shackles of the world. His freedom allowed him to develop the third perfection: energy, enthusiasm, and vigor to pursue his goal of freedom. This same Vigor enables us to find what constitutes freedom for us in the world of money.

A client I advised for a number of years came from a working-class background in an eastern mill town. Like all the men in his family before him, he went into the factory at age fourteen. He was a man of extraordinary talent and energy, the kind who regularly put in sixty to seventy hours a week. By the time he was thirty, he owned the factory and had made a great deal of money. Understanding firsthand the harsh reality of the laboring life, he wanted to spare his children the same ordeal. Consciously he wished to take away the pain of the struggle he had known; unconsciously he robbed his offspring of the struggle they needed to find purpose in life on their own. He indulged his kids in the best of everything, from designer-label clothes, bicycles, and pets to exotic vacations, automobiles, and rock concerts whenever they wanted, whether they deserved it or not.

The results were disastrous. Today those children have grown into adults who spend down the assets of sizable trust funds, waste days in front of the television, and phone their now-aged dad to complain how rotten their lives are. He wanted to be kind and caring, yet he fell unwittingly into a pattern of action that robbed his children of Vigor.

Vigor centers on discovering purpose in life and putting one's energy into accomplishing that purpose. Vigor is centered in the fifth chakra, the throat, the place from which we speak with authority. Vigor concerns authority, in the sense of "authoring" our own lives, and it springs from a variety of practices and exercises we will explore in detail later in this book.

THE TWO STAGES OF AWAKENING: VISION AND ALOHA

Vision and Aloha are strongly related, the first stage being more external, the second more internal. In Vision we draw from practical knowledge, the opening of the heart to feelings, and the sense of life's purpose to take effective, even prophetic action in our communities—whether they are as large as Earth itself or as small as a backyard. And as we grow in wisdom and achieve Aloha, our souls manifest themselves in small actions others may experience as blessings. The serenity, ease, and freedom that Vision and Aloha offer are the rewards of the Seven Stages.

VISION. This stage rests in the sixth chakra, the so-called third eye of yoga and Tantric Buddhism, where we see God everywhere. Once Shantideva had developed the energy to pursue freedom, he was able to follow the spiritual practice necessary to accomplish it. Shantideva described this perfection as the power to meditate one-pointedly. Vision matches this powerful inward focus with a powerful outward focus. Instead of seeing God everywhere, we see good to be accomplished all around us, and we have the skills to make the vision real.

Vision is all about seeing. It directs our sense of life purpose beyond ourselves toward the health and welfare of communities. Personal gain may be mixed in, yet the perspective of the whole is the driving force. For many people who grew up in steel country as I did, Andrew Carnegie remains an unpopular figure a century after his death. But his donation of hundreds of millions to endow thousands of public libraries across the United States remains a classic example of Vision. These days Vision manifests itself in the Internet and other technologies that connect communities across the face of the globe. Ted Turner's zeal to build CNN into a worldwide communications system is yet another example of Vision in action.

Vision, though, need be neither grand nor global. It may be as simple as preserving a small park threatened by development in a city that desperately needs its few remaining green spaces, or finding a donor to provide swings for a children's playground, or pitching in to serve Thanksgiving dinner to the homeless. We understand that we ourselves, not somebody else, are responsible for the things of this world. We take delight in having the tools to make a difference.

In Vision, we perceive that waking up to money really has had nothing to do with money per se. Instead, we have been allowing our souls to awaken, grow strong, and move into the world, as they are meant to do. Awakening is our birthright; it is the essence of freedom.

With Vision we understand further that money is a conduit through which our souls flow into the world. We have produced as much as we personally need. We discover within us a capacity to reach out farther than we have ever imagined toward meeting the needs of our families and communities. We find no obstacle between what we want to accomplish and what we do. If we have grown rich, we give it back to foundations and nonprofits (e.g., Rockefeller, Ford, Annenberg, Packard, Hewlett, etc.); if not, we give locally to our communities. We understand that nothing really belongs to us, even what we conventionally call "I, me, or mine." This understanding leads us to community service as a way of returning the gift.

ALOHA. The last perfections of Shantideva's *Bodhicaryavatara* are wisdom and generosity. Their chakra is found at the top of the head, the place where we merge with the divine. When you encounter this energy, you know exactly what it is.

My mother was a housewife, and the arena of her life's activity was her home and yard. She took her responsibility toward that space both seriously and lovingly. The one morning a week when Mr. Johnstone worked his way up the back alley to pick up the garbage at each house, she stepped outside to say hello. It was a meeting she never missed. Whatever she was doing, she dropped it to head out back.

There came a garbage morning during my teen years when my mother and I were engaged in one of those deep and serious discussions adolescent boys have with their moms. Right in the middle of this earnest talk, the clatter of cans announced Mr. Johnstone's coming. My mother's ears pricked up.

"I have to go out," she said. "I'll only be a minute."

"You don't have to go," I said. "The garbage is already out. You can stay."

"No, I have to go," she insisted, and she was out of the house before I could protest further.

Years later, at my mother's funeral, a small African American man with gray hair came up to me. "I'm Mr. Johnstone," he said. "I used to pick up your garbage when you were only a child."

I was stunned. I remembered Mr. Johnstone as strapping, tall, and strong, a lion of a man. Age had withered him, yet I felt his strength when he shook my hand. In that simple touch he bridged the divide between us: a poor, now-old black man connecting with a younger, better-off white.

"Your mother was a wonderful woman," Mr. Johnstone said.

"I know," I said.

"No, you don't," he countered, his eyes flashing both ferocity and kindness. He took my right hand and cradled it between his two palms.

"Let me tell you something about your mother," he continued. He poured his eyes into mine. "I never left her backyard without feeling I was a better person than when I went in."

My mother's gift to Mr. Johnstone and his to me were acts of Aloha, generous and selfless blessing that transcended the economic differences between us. Aloha is a word I've borrowed from the native Hawaiians I know from living part of each year on Maui. Tourists learn that "aloha" stands for both hello and good-bye in Hawaiian. Actually it has a deeper, richer meaning. Aloha conveys kindness, generosity, at-one-ness, and compassion.

Practicing Shantideva's perfections of generosity and wisdom, we give without expectation of return, understanding that living is giving. We know both the limitations and the power of money, yet money no longer agitates us. We rest calm before it. In that calmness we can serve one another from the natural generosity that lies within and waits to be offered to the world. Aloha does not arise from clinging to childhood messages about generosity. Rather, it is the natural consequence of facing the world as it is and connecting wholly, deeply, and truthfully with its reality.

LOOKING FORWARD

The Seven Stages of Money Maturity will guide you chapter by chapter through the steps leading to Money Maturity, showing the pattern by which each of us grows toward freedom. As you read through this book, you will discover yourself awakening as a person. You will discover too, as participants in my seminars do, that you feel energized in each of the Seven Stages and that you have discovered seven powerful new ways of working not only with financial issues but also with the whole of your life. Like Shantideva, you will set yourself on the pilgrim's path to freedom.

part one

CHILDHOOD

chapter 2

INNOCENCE:
WHAT WE CLING TO

When the voices of children are heard on the green
And laughing is heard on the hill,
My heart is at rest within my breast
And everything else is still.

William Blake

Dear God,
Is Reverend Coe a friend of yours, or do you just know him
through business?
Donny

Children's letters to God

When Mahealani Sapolu was growing up poor in a rundown section of Honolulu, long miles from Waikiki's elegant high-rises, her father told her where money came from.

"You get it from working," he said. "Working hard."

And work hard he did. Whenever he had a job—as a deckhand on a glass-bottomed boat, a gardener for a tourist hotel, or a busboy at a beachfront restaurant—he was up before the sun and out the door. But Mahealani's father was uneducated, and there were many times when the demand for unskilled labor dried up and no jobs were to be had.

At those times Mahealani's mother stated her deepest belief about money: "You have to trust. If you need money, it will come."

She had a point. On the first of every month when her husband was unemployed, a welfare check appeared in the mailbox.

Among the native Hawaiian community, Mahealani's mother's point of view was more favored than her father's. "Money is the white man's invention," an elder told Mahealani. "They came up with it just to make sure we lose. Trust your own people, not money."

Mahealani found the open-hearted beliefs of her mother and the elder more congenial than her father's cold-eyed view of the world. When she married and left home to live in a small town on the windward side of the island, she continued her easy attitude toward money.

"We're short, we borrow," she said to Ricky, her husband. "So what? When we really need the money, we'll get it and then we'll pay the loans back. You've got to trust."

Debts mounted and mounted. Still, Mahealani shrugged off the $20,000 she and her husband owed as nothing of any particular importance, a problem they'd take care of one of these days. After all, Ricky had his own one-man furniture-refinishing business, and she was good at picking up odd jobs. Still, they made just enough for food and rent, with nothing left over to pay down the still-growing debt.

Then Mahealani discovered she was pregnant—with no health insurance. A couple of days later, Ricky came home to tell her a bill collector had shown up at work and harassed him about the money they owed.

"We're in more of a bind than you think," he said, clearly shaken. "If we don't get this debt thing straightened out, we could lose it all. And we don't have enough to lose any of it."

Mahealani felt her blood run cold. "I didn't want to admit it, but I knew Ricky was right," she said to me later. "And a lot of the pickle we were in was my problem."

Derrick King enjoyed a solidly middle-class upbringing in Southern California during the years when there were still orange groves scattered among the expanding home tracts. His aerospace engineer father spent too little time at home, however, to even notice the sweet scent of the orange blossoms. Working long and hard, weekends as well as weekdays, Derrick's father was committed to his job.

"Money makes the world go round," his father said to Derrick when he was small. A jolt of energy ran through the boy at the statement. Somewhere he had heard "Love makes the world go round," and his father's contradiction surprised Derrick. Still, the shock of it seemed right to him. His heart wanted love, yet this new notion of money offered something masculine, something strong and powerful. Derrick could learn about money, count it, control it. It was something he somehow already understood.

Derrick's father explained further that money was the only way to gain entry to a good life. "I want you to go to USC because it's the best," he continued, "but it's going to cost a lot."

As Derrick grew into adolescence and USC loomed nearer, his father shared more of his philosophy about money.

"When you get down to it, it's a game," he said. "Money is the way we keep score. It's how we tell who wins."

Derrick's mother paid no attention to money, letting her husband handle all matters financial. She saw his hard work as the result of the family's Christian heritage. "Above all else, you have to take good care of your family," she said. "That's what your father's doing. That's all that matters."

By the time Derrick enrolled at the University of Southern California, he was certain about three facts of life. Hard work guarantees success. More money is always better than less money. And women don't have to know about money; men do.

After earning an engineering degree and feeling a need for adventure, Derrick took a couple of years off to join the Peace Corps, where he spent two years on a construction crew building schools in North Africa. When he returned to the United States, he completed an MBA, then took a job in the then-small personal computer industry. His diligence and hard work pushed him rapidly up the career ladder. By the time he became the marketing director for a well-known PC manufacturer, he had also acquired a wife, two sons, and a comfortable home near Silicon Valley.

Yet, for all his outward success, Derrick's life was leaving an increasingly sour taste in his mouth. His wife, Alexandria, had never held a job in her life, clipped coupons to save on grocery bills, and depended on him for every decision about money—a fact he realized she resented more and more with each passing day. As for his sons, Derrick never attended their Little League games, swim meets, or parent-teacher conferences because he was always at work, slogging away to earn enough money to send them to the prestigious East Coast colleges he was sure would guarantee them access to exceptional careers.

"Sometimes I wonder what I'm doing," he said to me. "I've been a success so far, but for what? We have money, but Alexandria is unhappy. I wonder if deep down she resents or even hates me. I see my kids so rarely I practically have to ask their names when I come home. I work my butt off to give them the best, but when it's all over, I wonder if we'll even know each other. I always believed hard work was the best way to be a success and provide for my family. Now I'm worried that I could be losing them all—and myself—in the process."

When I first met Susanna Swartz, she was living in a cramped apartment in a gritty blue-collar neighborhood of Boston. Despite her living conditions, she was worth more than most of us can even dream about—even though she had already lost a substantial portion of her massive inheritance.

"Money," her father told her when she was growing up, "is one thing you'll never have to worry about."

Still, for something that was supposedly worry-free, money drew unending attention—at least as far as the men of the family were concerned. Susanna's father was away more than he was home, managing the many industrial and commercial real-estate holdings that formed the family business. He groomed each of his three sons for money-oriented careers—one as an accountant, another as a lawyer, and the last as an international banker. He told Susanna she'd make a good wife and mother.

In comparison to all the money she would one day inherit, Susanna felt small, trivial, inconsequential. She wondered what she had ever done to deserve such wealth. And when her father and brothers engaged in long debates around the dinner table about which way the stock and bond markets were heading, they ignored anything she had to say.

Susanna seethed against such facile dismissal. She resented men and their money-oriented ways and the giant corporations that made and protected their wealth. Goodness rests not with those who have money, she was sure, but with those who don't. And she found herself on the wrong side of virtue's divide.

Susanna married soon after graduating from college with a degree in art history. Her husband came from a family with much less money than her own, but his heart was in the right place. He was as socially committed as she was, dedicated to reversing the fortunes of the downtrodden at the expense of the wealthy. Since Susanna had so much money, neither of them really had to work. Her husband used his new law degree to help a number of political action groups, while Susanna raised three children to adulthood and campaigned for any cause that identified large corporations as the source of all wrongs and injustices.

One day her husband didn't come home. A younger woman, he explained through his attorney. After the dust settled from the divorce proceedings, Susanna discovered she was worth much less than she once had been. Her husband had taken possession of much of her inheritance, entirely legally, and there was nothing she could do about it.

"I always knew it was men and their money ways that spawned the evil in this world. Then it happened in my own life," she said. "I moved to this neighborhood because I wanted to be on the right side of the tracks for a change. I have a lot to learn."

When we enter this world at birth, money has no meaning. As newborns, we live in a world defined by simple physical needs for food, warmth, and touch. We exist in a blessed unknowing that creates a special freshness and wonder. All of us know this Innocent state of being, replete with the honesty, directness, and wisdom that draw us to small children and their uncorrupted ways. Yet at some point this primal state breaks down, not because it is wrong or the world flawed, but because life draws us down its path. As we grow, we learn—and one of the realities we must learn about is money.

CLINGING TO BELIEFS BEGETS INNOCENCE

I grew up in an Appalachian village in the Ohio River Valley, a little place called St. Clairsville. My father was an attorney who ran a country practice in Martins Ferry, the nearest "big" town, across the river from Wheeling, West Virginia. My father was a hardworking man. He logged long days in his law practice, and he often worked on Saturday mornings. On rare occasions he even brought work home on the weekends. He spread his papers across the dark mahogany table in the dining room, sat rigidly in a straight-backed chair, and made notes in pencil or fountain pen.

"What's he doing?" I asked my mother.

She answered solemnly: "He's making money."

I crept silently into the room to watch. He was too focused on the matter at hand—a will perhaps, or a commercial contract—to notice me as I stood on tiptoes to peer at him over the papers. To my child's eyes, my father painted the perfect picture of discomfort. His lips were pursed, his face pinched, his back rigid. Now and again he rolled up a hand, squeezing it into a tight fist. I watched him until I couldn't stand it anymore, and then I burst from the room in wild escape. I crashed through the back door and ran for the meadows and the hills, where the air was free and the sunlight bright and yellow butterflies winged over fields of nodding goldenrod.

For long, long years after, I held on to that vision of my father engaged in the task of making money on the dining room table. In my Innocence, I had come to believe that earning money, even for a purpose as worthy as supporting your family, was, in contrast to my day in the fields, like volunteering your body to an Inquisition torture chamber. I wanted nothing to do with it. Even after I graduated from Harvard, I spent the better part of the next decade resisting and rejecting the idea of a career, setting aside my natural aptitudes in financial affairs for a vain attempt to become an artist, losing myself in evenings of fantasy, television, or despair. I was determined never to take on my share of my father's suffering. Even then I knew I was clinging to Innocence. I used to tell myself that if I lost my Innocence, I would lose my life.

As soon as we become aware of money, we develop beliefs about it—beliefs we cling to, sometimes for the rest of our lives, often at the cost of our souls. Innocence represents the beliefs, thoughts, stories, attitudes, and assumptions about money we will hold on to no matter how clearly the world demonstrates their untruth and no matter how much harm they cause us and those around us.

Holding on to patterns of thought created in the experience of seeing my father making money at the dining room table kept me from developing a sense of Vigor around work and a financial plan for freedom until I was well into my thirties. We have all had experiences like this. This is the trap of Innocence—we hold on to a body of beliefs with such fierceness and misplaced loyalty that they block us from the experience and pursuit of freedom, often for years, sometimes for our whole life.

The consequence is the same whether we accept a belief or reject it. The stories of my three clients described at the beginning of this chapter all turned on beliefs born in Innocence—some accepted, some rejected. For Mahealani Sapolu, money was something dangerous that got in the way of a heartfelt life. She rejected her father's puritan ethic of hard work and held to her mother's belief that money would magically appear when needed—until she discovered herself teetering on the brink of bankruptcy. Derrick King incorporated his father's ethic of hard work in the supposed service of family until he felt his life cracking underneath him. Susanna Swartz thought she had rejected her family's money-centered lifestyle, yet she found herself in a dilemma of divorce and deception where money took center stage and pushed all else aside.

THE PROMISE

I've never encountered a money dilemma in a client, friend, or student where some misguided belief system didn't lie right at the root of the problem. Mastering the stage of Innocence promises to remedy that, allowing us, for the first time in our lives, to see money issues as they are rather than through some filter we've held on to since childhood. Every money message we hold on to contains a fatal flaw; it imprisons us in an incomplete world. If you are sabotaging yourself around money anywhere in your life, you can bet there's a message, story, or belief system behind it. If you could just let go, your problem would begin to resolve. By learning to let go of our stories around money, we can accomplish whatever we want to, and we can experience the ease and freedom we have always desired.

The rest of this chapter has two major themes. First we will look at a number of examples of how people trap themselves in belief systems, often unconscious, that put a curse on their financial lives and how they have changed by noticing and then letting go of these messages. Second, we will look at how each of us can recognize and let go of our own internalized belief systems. As part of doing this we will create an inventory and classification of life experiences around money. Then we will learn techniques to let go of the messages and thought structures that block our freedom. In seeing our stories for what they are and understanding how they limit us, we can learn to become more flexible in our attitudes and approaches toward money and put an end to the dysfunctional notions that have plagued us.

THE TRAPS WE SET

Refusing to recognize our belief systems and remaining mired in Innocence has powerful consequences on our financial lives. The following examples illustrate some of the common traps people fall into because of their unquestioned financial beliefs.

OVERSPENDING AND HOARDING. These are flip sides of the same coin, reactions to messages like "Diamonds are a girl's best friend" or "Your best friend is your bank account."

The highly successful financial advisor you met in the beginning of chapter 1, when he came to me because something was missing from his life was a classic hoarder. He just couldn't stop making money no matter how much he made. As I got to know him better, I learned that his father had drilled into him the message "No matter how much you've got, it's not enough." The advisor took his father at his word and just kept making money. His net worth was well up into seven figures, but he stayed at it, sixty or seventy hours a week, even though the cost to his personal life was mounting higher. Not long before he came to speak with me, his girlfriend of several years' standing had walked out after a bitter fight, one of many such conflicts. He was pushing her to bring home more money, while she felt he made more than enough for both of them and it was time to work on some life goals other than accumulating ever more wealth. Unable to let go of his belief or to relinquish moneymaking as his main source of self-worth, he let his girlfriend go rather than change. The world was sending him a message about his Innocence, and he wasn't getting it.

Giving up the message that had driven him for so long was difficult. Seeking me out was a sign he was hitting bottom; for the first time in his life he didn't know where he was going. As we began to look at the message his father had given him, it became clear that he was ready to reconsider his belief system about money, but like many people, he didn't have a clue about what to replace it with. In his case, it became important to pay less attention to financial matters and give more time to the soul. He engaged in a long search for meaning, a period of self-exploration, intent on changes. His life did change in many external ways, but what most impressed me was how he became a genuinely likable human being.

Mary, another client of mine, was an overspender for good causes. Raised in a pious family with the constant teachings that "It is better to give than to receive" and "The rich make their money off the backs of the virtuous poor," Mary worked hard as a secretary and lived a frugal lifestyle that gave her several hundred dollars left over at the end of the month. Still, she had no personal savings, because she gave all her extra to her church and to a number of charities active in her Boston neighborhood. Then Mary's older sister was diagnosed with metastatic ovarian cancer. Ever sweet and loving, Mary wanted to take time off to spend with her dying sister, who lived outside Miami, but she had nothing in reserve and could afford no more than a long weekend away. Her inability to do what she wanted, even when that desire was an act of loving-kindness, shocked her. She was meeting her own Innocence in a head-on collision.

Like the financial advisor, Mary changed over time, and she became a good saver. Another message began to replace the belief system of her childhood. "I want to be able to contribute as much as I can over my lifetime," she said to me. Her savings came to represent something new and generous to her. The money could provide her with more time to give to others or, when she died, to directly benefit her church and her community.

CHOOSING BETWEEN MONEY AND INTEGRITY. This choice is a dilemma many of us face in career and family. This was very much the issue affecting Derrick King. Building his life on his father's "Money comes first" dictum, Derrick knew, grudgingly, that something was missing. Still, he felt that this sense of deficiency was simply the price he had to pay for bearing up to the demands of being a good provider. His belief system allowed him to justify the way he took his family for granted. He figured that sending his sons to the "best" schools was a sufficient rationalization for failing to be around as they grew up and for paying his wife little or no attention as a person in her own right. Derrick was sacrificing integrity in his most intimate and important relationships on the altar of money. In some profound way, that trade-off was killing him inside.

As we will see in following Derrick's progress through the course of this book, only a major crisis could bring down his pattern of belief—but come down it did. Then was he able to rebuild his life based on its reality, not a body of inherited beliefs, messages, and attitudes that worked to his detriment.

DREAD, PANIC, AND DISEMPOWERMENT AROUND MONEY. Such feelings disturb many people on a daily basis. As children we were all disenfranchised around money. The anxiety and insecurity that arose from those experiences can continue to plague us even after we are grown. Typically, these feelings are born in messages about money that left us powerless to do anything except worry or panic: "Your man will take care of you," "I'm not made of money,"

"Do you think I'm your personal banker?" and "Don't even think about asking for anything." This kind of message leaves us feeling terribly alone, and it can lead to greed, hoarding, or an endless sense of defeat.

Defeat was the core belief I uncovered, almost by accident, in an apparently very competent and seemingly ambitious young woman named Dolores. She had just come to me as a client, and I was taking her through the questions I pose to discover goals and values. Like me, Dolores had majored in English in college, and she had joined a Fortune 500 company in marketing communications. She was making a good salary, but she was unhappy with the job and the direction her life was taking. I started with asking her fundamental objective, trying to uncover the source of her dissatisfaction.

"I want to make a million dollars," she answered.

"That's a lot. What would you do with your life if you had that million right this minute?" I asked.

She seemed stumped. "I really don't know," she said.

And she really didn't know. I asked question after question, trying to elicit the deepest goal in her life. I wasn't hitting it; in fact, I wasn't even getting warm. Stymied, unsure what to ask next, I asked her, "You majored in English. Do you want to be a writer?"

"Yes," she said, "a writer, that's it. I want to be a writer." A look of relief filled her face, then she fell into a silence that lasted a minute or two. Suddenly she burst into tears.

"No," she said with streaming eyes, "I don't want to be a writer. What I really want to do is run a clinic, a place where people come to get better. I've always assumed I could never possibly do it."

"Why's that?" I said, surprised at the depth of emotion emerging from her.

It took a while to get an answer to that question. Dolores came from a big family that had little money, and her mother was, as Dolores described her, "positively ditzy about money or even getting out of the hole we were in. She kept telling me she was an idiot, except at school, and she expected me to be the same way because I was female too."

Dolores's mother was surprised when her daughter got into college, doubly surprised when she graduated. "But she didn't really change her mind," Dolores said. "She kept telling me how women can't have what they want. I must have soaked that up and taken it for granted."

Building on the clarity of this emotional breakthrough, Dolores and I explored her career direction together. The way she saw it, she'd have to earn a Ph.D., amass a great deal of work experience, and pick up a master's in public health along the way. We toted up the time it would take.

"Twenty-five years," I said. "No wonder you feel discouraged and you've buried this dream. Waiting that long for anything besides grandchildren seems foolish to me."

"You see, I can't do it," she said, already resigned to impossibility. "What I want is out of my reach."

The more we talked, though, the more I came to realize that the clinic she envisioned was something out of the ordinary and the traditional. She was interested in acupuncture, massage, tai chi, naturopathy, and nutrition.

"You don't need a Ph.D. for that," I said. "You could start right now."

"Really?" she asked.

"Really," I answered.

Together we began to chart a five-year plan toward creating the clinic she wanted, building on the entrepreneurial skills she already had and the network of alternative healers she knew. What had seemed impossible became possible, and she did in fact launch the clinic—in only three years.

This story illustrates how belief systems work on our lives even when we are long past early childhood. Dolores had received the clear parental message that what she wanted she could never have. She internalized this belief, then structured her life to follow its dictates. Bringing these beliefs into consciousness, as Dolores did, is the first step toward the freedom of Money Maturity.

INABILITY TO ATTEND TO PRACTICAL NECESSARY FINANCIAL TASKS. This inability affects most of us to some degree when it comes time to do tax returns, fill out insurance forms, even pay the bills. Some people take this tendency to an extreme.

As Denise was growing up, her mother inculcated her with two basic financial messages: "Money's not important" and "Your man will take care of you." Denise took her mother at her word. When I met her, in her mid-thirties, she had never in her life so much as balanced her checkbook.

"Oh," she said, when I asked, "I just tossed those things that came from the bank."

"Your statements?" I asked.

"Right, the statements," she continued. "Well, I put them in this box, and then the box got full. I figured I'd get around to balancing my account one of these days, but one of these days just never happened, and that box was getting awfully heavy and dusty. So the last time I moved, I just put it out with the trash."

She tossed a puzzled look at my obvious consternation. "It's nothing to get excited about, George," she said. "After all, money's not what's important."

Denise's other chicken came home to roost when her live-in boyfriend met someone he liked better than her and moved out suddenly to take up with his new love. If another man had come into her life right away, Denise might have returned to her childhood messages as sources of unshakable wisdom. But that was not to be. Reality made money important to her in a hurry, and the independence Denise developed from learning that she could take care of herself made her a good partner when the next relationship came her way.

INVESTING IN THE LATEST GET-RICH SCHEME AND MAKING POOR INVESTMENT CHOICES. Patterns such as these are more common than one might think, given all the media attention to good investing. My friend Harris is a good example. Harris has an infectious optimism and good work habits. Whenever he had a windfall from work, however, or managed to save some money, he figured it was time to make his fortune. He chased investment ideas as if they were fashion crazes. He bought shares in a blue-green algae company that promised to double in size in six months (it went bust in three), became a limited partner in a plan to raise cattle in an area of Zimbabwe infested with tsetse flies (which give cattle a fatal disease), and in a conservative moment let an investment "advisor" talk him into an unfortunate annuity. The spreadsheets of numbers the "advisor" showed boasted rates of return twice as high as what Harris ultimately received. When I worked through the mathematics of the contract at Harris's request, I discovered that the only thing high about the annuity was the undisclosed commission paid to the "advisor."

His mother's favorite, Harris heard her say again and again to him, "You'll strike it rich someday." Slow and steady work was never part of this picture. Making a fortune was as instantaneous as striking a match against its box. It was just a question of finding the right match and the right box.

Beliefs that rob us of our power to invest intelligently are often less dramatic, but no less destructive, than Harris's. People who allow themselves to be talked into investments they don't really need—such as tax shelters for individuals of modest income who don't require tax shelters or life insurance for people without children, families, or businesses to protect—are clinging to a belief much like Harris's, one that blocks them from investigating exactly what an investment is and what the alternatives are.

These messages can be very deep-seated. Harris was well into his forties before he began to question his belief that he would strike it rich and recognized instead the small fortune he had made over the years and thrown away.

TRY THIS: YOUR LIFE IN MONEY—INNOCENCE

This is a good point to stop and reflect on the beliefs, assumptions, and attitudes about money you learned as a child and still follow. An exercise I have used profitably with many people is writing an autobiography that focuses on the role money has played in our lives from first memory to current moment. In the course of each of the Seven Stages, we'll focus on a different aspect of this task, beginning here with Innocence. Since you'll have the opportunity to add to this self-recorded life in money as we proceed, you might want to write in a notebook reserved for this purpose or set up a separate file on your computer.

The assignment is simple—record the messages, lessons, and stories about money you heard in childhood. Answering the questions that follow will help your understanding of how money messages have affected your financial life.

What are your three earliest memories of money?

When and how did money first enter your relationship with your mother?

When and how did money first enter your relationship with your father?

What is your first memory involving money and a close relative? A shopkeeper? A neighbor?

What were your family stories about money (e.g., about Grandpa losing the farm in the Depression, or the time Auntie Mae had to go on welfare)? Were these stories told with an air of approval or disapproval?

What did your mother have to say about money?

What did your father have to say about money?

Did you ever worry about money? What did you say to yourself when you were worrying?

What are all the one-sentence lessons you learned about money while growing up? Who spoke each of these lessons? Which ideas did you accept? Which did you reject?

What were your first money experiences with cars, homes, insurance, stocks, bonds, lawyers, brokers or financial planners, legal papers, and banks? What messages did you carry out of these experiences? Do you respond to the same messages today?

It's important to keep in mind that Innocence is not only a state in the past. It arises now, in the act of clinging to old ideas as a way of protecting ourselves against reality. So take a moment to answer and reflect on these questions pertaining to your adult life:

How have your beliefs about money hurt your life and caused suffering?

How do you still make choices based on beliefs right now, at this very moment? List the ways. Do you continue to want to live by these messages?

Now that you have recalled events from your past, see if you can summarize the major belief systems you have adopted over time in one-line messages, such as "Don't lend money to relatives" or "We'll never have much money." Were these messages your family tried to give you, or did you take on an opposite message in reaction to what you didn't like in your family's relationship to money? And what happened to the message opposite the one you took on? If you have rejected it, have you left out a part of yourself in doing so?

THE WISDOM OF THE OPPOSITE

Innocence reminds me of the age-old nursery rhyme about Humpty-Dumpty. Humpty-Dumpty sits on his wall, round and whole as we are in our earliest days. Then money and its contradictions come into our lives. Our father says, "Time is money," when all along we'd been thinking time was for play. A teacher quotes, "A penny saved is a penny earned," then a friend calls us a penny pincher. Our mother advises that "Money isn't everything," but we remember our father telling us "Money makes the world go round" and if it does all that, what else can there be? Yet another teacher says, "You'll never make a million dollars," while grandfather tells us to "go for broke." Suddenly we have met contradictory and often unpleasant interpretations of money. Like Humpty-Dumpty, we suffer a great fall onto reality's hard surface and we shatter. And, no matter how hard we try, we can't put it back together again.

The shattering happens because the beliefs we hear don't completely fit the real world and because they contradict one another. Many of us, adults and children, don't want to face the complications of money's world. Rather, we prefer to cling to a message that makes the world simpler than it is.

Take as an example a common maxim like "A penny saved is a penny earned." We all know it's true. Restraining the desire to spend money in the immediate moment creates a reserve that can be called on in the future. Yet that same maxim contains an insidious message as well. The child feels scolded against spending on self. Better to deny yourself today, the maxim says, and put it aside for the future. For a child with little sense of the future or a feeling of impoverishment relative to what peers have or what he or she sees on television, "A penny saved is a penny earned" may leave a lifelong habit of resistance and resentment toward saving. The child clings to the opposite of the saying as a way of rejecting additional self-denial.

The beliefs about money we learn as children are true—but only part of the time. They arise as accurate representations of particular segments of experience, but they do not fit each of life's many different moments. "Time is money" holds true in business planning, though not in matters of the soul. "A fool and his money are soon parted" warns us about the dangers of gullibility and openness—which at times are attractive human characteristics. "Don't look a gift horse in the mouth" reminds us to be grateful for what comes unearned, yet at times the exact opposite can be true. It pays to be skeptical about who is giving what to whom—as the Trojans learned when they unquestioningly wheeled that wooden horse full of Greek warriors within their walls.

What breaks Humpy-Dumpty is the fact that each belief contains some kernel of truth, but not the whole truth. We cling to partial beliefs and reject anything that doesn't fit the worldview we construct inside ourselves. Innocence becomes ignorance, and we sacrifice the very wholeness we want so much to find.

Take Mahealani Sapolu's parents as an example. Both father and mother had a point. Her father argued rightly that people who work hard are more likely to make money than those who don't. Yet his pronouncement ignored the equal truth that hard work alone is often not enough to build success. Mahealani's mother also had a point. A deep trust in the cosmos providing for our needs is a virtue embodied by revered figures like Mahatma Gandhi and Francis of Assisi. Yet for those of us who have to live in a more practical and less saintly world, trusting to providence can simply be a fancy excuse for refusing to develop the move toward Money Maturity.

Both of Mahealani's parents gave expression to an important aspect of living, yet neither one stated the whole truth. Holding to one belief over the other maintains us in a state of false Innocence. Understanding the truths behind both is a stepping-stone on the path to Money Maturity. Clinging to only one such truth over the others prevents us from growing up around money. Each message—as well as its opposite—is a crack in Humpty-Dumpty's shell.

Recently I made a list of many of the maxims, aphorisms, proverbs, and family pronouncements I've heard from family, clients, and students. Then I wrote out each statement's point and its opposite. As you will see, both are true—at least some of the time.

BOTH SIDES OF BELIEF

As you read through this list, check off those that ring true to you. Which of these beliefs have you lived by? Which have you rejected? Did messages other than these establish your responses to money? Becoming familiar with your own belief structure around money is the first step toward Money Maturity

A bird in the hand is worth two in the bush.
> On one hand: What you have before you is worth more than some potential out there where you can't grab it.
> On the other hand: If you focus only on the present and don't plan ahead, you'll end up with nothing down the line.

A fool and his money are soon parted.
> On one hand: Believe everything you hear, and you'll be a sucker for every con artist who comes along.
> On the other hand: Openness, credulity, and a sense of wonder are the stuff of saints.

A penny saved is a penny earned.
> On one hand: The capacity to put money aside is the most powerful tool each of us has for accumulating wealth.
> On the other hand: If all you do is save, how can you take care of your present needs and wants? And how can you be generous?

All work and no play makes Johnny a dull boy.
> On one hand: Many of the activities that shape our lives most deeply happen outside work, in family, song, poetry, even baseball.
> On the other hand: Why not make work as nurturing as sports, literature, family, and music?

Daddy will always take care of you.

On one hand: There's no substitute for security.

On the other hand: Depending on someone else undercuts independence.

Diamonds are a girl's best friend.

On one hand: Look for what's lasting in any relationship.

On the other hand: There's a lot more to a good relationship than what you can sell from it.

Don't count your chickens before they hatch.

On one hand: A prudent, thoughtful approach to investing and saving will protect your nest egg.

On the other hand: Failure to take risks will cut you out of the most productive investments.

Don't look a gift horse in the mouth.

On one hand: We should be grateful for what comes our way.

On the other hand: Gifts can contain hidden handcuffs.

Don't put all your eggs in one basket.

On one hand: Skepticism and diversification are excellent protection for your investments.

On the other hand: Commitment—to a person, a way of life, the pursuit of freedom—requires all of you, not just a part.

Hard work always yields success.

On one hand: Success is ten percent inspiration, ninety percent perspiration.

On the other hand: There's more to gain than pain.

Marry for love, not money.

On one hand: Relationships have value beyond dollars and cents. Besides, money can't buy you love.

On the other hand: When you make a lifetime commitment, be sure you know how you're going to pay the bills.

Money doesn't grow on trees.

On one hand: It takes work to get money.

On the other hand: The most important parts of life don't carry a price tag.

Money is the root of all evil.

On one hand: Money spawns all sorts of wrongdoing, from cheating on income tax returns to killing parents for inheritances.

On the other hand: Money isn't the problem. It's the greed, ambition, and hunger expressed around money that cause trouble.

Money is a sign of success.

On one hand: People with money got that way by working hard and smart.

On the other hand: Not if it was handed to them—particularly through inheritance. And what about drug lords, financial manipulators, and white-collar criminals? Remember, too, our friends who have little money yet live wonderful lives.

Money isn't everything.

On one hand: Money is only a small part of life.

On the other hand: It may be small, but money can nourish or destroy everything else.

Time is money.

On one hand: You have to husband your resources for the most financially rewarding activities and set priorities carefully.

On the other hand: Thoreau said, "Time is a river in which I go fishing." That's a better way to live.

You only get what you pay for.

On one hand: Good stuff is more costly than junk.

On the other hand: Air and water are free. So are many of life's most valuable gifts—and you never have to pay for them.

Your best friend is your bank account.

On one hand: Saving for a rainy day means you'll have money when it clouds over.

On the other hand: Money is no substitute for love and friendship.

FINDING A BALANCE POINT

One of the key ways of confronting and understanding beliefs is to examine their opposites for the truth they can hold, just as we have done in the list above. Often the opposite of a message we have clung to holds a key to some important part of ourselves we have rejected or hidden.

A good example of the value of this technique is Sheila, who came to one of my seminars in her late fifties as part of an effort to decide what to do next with her life. As I got to know her, she told me that her family's mythology of money had revolved around Ben Franklin's proverbs: "A penny saved is a penny earned," "Time is money," and "A fool and his money are soon parted." She experienced these aphorisms as cold calculating messages that horrified her. Disheartened, discouraged, and disempowered around money, she decided early in life that the financial world could get along quite well without her. She married immediately after college, quickly had three children, and devoted herself to raising her family. Fortunately Sheila had chosen a good man, and the two of them built a strong life focused on their children. Yet, as deeply as she felt connected to her family, Sheila experienced herself as disconnected from the wider world. Slowly she became aware of a deep desire, one that stretched back into childhood, to act in the world in a way that blended power, grace, and generosity. Recognizing that her own fear of money was holding her back, she resolved to take an opposite tack and engage the world of money head on. As soon as her youngest child was off to college and she had more time to herself, she enrolled in an MBA program, completed the degree, and took a job with an investment banker.

"I worked my tail off for almost ten years," Sheila told me, "and I did well, even though I had started my career in my late forties rather than my twenties. Still, I realized that all this work wasn't leading me where I wanted to go. I had learned a great deal about my personal power and I had increased my base of skills and knowledge, but I was spending my days putting together acquisitions and mergers. I thought, 'Where's the generosity in that, the grace?' So I quit."

Sheila was looking for a balance point between the two extremes created by her early learning. She was seeking to find a lifestyle that allowed her to look at both sides of her own coin. She was seeking to put the belief systems of Innocence behind her and move toward the self-knowing balance that underlies Money Maturity.

MECHANISMS OF DEPENDENCE

Innocent people are, like children, dependent. Sheila saw that. She realized that the belief systems she learned from her family made independence and freedom impossible, so she moved against them. Yet simply moving in the opposite direction took her only so far. She had to look at herself more deeply, uncovering those mechanisms by which she trapped herself in a relationship with money.

One of the ways of uncovering the belief systems you have internalized is to look for the mechanism by which you encourage dependence on forces outside yourself. In the course of my work, I have found that we use any of a number of ways to hold on to the partial truths that keep us out of balance. Each of them prevents the self from developing its own essential independence and freedom.

RESENTMENT AND BLAME

Of all the snares that catch and bind us to Innocence, resentment and blame are the most common. Susanna Swartz offers a good example. While her resentment of corporate America was obvious, that feeling was rooted in her childhood experience of her father trivializing her around money.

"He told me that since I was a girl, I didn't need to understand finance the way my brothers did," she said to me early in our work together. "He was always educating them in the stock market, and he pushed them into business and law majors in college. When it came to me, he clammed up. Jeez—for years I thought the Dow Jones average was some kind of baseball statistic. So I studied art history, because it seemed like a good thing for a girl. I never did learn about money. I'm really ticked at him because of that."

"Why don't you go back to college for a year or two and study economics and finance?" I asked. "You have the time and the money."

"No," she scoffed, clearly amazed at my suggestion. "My father would roll over in his grave if I did that. It's too late to start now." She threw up her hands.

Susanna was only in her forties, and it was far from too late. In fact, it's never too late to remedy your deficiencies around money. However, Susanna preferred to blame her father for her financial ignorance. In essence, she was choosing to use blame to maintain her childhood beliefs rather than take responsibility for herself by embarking on her own path toward freedom and independence.

And why? Because holding on to the blame continued her Innocence. It allowed her to maintain a carefully cultivated vision of what had been—even at the expense of who she was now. As so often happens, she was clinging to a belief when the price of clinging was ignorance. She knew it had done her harm. Yet she held on to it anyway.

We have to sacrifice ourselves in order to maintain the naive belief, which in turn maintains a childish dependence. This destructive dynamic is Innocence's dark side.

Resentment and blame can be directed at all sorts of targets, from corporations to current and former spouses, parents, age, or a bad back. Other candidates include foreigners (illegal aliens are a popular choice), unions, the Internal Revenue Service, the federal government, and either major political party, among others on this endless list.

CONSPIRACY

Sometimes resentment and blame puff themselves up into a theory of large-scale conspiracy. Dave and Miriam, a couple I've known for a long time, subscribed to a conspiracy theory to maintain their financial belief system. They labeled saving "bourgeois." It wasn't only unhip; it was also politically incorrect, for reasons I never quite understood. Although the two of them made less money than I did, they always drove a newer car and lived in a bigger house. They spent every penny they made and borrowed more. Now financial reality was closing in on them as their two children neared college age and they wondered how they'd ever afford tuition.

"When I was younger, I thought by this time in my life I'd have enough to kick back and write a novel. But I don't," Dave told me. "Everybody knows the working stiff can't get ahead. You understand why, don't you?"

"Tell me."

"The Trilateral Commission."

"The Trilateral Commission," I repeated. I wanted to be sure I'd heard right.

"David Rockefeller put it together in the early 1970s to represent the global financial interests of the United States, Japan, and Western

Europe. These guys run the world—and they're the number-one reason why I've worked this hard all my life and I don't have any real money to show for it."

Dave continued his tale, telling me how the two hundred or so corporate leaders who make up the Trilateral Commission set the rules of the economic game and make sure people like him can't accumulate wealth. They had joined forces to ensure that middle-class families remained economic slaves.

Whatever the truth of the Trilateral Commission's power or lack of power in the world's financial markets, Dave was engaging in a classic expression of conspiracy theory. As he saw it, his own lack of success was due to overwhelming outside forces arrayed against him. His belief made him the victim of the actions of a group of people who did their evil deeds at great remove. Dave was subject to their whims, and, as a pawn caught in a global scheme of control, he was powerless to escape its grasp.

Most important, this belief kept him from looking at his own complicity in his situation. With college expenses approaching, Dave found himself financially short for the simple reason that he had failed to plan ahead. He refused to see that. Blaming the Trilateral Commission for all life's ills let him sidestep personal responsibility— and mired him in the dependence that characterizes Innocence.

The Trilateral Commission is only one popular candidate for conspiracy theories. Others include the United Nations, international Zionism, the Masons, and any and all multinational corporations. In each case, the dynamic is the same—holding on to Innocence by laying the fault at the feet of some all-powerful outside force.

OBLIVION AND ADDICTION

Oblivion is the behavioral version of "ignorance is bliss." Some people who practice oblivion do it by simply ignoring money. They act as if money doesn't exist or, at the least, is completely unimportant.

The mother of a client of mine told her when she was a child, "You'll never have much money. It doesn't run in our family." Reacting against this pronouncement, she decided to ignore money and act as if it didn't exist. Better, she thought subconsciously, to turn away from money rather than face the difficult feelings aroused by admitting bad genes of financial incompetence. As a result, even though this woman was quite competent, she was always poor, felt powerless, and failed to cultivate a sense of purpose in her life.

Oblivion plagues the wealthy as well as the poor. I've worked with a number of rich clients who chose to be oblivious to their inheritance, often out of complex feelings of guilt or shame over having so much for doing so little. Often these people express their oblivion through a history of choosing financial advisors distinguished only for their incompetence or fraudulence.

Maria acted as trustee for her elderly mother, whose substantial fortune she would inherit upon her death. I met her briefly as a client when she suffered momentary distrust of the man she had selected as financial advisor in the administration of her mother's sizable assets. Her distrust should have been much more than momentary. Even though this man worked with one of America's top-ranked brokerage firms, his approach was costing Maria and her mother dearly in terms of exorbitant fees and poor planning resulting in high income taxes. (For those of you who are financially knowledgeable, the broker was actively trading stocks, nearly matching the returns of the Standard & Poor's 500 Index. But the active trading meant that Maria's mother was paying taxes neither she nor her estate would have had to pay had the broker simply bought stocks and held on to them.) I laid all this out for Maria and suggested that she find another advisor. She said she'd think about it. When I called a week later to follow up, she said, "I've thought it over and I'm staying with him. He works for the best, and that's good enough for me." Maria paid dearly for her oblivion. By the time her mother died, the estate was worth half of what it should have been, a decline due entirely to incompetent management and Maria's supportive belief system.

Addiction helps in the pursuit of oblivion. The most powerful financial addictions are gambling, overspending (chronic indebtedness), and controlling behavior. One of my clients had a father who excelled at both gambling and controlling behavior, which was driven by a fear that someday somebody would figure a way to take all his money. He kept his poker winnings in cash and stashed them away in safe deposit boxes all over the country. "Don't worry," he told my client, "you and your mother will never have to be concerned about money." Then the father was killed suddenly in a hunting accident when my client was only fifteen. He left no insurance and no list of his many money caches. The funds were never found. In spite of the father's best intentions to care for his family, the son and his mother ended up on welfare.

Clinging to old patterns and habits around money, like gambling and safe deposit boxes full of cash, helps the addict keep from facing the actual poverty of his or her life or relationships. As long as our habits are so firmly in place that they are all we see, we think there's nothing wrong and we never hit bottom. We also never have to do the spadework of adulthood that strengthens and frees us. Other addictions can contribute to this pattern—overeating, alcohol, cocaine, marijuana, even television—all of them contributing to keeping financial reality at arm's length and preventing us from working with money as a set of needed skills. In fact, addictions often arise in response to attitudes about money. One of my clients, who was seriously overweight, connected her eating compulsion with a childhood message: "Buying clothes for you is a waste of money. You'll just gain weight." Understanding the link between belief and behavior, she was able to change her diet. Likewise, attitudes of hopelessness about making enough money have lain at the core of marijuana and alcohol addictions in some of the people I have worked with.

MAGICAL THINKING

Practically everybody knows somebody who believes that it's only a matter of time until the lottery comes up with his or her numbers. The same kind of fantasy wish affects serious investors too. At least once a month I get a call from a current or potential client who has heard about some wonderful new investment scheme with guaranteed monthly earnings of 2 to 10 percent—that works out to an incredible 27 percent to 214 percent per year. These people don't even bat an eye; they assume it's true. They tell me rich people have made money this way forever and someone is finally letting them in on the secret. All they have to do is get in on the ground floor, sit back, and the money will come rolling in, all by itself.

Lotteries and no-risk investments are examples of magical thinking. We exchange all common sense for a fantastical belief that the world will turn in some miraculous manner that rewards us magnificently.

Magical thinking need not be so grandiose as an infusion of huge riches. It can be ordinary or day to day. Mahealani Sapolu's mother's belief that money would appear whenever needed is an example of this ordinary form of magical thinking. Once Mahealani came to understand her own money background better, she was able to see how the magical thinking got in her way.

"Believing that made my family look to someone else for security," she said. "If money just showed up when we needed it, we didn't have to do anything but wait. I could have been out looking for work, trying to make money. Instead, I was sitting around, waiting for the welfare check."

Like all forms of Innocent belief, magical thinking cultivates dependence. It locates the onus for one's condition in the outside world, not in one's own body, heart, and soul.

Bette, originally a seminar student, had held to a New Age belief that money is a flow, she'd always have as much as she needed, and money was something she'd never have to worry about. The belief seemed to work until her husband's business went down in flames and her marriage burned up with it. Bette looked for a new man desperately, took self-improvement classes in everything from rock climbing to fire walking, and hopped from one dead-end job to another. Whether she had a little money or a lot, she spent it all, saying to herself over and over "It's a flow, it's a flow. Let it go, let it go."

Bette was difficult to work with, and I wasn't sure I was getting anywhere with her. Then one day, not long after quitting still another job and coming home yet again to find nothing in her refrigerator and less in her bank account, she came in to see me utterly transformed. During a long weekend that involved plenty of soul-searching and no self-improvement, she had come to understand the pattern of her life from a new perspective.

"My old messages don't work, but I've been holding on to them while I've also been trying to change. It's like cutting off my own legs when I want to walk," she said. "I've been chasing every man I meet trying to find one who'll support me, and all the courses I've been taking tell me it's a flow. That's a crock. What I really need is to learn how to be more intentional about money. I need to be in control, not out of it. I have to learn how to be more practical and measured around money. You've helped me see what's going on psychologically within myself, but I've been ignoring your practical advice about saving and budgeting. It's time for me to pay attention to the practical and get my life in order."

Only when Bette had let go of the belief systems that made her dependent and mired her in magical thinking could she develop the external focus she needed to get her financial house in order. And, in time, she did exactly that.

TRY THIS: OBSERVING THE MOMENT

Meditation is the best technique for learning to let go of habitual thought patterns, because virtually all meditative techniques build on simply letting go of thoughts. Meditation is also ideal for coming to a heightened awareness of unconscious messages about money. The practice of meditation asks us to develop an awareness of all the mental processes occurring inside us moment by moment. After all, the purpose of meditation is to wake up.

If you practice the following meditation anywhere from fifteen minutes to an hour every day, you will find that you are better able both to notice your money messages and to let them go. And you will achieve greater flexibility in all your financial circumstances. But— and this is a big but—if you cling to this goal, your meditation won't go well. Meditation is about learning, among other things, to be open, unobstructed, and clear. Just enjoy the process and let your expectations go. Clinging, as we will learn after the meditation, blocks the path to freedom and leads only to Pain.

MEDITATION: LETTING THOUGHTS GO

Assume a comfortable posture, preferably sitting in a chair with your back straight and feet flat on the floor. Close your eyes. Let your body relax, starting with the soles of your feet and proceeding to the top of your head, freeing yourself of tension. Pay attention to your breath, how it passes in and out of the body, through your nostrils down into your belly and back out.

As you relax, observe the thoughts passing through your mind. Without attaching to any one of them, note how they flit past, like migrating songbirds or cars speeding along the freeway. It is as if they have lives of their own, each one lasting only an instant. Whenever you notice a thought, simply let it go and return to your breath. The next time you notice a thought, let go of it and return gently to the breath without judgment. Continue this practice for at least fifteen minutes at a sitting.

LETTING CLINGING GO

Clinging is the key issue in Innocence. Reality moves past us in its own rapid swirling way, ever changing, ever new. Innocence leads us to ignore the mutable aspect of the real and cling to a false notion of permanence, turning what is into what we believe it must be.

William Blake, the eighteenth-century English mystic poet and artist, understood this fact deeply, as he shows in these exquisite lines:

> *He who binds to himself a joy*
> *Does the winged life destroy;*
> *But he who kisses the joy as it flies*
> *Lives in eternity's sun rise.*

Blake says that holding on to an experience or thought beyond its natural lifetime kills that thought. The key to living fully and deeply is to allow experiences to move through us in their own time while fully aware of each one as it passes. Indeed, we will discover later in our progress through the Seven Stages that letting go of thoughts and allowing feelings to be is key to opening our hearts around money and everything else in life.

While teaching us the passing nature of thoughts, the following meditation also exposes the danger of clinging to Innocence. It is a simple act of focusing on thinking and watching how it progresses.

Once again, assume a comfortable posture and relax yourself from feet to head. The next time a thought comes past, take hold of it. Better yet, if you can think of a profound thought about money, yourself, or this world, grab it. Imagine that you have mental hands. Seize the thought and cling to it past the microseconds of its natural life. See if you can keep the thought with you for a few minutes. Pay attention to what happens inside yourself, particularly to your feelings, as you grab hold and cling to the words.

Whenever I repeat this exercise for myself, I am reminded of important realities about the way our minds work. To begin with, my notion of the profound changes. What happens to my thought is far more profound and fundamental than the thought itself. If the thought were truly profound or if it were really mine, it would stay with me. But in fact it flits away the very moment I think of it. Thoughts last but an instant, and they move through us in infinite variety again and again. One thought can spawn whole multitudes of related thoughts, all of which mirror the original thought. To get the original thought back, I have to repeat it to myself, an action that takes considerable energy. Yet, after a while, I can't relate to the thought any longer. If I cling to the thought itself and not the feeling that underlies it, the thought becomes empty, as if it belongs not to me but to someone else. The longer I hold on to the thought, the more energy this clinging requires, and the more unpleasant it becomes to hold on.

It is the nature of thoughts to arise and pass away instantaneously. Thoughts themselves are already free, yet our clinging nature seeks to imprison them. And, as we discover from this exercise, clinging jeopardizes our freedom because we experience it as suffering or discomfort.

This exercise leaves us with two great teachings about money, ones that we often forget. First, nothing in the world truly belongs to us, not even the thoughts we consider our most profound. Second, greed and miserliness toward what we think of as ours make us uncomfortable. The longer we cling, the more the discomfort heightens toward suffering. We discover how, in the momentary act of clinging, Innocence gives inevitable way to Pain.

chapter 3

PAIN:
THE BELL OF AWAKENING

I wander thro' each charter'd street,
Near where the charter'd Thames does flow,
And mark in every face I meet
Marks of weakness, marks of woe.

In every cry of every Man,
In every Infant's cry of fear,
In every voice, in every ban,
The mind-forg'd manacles I hear.

William Blake

Judas . . . was filled with remorse and took the thirty silver
pieces back. . . . "I have sinned,"
he said . . . And flinging down the silver pieces
in the sanctuary he made off, and went and
hanged himself.

Matthew 27: 1–5

As Mahealani's mother promised, the welfare money always showed up—only there never was enough of it. Clever at stretching dollars and food, the elder Sapolu kept her large family fed for three weeks, sometimes even a day or two longer. Then, with another week to survive till the next check came, it was beg, borrow, steal—or go hungry.

Mahealani's father was too proud for anything but hunger. His stomach growling, he hit the streets looking for work, any work. Sometimes weeks, even months went by before he hooked up with a boat crew in need of a deckhand or a landscaping company wanting another strong back.

"I remember how it was when he came home after a day of looking with no luck, particularly when there was wasn't any food left in the house," Mahealani said. "Something in him was broken. It was like all the sadness in the world came down on his shoulders and he couldn't hold it up anymore. It hurt me to see him like that, a proud man beaten low."

Mahealani's mother made the best she could of a bad situation. Sometimes she borrowed food from a neighbor, with a promise to repay after the first of the month—a promise she always kept. Sometimes she let people know she was in need, and a friend or relation would hear about her predicament and drop off a few fish hooked that morning. And sometimes nothing worked, so the family lived on powdered milk and stale bread from the day-old store for the final few days of the month.

"Then my mother looked the same as my father. All the stuffing just drained out of her," Mahealani said. "She was a strong woman, but being poor was stronger than she was. I could see the humiliation, the shame in her face. I wanted to help her, but there was nothing I could do, I was just a kid. Inside all I felt was hurt, like a fire burning."

It was on a Sunday, the one day of the week his father took off work, that Derrick King first noticed the fatigue written into the older man's face. He was gray, ashen; even the pupils of his eyes lacked color. Derrick wanted him to come outside and play catch in the front yard. When his father said, "No, kiddo, I'm too tired," and reached for the Sunday *Los Angeles Times*, more as shield than reading material, Derrick knew better than to push.

"First I thought, 'Ah, he's just old.' But he was only about forty. Then it hit me. He worked so hard he was always completely shot. He didn't have energy to do anything else, even things he liked, and he liked baseball. I remember thinking 'Is this what it means to work for a living? When I grow up, am I going to have to do the same thing?' This bolt of fear shot through me like lightning."

Not that Derrick's father complained about his lot. He was stoic, laconic, long-suffering. He kept his fatigue and his feelings down, as far out of sight as he could manage.

Emotions were Derrick's mother's role in family dynamics. She cried at movies, funerals, and weddings, while her husband sat silent beside her, his eyes dry. It was clear to Derrick that his parents liked it this way, that they had divided up the psychological territory in a way that made sense to them.

"I think one of the reasons why my father worked so hard was that he wanted to keep my mother's love," Derrick said. "He acted like he felt he was only as lovable as his bank account. My mother didn't demand that he work so hard. She wasn't acquisitive, and she didn't expect him to be wealthy. Yet she took a kind of quiet pride in his steadiness, the way he always brought home a good living."

When Derrick was in his early teens, his maternal grandfather was hospitalized for rheumatic heart disease. He needed open-heart surgery, a then-experimental procedure health insurance wouldn't pay for and the old man couldn't afford on his own. Derrick's mother wanted to help, and she turned to her husband.

"My mother was crying. She was afraid her father would die without the surgery, which cost a medium-size fortune at the time," he recalled. "The emotions were playing across her face, waves of grief, fear, hurt. My dad was doing his stoneface routine, which was all he knew how to do. He was telling her he only had so much money, he could help just a little, he couldn't pay for the surgery all by himself. That made my mother cry harder.

"I could tell what a bad place both my parents were in. My mother needed to help her dad, but she had no money of her own. My father came up against his own limits, and that hurt him. I knew no matter how hard I worked, I could end up in the same spot they were in—unable to do what I felt like I had to do. Then all this deep despair swept over me."

Susanna Swartz's father liked to make her mother beg for money.

"He took some kind of perverse pleasure in having her grovel before him," she told me. "He put her on a household allowance that she always overspent. Then she went to him for more. He had it of course, and she knew he had it. But he wanted to make her beg before he gave it to her. It was a game between the two of them, and it was unholy."

One time Susanna happened across her parents in the garden and watched them from behind a hedge. Her mother, dressed in gardening clothes, was down on her knees, a discarded trowel lying on the flower bed, holding out her now-empty hands like a religious supplicant. Her father stood above his wife, feet wide, arms folded across his chest.

"He was smiling. He always gave her the money, but he wanted to humiliate her first," Susanna said. "My mother was saying 'But I really need the money this time.' My father had this wicked grin on his face. 'Then ask nice,' he said. 'First you have to ask nice.'

"I already knew that women were powerless around money. Now I understood how much it hurt."

The shock of the incident deepened when her parents caught Susanna watching them. Susanna's mother seized her by the upper arm and breathed a threat into her ear: "You say a word about this, and you'll get the spanking to end all spankings."

The humiliation of women around money, and the shame it aroused in her, wasn't the only secret Susanna had to keep. Her mother and father were adamant that she never tell her playmates or school friends how much he made.

"Not that I knew how much money he was really bringing in or what it meant in the scheme of things, so I didn't understand why I had to keep silent about something I totally didn't know," Susanna said. "I had this feeling there was something dark, mysterious, and sinful at the core of our family. It was like one of those Gothic novels where a mad aunt is locked up in the attic and no one in the family dares breathe a word about it.

"Other people wanted the kind of money my family had, yet what I felt was shame and humiliation. It's funny, but inside I felt like the money made me dirty."

Pain is the other half of samsara, the counterbalance to Innocence. Buddhism describes samsara as a cycle, or wheel, that turns from birth to death and possibly to rebirth. This is the realm Buddhists seek to escape, because none of it is free. Samsara arises not from free choice but from habitual responses to suffering.

In the deepest understanding of Buddhism, birth, death, and rebirth are something other than singular events in a historical life. Rather, they occur in every moment of day-to-day existence at an unconscious level. Consider, for example, someone who is addicted to shopping as a response to suffering. Heading out for the next shopping spree feels like birth, while death consists of the mixed feelings—satiation mingled with guilt or shame—that come at the end of the splurge. Rebirth comes on the next trip to the mall.

Where Innocence consists of our belief systems, thoughts, and stories, Pain represents the wild, unbearable, chaotic feelings hooked to these systems, thoughts, and stories—emotions such as envy, greed, desire, frustration, anger, despair, fear, humiliation, boredom, and sadness—that great mass of unpleasant feeling we would just as soon avoid. Attaching these feelings to stories gives us a way of tolerating and explaining them. Because we don't like these troubling emotions and try to push them away, they attach themselves, seemingly permanently and often unconsciously, to our belief systems, thoughts, and stories. Then we go round and round with them, inventing endless variations of the old themes as new money circumstances present themselves.

Suffering is the Buddha's First Noble Truth. His Second Noble Truth is that suffering has a cause—specifically the self clinging to belief systems, thoughts, and stories. Money provides a perfect example of how the Second Noble Truth works. Money is something we measure, and as soon as we become conscious of money, we measure ourselves and others against it, clinging to the notion that our worth depends on money's valuation. Inevitably we suffer, no matter how hard we try to avoid the difficult feelings woven into Pain.

The mastery of Pain begins in noticing difficult feelings rather than trying to avoid them. We begin by separating feelings from stories and recognizing their emotional content as sensations passing through and residing in the body. We do not necessarily resolve our feelings, but we do know what they are, when they arise, and how they differ from thoughts.

MASTERING PAIN: THE PROMISE

In Buddhist monasteries bells are rung to signify the beginnings and ends of portions of the day and, more important, to awaken the monks to what is happening in this one precious moment. Pain does the same. It comes to wake us up; Pain is our bell of awakening.

Whenever Pain rings its bell, we face a choice. We can rush off after some old habit to cling to, like overspending. Or we can move forward into freedom and adulthood. Once we master Pain, learning to hear its ring allows us to choose what we haven't chosen before—action around money that frees rather than imprisons us. Pain tells us that we are out of balance around money. Once we recognize its ring, we can choose to move toward balance—by gathering sources of information about money, for example, getting out pencil and paper or spreadsheet and figuring out our finances, opening our hearts around money, gathering vitality to move forward, and getting financial help in areas where we can't do it ourselves. Or we can fall back into the old pattern of endlessly repeating bad habits around money. Pain hurts, yet it holds the power to wake us up.

A good example of the workings of Pain—and the benefits of mastering it—come from the story of Sherman, a client of mine. Like many of us, Sherman was raised to think money painful and mysterious. Sherman's father added an extra degree of difficulty to this basic lesson.

One day when he was a boy of seven or eight, Sherman went out for a walk with his father, and the two of them stopped at a local convenience store. "Why don't you get yourself some candy?" his father said. Like any kid, Sherman jumped to, found his favorite licorice, unwrapped it, and was chewing happily when his father came to the cash register with the various items he was picking up.

"You have the money to pay for that, don't you?" Sherman's father said, motioning toward the half-eaten licorice.

Sherman didn't have the money. In fact, he'd assumed his father was going to pay. He felt so awful he could barely manage to say "No."

"Wouldn't you know," his father said, turning to the store manager who was running the cash register. "The kid wants candy and he doesn't have the money. He's going to have to come back tomorrow and bring you what he owes. Don't worry, I'll make sure he does it."

And that was exactly what Sherman's father did. Next day he nagged Sherman until the boy walked back to the store and counted out the right price from his own meager store of coins. Sherman hated every moment of the experience. He had expected pleasure and pride, that wonderful feeling spawned by generosity in his father, only to feel cut inside when what had appeared to be a blessing was transformed into a curse.

Similar incidents happened again and again, and not just at the candy counter. Whenever Sherman needed something that cost money, both his mother and his father responded the same way: "What do you think I am—your bank account?" And each time he felt that same humiliation, the same terrible sense that the world didn't have enough for him.

Sherman developed an intense fear around money, which he carried into adulthood. No matter how much he was making or had socked away, Sherman always felt insecure, anxious that some person or accident would pounce on him in the next instant and rob him of his money. Troubled and uncertain in working with others, he constantly worried, felt himself trapped inescapably in the rat race, and habitually overworked—all because of the deep-seated, childhood-rooted anxiety that there would never be enough, that a new round of humiliation by take-away lay just ahead.

"Sometimes I feel like I can't afford to live. When I think about having enough money, the only feeling I get is despair that I'll always fall short," he once said to me.

This difficult emotional predicament softened as Sherman began to explore, notice, and both accept and let go of the physical manifestations of these feelings during crises at work. "The trick for me has been to realize when I'm in a panic or racing around or frustrated or angry. When I notice that, I pause for a minute, recognizing my confusion. Then I remind myself of what I want to do or who I want to be. I might tell myself how I need to learn a particular task and get clear on the process, whereas a moment earlier I was confused. Or I might remind myself that I'm with other people. I used to see my coworkers as just job performers like myself, caught in the rat race; to me they weren't like real people. Now I want to be more open to who they are. Or I might just tell myself to get to work. Often I feel a touch of the humiliation or shame I experienced as a child, and I remind myself that that was then and this is now—and this is different. Reframing my emotions this way has improved my life at work."

This new feeling of mastery came to Sherman because, in our work together, he had opened himself up to the feelings planted during his childhood. He didn't find the process easy, but he did find it rewarding.

"At first I thought you were crazy for wanting me to contact my childhood Pain, to name my feelings and then feel them," he told me later. "When I really got into it, I was convinced you were crazy—at least for the first couple of weeks. I was angry with you 'cause I felt woozy and unsure of myself, as if I were going backward, not forward. Then I realized these feelings were telling me something about my situation that I needed to face up to and change. The anxiety, the rat race, the feeling of never enough—I thought all this was the way the world is and there was nothing I could do about it. I put it all out there rather than inside myself. By taking the feelings back, I've become a different person, more at peace with myself.

"It sounds crazy, doesn't it—more at peace from feeling the Pain. But that's the truth of the matter."

Like Sherman, you too can learn to became both more peaceful and more successful by noticing painful feelings and learning not to respond in old habitual ways. The payoff is enormous. Rather than shutting down, getting confused, making serious financial mistakes, launching an eating or spending binge, or reaching for a beer whenever difficult feelings arise, we can learn to see unpleasant emotion as a sign that it's time to come back to balance, to get to work—to make use of the skills we will learn more about in the upcoming chapters on Knowledge, Understanding, and Vigor.

Working on Pain helps address a number of problems around money:

- If economic differences between you and others bring up feelings of guilt, envy, or sadness so powerful that you lose your ease and presence of mind.
- If you feel pain or alienation in regard to your work situation.
- If you are one of those who feel caught in the rat race.
- If your life is marked by frequent bouts of money anxiety and money worry.
- If you find yourself shutting down when financial responsibilities like taxes, budgets, bills, mortgages, insurance, and jobs arise.

As you work on your own issues of Pain, you will find yourself able to get to work and accomplish your objectives around money. For example, you will discover that you can learn information about money you used to resist, feel more open and kind in situations that once got your goat, and experience energy to move forward in areas where formerly you felt at a loss. Indeed, you will be able to make more money, enjoy a greater sense of purpose in your life, and give more generously.

We will approach our work on Pain in two ways. First, I will help you see and identify the stories and patterns to which you attach difficult feelings. We will begin by exploring patterns in general. Then, building on the exercises in chapter 2, you will explore your own particular patterns of Pain, discovering how you get hooked in ways that are difficult to give up. Next, I'll share exercises that help you recognize painful feelings as sensations in the body and come to a place of ease around them. Once recognized for what they are, feelings, like thoughts, can be released and let go.

THE SOURCES OF PAIN

Everyone I know—every last person, bar none—feels or has felt similar Pain around money issues. Gender doesn't matter, nor does race, social class, or even poverty versus wealth. All of us have felt the Pain of standing defeated before the dollar.

As we grow out of the dependency of early childhood, we confront the difficult realities of living in a family and the larger world beyond our homes. In the process we encounter money as a faceless alien force whose great power rules our lives. Typically, these childhood encounters with the Pain of money are sharp, harsh, and sudden. They center on three basic kinds of experience.

The first has to do with the discovery of economic differences in the world, the difficult realization that arises when we understand we are richer than some people and poorer than others. I discovered this after sixth-grade Christmas, when I told my friend, the coal miner's son, about the gifts I had received, and he burst into tears at being given only a deck of cards.

This same Pain, but with the roles reversed, came up again and again during my teenage years, particularly whenever I heard the car songs, like the Beach Boys' "Little Deuce Coupe," that lauded the car-centered culture of the late 1950s and early 1960s. These songs centered on cars, but I knew what they were really about—girls, and how to get them. I didn't have the money to buy a car, so I felt as if I had little chance to meet and win the girl of my dreams. I resented my own poverty, and I resented the boys who came from families rich enough to buy cars and get girls. I resented girls too for responding to a symbol as shallow as eight cylinders sheathed in two-tone and chrome. This Pain of mine sprang from the same source as my Christmas gifts' emotional effect on the coal miner's son—the emotional realization that some people had more money than I did.

This source of Pain continues when we grow up. In fact, economic differences are central in most painful experiences around money, such as struggles against corporations, job situations, and money conflicts within intimate relationships. Even as adults, few of us can honestly say that an acquaintance's financial resources have no emotional import for the relationship.

The second primal source of Pain, one typically encountered in adolescence, arises in the understanding that either we will have to work for a living or we will have to secure money by other means—manipulation, inheritance, marriage, perhaps even crime. We encounter a shocking understanding that we will be paid not for who we are or what we want to accomplish in the world but for doing what someone else wants. Power drains from our souls. Despair at losing freedom itself and the freedom of our time saps our energy and diminishes our sense of self-worth. Feeling enslaved to the dollar, we question our integrity.

Like the Pain of economic differences, this source of hurt doesn't get better with time. More than twenty-five years out of college, perhaps a quarter of my classmates have told me they would rather be writing a novel than working for a living (and losing their emotional self-possession in the process). Many people I've talked with—from young people in their twenties and thirties to the aging Baby Boomers of my own generation—feel trapped by money. It may be that money holds them in a job they dislike, or perhaps it binds them in a relationship that guarantees a living yet comes with a price tag. In my workshops, woman after woman has told of the Pain of feeling as a girl that her only access to money lay in manipulating her father and then reexperiencing the Pain by repeating the pattern with a husband. Always one down around dollars, these women felt trapped and, as a result, sacrificed their integrity to win the money they needed.

One of the most profound, and difficult, stories connecting money with manipulation and entrapment was told to me by a young woman named Sophia. Her story, awful as it is, is all too commonplace.

When Sophia first came to see me, she was cross and querulous, complaining all the time that she wasn't getting enough money from her father. She seemed overly dependent on him for money, and she was clearly angry with him for making her feel dependent, typically by being haphazard and unpredictable in distributing money from a trust fund of which Sophia was a beneficiary. Sophia didn't make much on her own. She was dedicated to nonprofit and nonpaying occupations with organizations that espoused radical political views. She even condoned revolutionary violence under certain circumstances, and, speaking the language of oppressor versus oppressed, she was ever searching for truth and justice.

Since Sophia appeared unable to separate from her dependence on her father and the trust fund, I saw my task as strengthening her self-esteem around money. We had been following this tack awhile when one day, after a long bout of complaining about her predicament, she relaxed. Not thinking and wanting to lighten the mood, I bantered, "Well, despite all the bad stuff that went on in your family, at least you weren't abused."

Sophia didn't think the line was funny at all. She trembled for a moment, suddenly changed the subject and announced how angry she was at her mother. Then she blurted out, "From the time I was twelve till I went away to school at fifteen, my father abused me."

Now we both understood better what was going on. Even though Sophia's father had never explicitly used the money to keep her quiet, he impressed on her the lesson "If you're a good girl, you'll get money"—and good girls, of course, don't tell about the nasty things their fathers did to them. If she wanted money, Sophia had to bear the guilt, shame, and humiliation of being a victim of abuse all by herself. This connection of terrible, painful emotion with the money she needed to live on held Sophia in a crushing emotional trap.

Later, through work we started together and that she continued with a counselor, Sophia gave up all emotional investment in "her" trust-fund money and learned to recognize her painfully charged feelings toward money. This enabled Sophia to see clearly for the first time who she was as a person and what she wanted out of life. Even as she was acknowledging her feelings, she confronted her family over her father's abuse and launched legal action to secure her rights in the trust fund. Sophia also took her first real job, which gave her a feeling of independence from the tainted money her father doled out in unpredictable dollops. Having opened herself to career possibilities and issues of life purpose she was unable to look at before, Sophia is now preparing herself for law school. By reengaging the difficult feelings attached to money in her childhood, Sophia can now go forward into the world of finance as an adult.

The third source of childhood Pain around money comprises any of a list of difficult emotions. Sometimes Pain manifests as envy. One sibling saves money for a bicycle and buys it. The sibling without a bike, whose money has been frittered away on candy and soda, turns green because he doesn't have a shiny new Schwinn like his brother or sister.

Childhood Pain may turn on perfidy, treachery, or betrayal. A woman in one of my workshops told of a horrible episode when her mother, as usual, overspent the household allowance and didn't have any money left for groceries. She solved the dilemma by handing each of her children a hammer and ordering them to break their piggy banks and bring her the money.

"She never paid us back either," the woman said, hands shaking and voice wavering. "I'd been saving nickels, dimes, and quarters for years. It was mine and she stole it."

Her sense of personal violation and betrayal, even decades later, was palpable. She grew into an adult who couldn't trust anyone around money. She argued the price of everything and hired and fired investment managers the way other people change socks.

Adulthood contains its own sources of Pain. We learn, for example, that doing the right thing doesn't always work. You can be an ace at your job and still get laid off when a corporate merger makes you redundant. Marriages often fracture around money, as finances become a battlefield in which partners blame their personal pain on the other rather than seeing its source within themselves. Soaring or unexpected taxes, uninsured losses, divorce, lawsuits over money, soured investments, mortgage or rent increases all entail Pain. We may feel that no matter how hard or long we work, money anxieties never cease. In our despair it seems as if we've gotten nowhere. Then we discover that death is waiting for us and in the end our wealth won't do us any good. So what has all this hard work been for?

THREE STORIES

The question is an important one. And, I am certain, it has but one answer: We have to learn to mature around money. Here are three more stories illustrating the way Pain takes root during childhood and expresses itself as dysfunctionality in adulthood. They also show how useful recognizing Pain's feelings can be.

Patricia came from a wealthy Filipino family that lived in Vietnam, lost all its money during the war, and dispersed throughout Asia following the fall of Saigon. Patricia's mother had married an American, who aban-

69

doned her and her small daughter within weeks of bringing them to the States. Faced with a desperate situation, Patricia's mother took the only work she could find, in the sweatshops of Los Angeles, where she was known by her number, thirty-seven, not her name. Patricia and her mother were so poor that Patricia had to make one blouse last all year. Her mother washed, dried, and ironed it every night and patched the fabric whenever it became torn or worn.

Patricia knew the teachers and students looked at her askance for wearing the same clothes day in and day out. She compensated for her embarrassment at her poverty by deciding to show them up. Patricia excelled in school. A straight-A student, she caught the attention of a teacher who arranged for her to spend a summer on scholarship at an exclusive camp for rich kids in the mountains near Lake Arrowhead.

Some of the children at the camp got their kicks by stealing on a dare. Patricia saw this curious social custom as an opportunity both to get in with new friends and to replace the one blouse she was stuck with. She and her camp friend Molly shoplifted clothes from the expensive tourist shops in the resort towns around the lake. It all went well until the day Molly was caught. Patricia was already out of the store, but Molly turned her in.

Sitting in the police station, Patricia looked up to see Molly's well-to-do mother staring in her face, then turning to her daughter. "That's the last time I ever let you hang out with trash again," the woman said.

That comment stung Patricia in a way that nothing in her impoverished life had before. It produced a fierceness, a chip-on-the-shoulder attitude that impressed me about Patricia the first time I met her. She was successful in her work as a marketing executive, but she had never quite made the top tier she felt she should have. When she told me how the shoplifting experience with Molly had affected her, she said she would never forget being called trash.

"But how has that made you feel?" I asked her.

"I hate rich people!" she responded instantaneously.

As Patricia and I examined her career and explored this very clear feeling, it became obvious that although Patricia had done nearly as well at work as at school, she had let opportunity after opportunity to work with the largest, wealthiest clients slip by. The reason was clear: her ancient rage. Since coming to this realization, Patricia has advanced in her work. When the old feeling of hatred arises, she has learned to recognize it but no longer to respond to it. No longer does it dominate her. She notices the feeling, lets it go, and gets on with what she needs to do. Slowly the feelings, which remain present and can still make her flinch, have lessened. Her life with money has become more at ease and more successful.

Lucy grew up in a family that bounced from rags to riches and back, again and again. One year she and her family were living overseas in a poor country, where they had a house with servants in a posh neighborhood. The next, her father was waiting his turn in the unemployment line back home in the United States. Once her family lost its home when the bank repossessed the property for default on the mortgage. "Nothing you can do," her father said. "If they want to, they can take your home. One dollar is like $100 to those leeches."

Lucy's painful feelings around her family's ups and downs hit a peak when she was sixteen. Her father was doing well at the time, and he bought Lucy a car. She used the vehicle not only to get to her job as a babysitter for a wealthy family but to take the children to their country club for swimming and tennis. Then came the day when Lucy's father's car broke down and he had to use Lucy's to get to work, dropping Lucy off at the wealthy family's home on his way into the city.

"So, where's your car?" the children's mother demanded when Lucy came into the house.

"My dad's using it to get to work. His car wouldn't start."

The woman was livid. "How dare you show up here without your car! Just how do you think you're going to get my children to the club? And who does your father think we are to slight us like this. The impertinent fool!" She turned on her heel, leaving Lucy dripping with her splattered venom.

In the aftermath of that experience, set against the backdrop of her family's many economic ups and downs, Lucy felt confused, used, humiliated. She vowed always to look richer than she was. As an adult she was a dedicated and habitual overspender who, by the time we met, was in way over her head in credit card debt. Conventional wisdom about the need for a budget didn't sway her. Only when she admitted and accepted the load of envy, sadness, and humiliation she had been carrying since childhood could Lucy begin to get her financial house in order. Now she is living a genuine economic life rather than a life of pretense, and she has come to terms with the hard fact of financial differences.

Reggie's mother made his clothes. They were nice and they fit well, but they were out of style. Reggie took his unstylish garb as just one more sign of the poverty that plagued his family, like the dull stupid jobs they all worked. It was tempting to steal to get extra cash, except that he took from his grandfather. When his brother was caught for the theft, Reggie never owned up to his own role in taking the money. Still, he could not escape the guilt he felt at stealing, the shame at being poor.

As an adult, Reggie felt his own job to be drudgery of the sort his family had always had to accept. The difference was that Reggie, as a manager in a manufacturing plant, was making considerably more money than anybody in his family had ever brought home. His success didn't make him feel better. Rather, he felt guilt at doing better, as if he didn't deserve it. It was almost as if he were stealing from his grandfather again.

The core of Reggie's issue with his work wasn't the job itself. His guilt and shame were keeping him from getting even further ahead and from experiencing any joy or pleasure in his work. As Reggie slowly opened himself to all his feelings, he realized that he actually enjoyed aspects of his work and that he was getting in his own way. He set himself three goals: to make his job more enjoyable every year, to get paid more as well, and to find ways to bring some generosity and joy into his family of origin.

BELITTLED BEFORE MONEY

Whatever source it comes from, Pain reduces personal power and self-esteem. At the core of each experience of Pain lies a message to weaken even the strongest soul: "You are nothing. Money is everything. Before it, you count for less than dust on a windy day." This message—that, compared to money, we have no value—is the marrow of Pain.

A student in one of my workshops told me about her early childhood: "One of my first memories is my mother saying she couldn't afford me. My parents were very young when they got married, and my mother became pregnant accidentally, when they didn't have any money. Sometimes when I was growing up, I'd hear my parents fighting after I went to bed and they thought I was asleep. My father would slip into these rages around money, how he wasn't being paid enough and he was always short. I felt really bad about that. I figured basically it was my fault."

This young woman considered herself personally worthless. Every time her parents fought over money, she felt that she, their unplanned and unaffordable child, was the cause of all the hurt. Only if she had not been born, she thought, her parents' impoverished paradise would have lasted forever. By the time she grew up, her self-esteem could be measured in negative numbers.

This diminishment of the childhood self before money has powerful results when we reach our adult years. Tahira Hira of Iowa State University has conducted empirical research on the relationship between low financial self-esteem and money problems. She found that individuals in financial trouble saw themselves as insecure, unable to do anything well, worthless, and afraid of success. Some also reported depression, and over half of the people studied considered themselves impulsive or compulsive gamblers. Hira's findings are consistent with other studies revealing that shopping addicts are trying to compensate for low self-esteem or a burden of unexpressed feelings.

Ideally, Pain is addressed directly in childhood, but, as so often happens, we carry these experiences into adulthood. Recovering the self-esteem lost in childhood depends on facing our feelings and then developing our skills in the three stages of adulthood. Without accomplishing this task, we are doomed to repeat the same unpleasant experiences of failure, entering again and again into the same old Pain.

THE CYCLE OF PAIN AND INNOCENCE

As we grow out of childhood and the original wholeness of Innocence fades, we take up beliefs regarding money as a way of holding on to what we are losing. Beliefs allow us to cling to an idea of the world as it should be. Of course the world isn't the way we would like; it sends us continuous, disturbing, even tragic reminders that it is something other than what we imagine and wish. Pain is our Innocence beseiged—the disjunction between what we want to believe out of our desire to cling to childhood and the reality we must confront.

Mahealani Sapolu wanted desperately to believe that the world was as beneficent and trustworthy as her mother made it out to be—despite the periodic hunger that told her otherwise. Her Innocence required belief in a kinder, gentler cosmos. Then she saw the hurt and fatigue in her father's face when he spent day after difficult day pounding the pavement for jobs that always seemed to go to someone else. She witnessed too the frustration that overtook her mother when the last of the money ran out and there was nothing to eat but powdered milk and day-old bread. The discovery that the world was treating her parents—and, by implication, herself—more harshly than she believed it should caused Mahealani deep, shocking Pain.

Mahealani did what we all do when we encounter Pain. She built a new, Innocent belief to counter it. She made a vow: "I told myself when I grew up, I'd never live like this, hand to mouth, not knowing where the next meal was coming from."

Clinging to that belief laid the groundwork for another cycle of Innocence and Pain. Married, on her own, and committed to never ending up as short as her parents did month after month, Mahealani borrowed and borrowed and borrowed. In credit cards she found a money source to ensure that she didn't have to live the way her parents had. She failed to notice that the money bore a huge price tag. Someday it would have to be paid back, along with a heavy burden of interest. In her Innocence, Mahealani ignored that fact, until the day Ricky came home shaken by the bill collector's visit and she realized the financial implications of her own pregnancy without health insurance. Now she experienced a new Pain created by her current round of Innocence.

Precisely the same cycle appears in Derrick King's story. On that Sunday when he recognized the fatigue in his father's face from endless hard weeks at work, a shock of terror went through him. He felt himself pale before the need to make money, and he understood the cost this demand exacted on his father. Yet he saw too that his mother and father loved one another and how the one's hard work was rewarded with the other's affection. Innocently he believed that work brings love. Then a second emotional shock hit when he came to terms with his father's inability to pay for open-heart surgery. Derrick saw the commitment he had to make: "I knew then that, for all my father's work, there was a limit to what he could do. I told myself I was going to have to do even better."

Like Mahealani, Derrick took a vow. Like Mahealani, he too set the stage for a new cycle of Innocence and Pain.

Derrick, in fact, did better than his father, rising in the personal computer industry to a well-compensated management position. True to his background, he was a decent man with a reputation for being results-oriented but fair and even-handed. The work side of Derrick's life was a clear success. It was at home that the new round of Pain began. He expected in his Innocence that his career and financial success should guarantee him his wife's love and affection, but it hadn't. She resented his tight control of family finances, and, with no career of her own, she was growing increasingly frustrated over her feelings of economic powerlessness. Derrick worried too that he never made sufficient contact with his sons. He feared that they would be grown up and out of the house before he ever really knew them. This Pain was keeping him up at night, turning inside him like a cold knife, gutting his Innocence.

Susanna Swartz came to blame money itself for the degradation and humiliation her mother had to endure. Although she distrusted her father, she felt she needed to love him, even when he made her mother grovel. Yet, as a young woman herself, Susanna identified more closely with her mother, and it caused her Pain to see her mother down on her knees begging for money. If money could do that to people like her, Susanna wanted nothing to do with it. In Innocence, she turned away from money, indicting it as the cause of such suffering.

Her beliefs were reinforced by the need to keep secrets about her mother's humiliation and her father's wealth. Money forced people to their knees; it stripped them of their right to speak. In the Pain of these revelations, Susanna sought escape into Innocence. She said to me, "My father's god was money, and I could see the awful gifts this god demanded. I knew money wasn't for me."

Each of these three lives—indeed, all of our lives—reveals this constant cycling between Pain and Innocence. Some experience shocks us deeply, cuts our current Innocence to the core, sends Pain through us.

In response, we build new belief systems that we hope and pray will hold us safe against the feelings we have just experienced. Then a new Pain strikes, different from the first one but equally destructive, equally excrutiating. And again we create a new Innocence, once more setting the stage for Pain, the two joined together by the hinges of the vows and commitments we make.

Money is not the issue here. Instead the issue is the way we react to Pain and cling to Innocence, a mental recycling that we do unconsciously to ourselves in the realms of samsara.

The cycle of Pain and Innocence is a habitual response that feels natural to the untutored mind of a child. But it enslaves us in samsara and holds us back from our true freedom. Deep inside each of us lies a uniqueness, a bodhicitta, a mind of awakening, a special and irreplaceable nature that longs to be free. All too often we lose this uniqueness, binding it under the layers of fear, resentment, blame, and regret spawned in every round of Innocence and Pain's constant cycle. We long to fly free, yet we chain ourselves fast to the ground.

When this reality hits me full in the face, I think of William Blake, who described the cycle of Innocence and Pain eloquently in his *Songs of Innocence* and *Songs of Experience*. I conjure an image of him walking the streets of eighteenth-century London and paying, as poets do, observant attention to the face of each person he passes. He understands where the Pain he sees comes from:

> *In every cry of every Man,*
> *In every Infant's cry of fear,*
> *In every voice, in every ban,*
> *The mind-forg'd manacles I hear.*

We bind ourselves, Blake says, with handcuffs forged by the workings of our own minds. We look to money as the cause, but we are pointing the wrong way. The root of it all lies within us.

TRY THIS: YOUR LIFE IN MONEY—PAIN

Advance your financial autobiography by adding to it the Pain you have experienced around money. Essentially, Pain covers the same ground as Innocence, but from the perspective of feelings and emotions rather than beliefs and thoughts.

Go back and review what you wrote about Innocence following these steps. First, take all the messages, stories, and belief systems you uncovered in chapter 2 and identify the feelings associated with them. Second, see if you can find patterns of feeling associated with thoughts that have repeated themselves in your life and thus constitute ongoing cycles of Innocence and Pain. See if you can understand how the story and the feeling get linked to each other—what's the glue binding the one to the other? Does it have anything to do with a process of identification, of taking things personally as "I, me, and mine."? What are the financial and personal consequences of your identification? Are you ready to let these structures go?

You can use these further questions to help guide your memory-plumbing and writing:

What are the feelings attached to your three earliest memories of money: elation, satisfaction, humiliation, shame, guilt?

When and how did money first enter your relationship with your mother? How did it change the emotional tone between the two of you?

When and how did money first enter your relationship with your father? How did it change the emotional tone between the two of you?

When you heard family stories about money, what feelings arose in you: pride, joy, fear, resentment, blame, guilt, shame?

What feelings did your mother express toward money?

What feelings did your father express toward money?

What form did your worry about money take?

Look at the list of one-sentence lessons you learned about money while growing up (e.g., "Money makes the world go round," "A fool and his money are soon parted," and "All that glitters is not gold"). What feelings arose in you when you heard these lessons? What feelings arise in you now as you read them?

What were your first money experiences with cars, houses, insurance, stocks, bonds, lawyers, brokers or financial planners, legal papers, and banks? What feelings are attached to them?

When did you first discover that you were richer than some people and poorer than others? How did that discovery feel?

When did you realize that you were going to have to work for a living, marry money, angle for a big inheritance, or lie and steal your way to wealth? Or have you given up on money out of resentment or despair?

As you were growing up, did you ever make a vow about money ("I'm going to do better than he did," "I'll never let that happen to me," "Someday I'll have piles and piles of money and they'll have to respect me")? What incident gave rise to these vows? What feelings flowed through you at the time? How long did you keep repeating those vows? Did your feelings change over time in relation to the vows? What feelings come up in you now as you recall these incidents and the vows you made?

Pain belongs to the present as well as the past. Think about these further questions pertaining to Pain in the present:

How has Pain around money hurt your life and caused suffering?

What difficult feelings do you experience about money in your current life?

How do you feel when you:

Watch a TV commercial for luxury cars, say, or mutual funds?

Are solicited for a contribution by a charitable group?

Walk into an auto dealership and a salesperson confronts you?

Negotiate who pays for dinner, the movie, theater tickets?

Have to go shopping for groceries, clothes, a new pair of glasses?

Find a pink slip on your desk at work?

Realize you'll have to turn to welfare or food stamps?

Consider the financial consequences of divorce or your children's education?

THE STONE OF SUFFERING

The beliefs, thoughts, and stories of Innocence are like a great stone we feel we simply must push up a hill. We push and shove this immense rock, sweating every inch of the way. We act as if weight equaled meaning, and we are attached to this meaning. We cling to it, afraid to let go even when the stone breaks free and rolls back over us, causing immense Pain. We push again and again up the hill despite repeated disappointments. Each time we start over again we give the stone a different meaning, making each fresh attempt a new project, a new adventure, a new heaven. Then the stone falls back on us yet again.

We cling to Innocence's great stone because the beliefs it represents express some essential aspect of life, something we fear to lose. Yet inevitably the stone tumbles back downhill and crushes us beneath it, re-creating Pain's hurtful presence. Still, we don't give up and try something truly new. We find a new handhold on Innocence and heave our shoulders into the same stone yet again.

Clinging to the stone with its repeated rolls through Innocence and Pain isn't like touching a hot stove. The physical pain of being burned sends an important lesson: Don't do that again. And we don't. From that point on, we check stoves before putting our hands on them.

Pain is different. There is something so seductive about the emotions attached to a given story that we never learn to let go of it. As soon as we identify with Pain and attach it to our stories, our lives feel dramatic. No matter how much sorrow we suffer, we cling—which initiates suffering, the price we pay for feeling the drama.

To our childlike minds, Innocence represents divine secrets, some quality of being held, cared for, and recognized even in the face of forces as impersonal as money. Innocence feels as if it is who we are. It is freighted with our identities, with everything that makes up I, mine, and me. If we let go, we fear we will lose our very selves.

Yet clinging is the source of suffering. Suffering occurs when clinging hooks the stories and beliefs of Innocence to the physical feelings of Pain. Until we awaken, we are condemned to doing the same old thing again and again, spending our lives repeating forever the very same pattern of suffering.

The cycle of Pain and Innocence represents the suffering of samsara, what Christians call Hell. The poet William Blake named it experience, and Shakespeare made this ever-turning wheel the twirling force of tragedy. The reality is the same: Either we go round and round forever, pushing the stone up the hill repeatedly, or we awaken and learn not to cling to the stone.

HELL AND THE HUMAN CONDITION

One of the gifts I received from my mother was a lasting appreciation for Christian mysticism. Lately I have been rereading Dante's *Divine Comedy*, a work she introduced me to. Besides being a superb artistic achievement, the poem offers an insightful look at the many layers of the human self. The first section of the poem, titled *Inferno*, is the poet's portrayal of the human condition of suffering, the world of sin, all the problematic aspects of the reality we are born into. Guided by Virgil, the great Roman poet, Dante journeys down through the layers of Hell, meeting group after group of lost souls damned for various sins, until he reaches the underworld's lowest point. There he discovers those who have been condemned for eternity because they had committed the most grievous sin of all, a wrong even more horrific than acts of violence: treachery and betrayal.

Dante wasn't writing directly about money in *Inferno*, but he could have been. In placing treachery and betrayal at the center of sin and suffering, he understood how we get ourselves into a predicament where all hell breaks loose and Pain lasts forever. In the very interweaving of Innocence and Pain, we betray our own beings and give ourselves away. Like the lost souls in Hell's deepest, hottest pit, we have betrayed who we are. And money often provides the setting.

The discovery that we will have to work for a living—a revelation we acknowledge as we approach adulthood—ignites the painful fear that we need to trade our souls for money. We start to feel like Judas, who has sold the best part of himself for a pittance and realizes, too late, what a bad deal he made. It is an experience I myself know all too well.

When I graduated from Harvard, I knew I had to do something to make a living, but the very idea of taking a job filled me with Pain. My Innocent impression of work came from my childhood vision of my father. To my childish eyes he looked to be chained to the dining room table, hard at the work of "making money," while outside the breeze blew fresh and the sun shone gloriously. Doing the same sort of thing felt like giving over to death, a betrayal of myself to the forces of darkness. After all, I had majored in English literature. I knew how to read books. I loved sharing ideas. I had a soul, and I wasn't about to sacrifice it in any pursuit as unfulfilling as a "job."

When I married, my wife and I made a deal. First she would support me for two years, while I pursued my writing and artwork and studied the soul. Then I would return the favor.

I loved those two years. Inspired by Blake and Dante, I worked diligently on my own epic poem, accumulating five hundred amateurish but committed pages of storyline and character sketch. I drew and painted and exhibited my art in small shows. I studied world religions and dedicated myself to contemplative practices. I felt myself growing inside, like a plant turning spring rain into leaf and flower.

Then my time ran out. My two years were up, and my wife claimed her half of the bargain. Again I faced the demand of earning money. The old suffering came back in all its agony. I was clinging to my belief in work-as-torture, and I suffered in every fiber of my being at the thought of entering that death-filled world.

Maybe I could be a farmer, I thought, and raise organic vegetables half time and use the other half of my days to write, paint, and study. My father took me out to meet a farmer he knew who worked one of the hollows in the hill country surrounding our hometown. This old man had a hard leathery face and horny hands that, no matter how hard he scrubbed, could never lose all the dirt ground into them.

"How many hours a week do you work?" my father asked.

"Don't know. Never thought about it," he said. "When the sun's coming up, I'm already working. When it's going down, I'm still working. What that's add up to?"

Somehow his answer didn't make farming seem quite like an easy job with plenty of free time. And there was more. As we were leaving the farm, my father said to me, "How old do you think he is?"

"Close to seventy," I said. "Maybe more."

My father laughed. "He's five years younger than me. I'm fifty-three."

The death of my farmer fantasy occasioned a new round of agonizing suffering. My mother came up with an idea.

"You've always been a whiz at math," she said. "Why don't you study accounting and do people's taxes?"

I looked at her as if she were crazy. Accounting? Taxes? What could be farther from my soul? But she was serious.

"You'd only have to work part of the year, from January through the middle of April," she said. "Then you could do your writing, art, and study the rest of the time."

At first, the very thought of accounting made me cold inside. It was too close to what my father did as a lawyer—which, in my Innocence and Pain, I feared deeply—and it was too far from the artistic and spiritual pursuits I considered my heart work. I was afraid that if I followed that route, I would somehow lose my own life. Yet I faced a reality: I had to make a living and hold up my end of the bargain with my wife. Reluctant and suffering, I signed up for graduate accounting classes. Soon I was doing taxes—unhappily—for professors I had known at Harvard.

When I look back at this time of my life, I both chuckle at my Innocence and Pain and relive the suffering I felt in cycling back and forth between them. The painful reality I faced was one all of us must deal with: anxiety, confusion, and despair over how I was going to make a living. I had no wealth of my own, no rich relatives to inherit from, and no skills to use in earning money. My choices were find work, starve, or take welfare.

Rather than face the difficult feelings confronting me, I clung to two deeply held and highly personal beliefs. The first was the notion that a job meant losing my own life. It seemed to me inevitable that if I signed on to the world of work, I would end up in some horrific prison of my own making.

This particular Innocence is commonplace, a belief many of us hold on to. A student in one of my workshops put it this way: "My father taught me I had to work in order to have a life. What mattered was what happened outside the job. It never occurred to me that I could make my job *part* of my life." I felt the same way. Life was one thing; accounting was something quite different, more like dying than living. Surrendering to the need to make a living via accounting was like digging my own grave and jumping in.

This particular Innocence was connected deeply to the second belief I clung to. I was convinced that my relationship with my soul was just fine. I knew what fed me—literature, art, and spiritual practice. Making money got in the way. It ate up time and took away energy. My heart wasn't the issue. Money was.

Blame and resentment boiled in me. Life shouldn't have to be like this, I told myself. It was the fault of society, government, big corporations. In a way I blamed money itself, for getting in between me and my soul.

This separation of money from soul—the Innocent belief by which we make the two distinct and different—is right at the core of Pain. Yet the truth of the matter is that our feelings of Pain around money have nothing to do with the nature of money itself. Instead, they arise from the way we address meaning in our lives. Pain tells us that we are pulled in two directions, like a person standing with one foot on a dock and the other in a drifting rowboat. We are stretched between the demands and realities of the outside world on the one side and the needs and wants of our inner selves on the other. Our relationship to money is a projection of our relationship to our souls. Pain is a sure sign that we are divorced from our souls and projecting our own lack of meaning onto money. We are evading the central purpose of our lives—to deal directly with our own deep selves, to gather strength to develop skills, to become better people. Instead of confronting the issue of connecting our souls meaningfully to the world of money, we use blame and resentment to support our Innocence—and, with it, our Pain.

SEX, MONEY, AND MEANING

Given the intimacy of our painful experiences around money, it is hardly surprising to realize that money and sex are profoundly interwoven. Both money and sex arise as powerful issues during adolescence and early adulthood, the period of life when our identities are most in flux and formation. Although both sex and money attract us, they are laden too with longing and Pain. In fact the chakra, or energy center, associated with the Pain of money is the sexual chakra. The Pain around both is so intense that sex and money are the two most common causes of divorce. They are also frequent subjects of internal fantasy and thought. Remarkably, we actually think about money more than sex.

Since 1972 *Money* magazine has been conducting its "Having It All Survey," an annual nationwide opinion poll on what Americans are feeling, thinking, and doing about money. The findings are revealing. In 1997 respondents said they thought more about money than sex by a margin of 47 percent to 19 percent (up from 44 percent and 16 percent in 1996). This means that by a ratio of almost 2.5 to 1, Americans put concerns about money ahead of concerns about sex. How can this be?

In a profound way, money concerns intimacy more than sex does. It speaks to our relationship both with ourselves—in terms of identity and purpose in the world—and with others—in terms of family, love, and friendship. Respondents in the *Money* survey rank money ahead of sex not because they are craven slaves to materialism and acquisition but because it connects their inner space to the world at large.

Money is the critical link between the interior and the exterior. If we have a poor relationship with money, it is likely we also have a poor relationship with our inner beings. When I was a young man considering accounting and telling myself that my soul was just fine while money was the problem, I was engaging in self-deception. I had a problem with money because I had a problem with my inner self and its mode of connection to the outer world.

I have guided countless clients toward a more healthy relationship with money by helping them see that their Pain around money arises from unmet intimacy needs, from a thwarting of the drive within us that creates identity, purpose, and family and connects to the world at large. The more these needs are unmet, the more Pain we feel around money.

Many people pursue what they think is a logical solution to the problem—they earn more money. This, though, can lead to a new issue: The obsession around earning grows so great that money becomes a substitute for intimacy. All the fears of childhood are left unresolved, and they manifest themselves in a never-ending pursuit of money in a world where everyone is alienated from everyone else.

FILLING THE HOLE

Whenever I am speaking to an audience, I ask, "How many of you live within five minutes of where you were born and raised?" If it is a national group, such as a professional conference for financial planners, no more than one out of ten people will raise their hands. Even in a local audience, the number has never exceeded one in four. America is a nation of the rootless, a country of people constantly picking up and moving on.

We have lost much of family and community and the sense of place, belonging, and intimacy they bring. Money and the things we buy with money have taken their place. Where we used to gather meaning and value from walking the streets of our town and saying hello to all the people we recognized—and we probably knew almost everyone—now we harvest VCRs, designer jeans, and the latest top-of-the-chart CDs at the mall. Money exchanges as simple as filling the car with gas used to entail interaction with people we knew at least in passing. Now we slide a credit card into the gas pump and fill up without saying a word to anyone.

In the changes that have transformed our society, particularly in the last few decades, money has taken on a new role. We rush to fill our souls with accomplishments and acquisitions, perhaps neglecting more traditional ways of connecting. Uncertain who we are and where we belong, our Pain leads us to look to what we can accumulate, particularly money, as a measure of meaning. Are we attempting to replace the depth and wisdom of generations of family and community life with automated teller machines, 401(k) plans, and brokerage accounts? It doesn't work—not because accumulating money isn't healthy, but because it's not enough.

A businessman friend of mine is devoted to sailing in his time off. Almost every weekend the weather allows, he takes his ketch out of Boston harbor into the open Atlantic and cuts blue water. He loves that boat and every moment he spends on it. He also knows how much it costs him.

"George," he said to me after a sunny afternoon of sailing. "Do you know what a boat is?"

I knew he had a punchline up his sleeve. "No," I said.

"A boat is a hole in the water you attempt to fill up with money."

Our souls are like boats. We feel this terrible hole deep inside ourselves, and we try to fill it up with money. But money can't keep a sinking boat afloat, nor can it sustain our souls.

Money in hand represents a store of purpose. It is payment for what we have earned with our energy and sense of purpose. But in our disconnected world, money changes into compensation for what we have lost. We are always making up to ourselves, scrambling to fill the vacuum within. No wonder we spend rather than save; no wonder we identify ourselves as a culture of victims. At the bottom we have lost an authentic sense of self, something money can never buy.

Pain is the energy that fuels the rat race. We keep chasing after money, hoping it will meet our deepest needs. We say we'd love to stop, but we are afraid to. If we stood still, difficult feelings might overwhelm us—and tell us things about ourselves we don't want to hear.

Because we ask money to do soul tasks it cannot do, few of us live money lives that are anything but split and alienated from our core selves. Money repulses us because it is unrelated to who we really are. We are cut off from our deepest selves because we chase after money relentlessly. It becomes easy to blame money for the problem, to say that money has nothing to do with spirit, and to agree with those who proclaim money as the root of all evil.

But money itself isn't the source of either evil or Pain. Rather, our Pain around money reflects a choice we make to face outward, rather than inward, to deal with our projections onto money rather than to seek out their roots within ourselves. We become obsessed with questions of more or less. Rather, we should be seeking to mature.

INEVITABLE PAIN, OPTIONAL SUFFERING

Pain happens. We bump into chairs and yell "Ouch!" fall ill and feel sick, and wince as despair runs through us. It is an Innocent illusion to think that we can live in a utopia where Pain can be teased out of the warp and woof of life. As long as we breathe, Pain remains with us.

Suffering is another matter. Suffering arises at every cycling between Pain and Innocence. And, since suffering has its source in the "mind-forg'd manacles" Blake saw in the faces of us all, we can do something about it. Pain happens, but suffering we manufacture for ourselves. Pain is inevitable; suffering is optional.

Pain is not our fault. It is our teacher. Whenever we feel difficult feelings around money, we can recognize them for what they are—a symptom of the suffering caused by the cycling of Pain and Innocence. Pain is a wake-up call, beckoning our hearts toward Money Maturity.

Every moment of Pain, whenever it arises, is our bell of awakening. Above all else, this single realization is the teaching of this book. Once we become observant, we feel each moment of Pain alerting and informing us of the patterns of Innocence we cling to. Pain increases our awareness of who we are and how we operate. It also shows us the way. With every twinge of Pain, we are presented with an opportunity to free ourselves from suffering by addressing the issues that need attention.

As you work through the exercises that follow, you will come to see better how Pain affects your daily life and where it arises in your body. Then ask yourself these questions: "Am I prepared to end suffering by devoting myself to the hard work of adulthood? Am I willing to open enough to Pain to let its feelings guide me to the skills I need to learn in order to bring suffering to an end?"

TRY THIS: PLACING PAIN IN THE BODY

Perhaps the most powerful tool for addressing difficult feelings is the capacity to observe and become familiar with Pain as it courses through the body. There is no more direct approach to this kind of observation than meditation.

Once again, assume the posture of formal meditation. Sit in a quiet place, with your back straight and your feet flat on the floor. Close your eyes, and focus on your breathing. If your attention wanders, come back to your breath, tracing its constant path in and out of your body. As you become peaceful, let go of your breath and begin to observe how your body feels. Pay no attention to stories, breath, thoughts, or other sensations. Bring your entire focus to bear on how you feel emotionally in your body. You may not feel anything. If so, notice the sense of emptiness. You may feel woozy, weary, frustrated, bored, or annoyed. Just keep looking at how that feels in the body. No matter what thoughts or imaginings arise, keep returning to the physical sensations of your feelings. Notice how they change or move about. When you mentally wander away, see if you can return to your feelings without judgment.

Continue this exercise for at least fifteen minutes at a time. Repeat it daily until you know exactly where you carry your difficult feelings in your body and you begin to feel some detachment and ease toward them. You will find this useful when we come to the healing work of chapter 7, on Understanding. And, for the time being, just noticing unpleasant feelings that block you will give you the strength to act more effectively when they arise.

TRY THIS: PRACTICING AWARENESS IN DAILY LIFE

Formal meditation, such as the preceding exercise, is a disciplined way of learning how to pay attention. As you go through your day and do all the things you need to do, use this heightened sensitivity to keep watch for every painful experience in regard to money. Look particularly for those patterns and feelings you identified in the autobiographical exercises. Notice the experiences that keep coming back. Pay attention to how feelings manifest themselves in your body.

Remember: Pain is the bell of awakening. If you become sensitive to it, you know that whenever it rings, it's time to wake up, do the work of adulthood, and move toward freedom.

part two

ADULTHOOD

chapter 4

ADULTHOOD:
THE HARD WORK OF DIGGING DEEP

When I was a child, I used to talk like a child, and think like a child, and argue like a child, but now I am a man, all childish ways are put behind me.

1 Corinthians 13:11

My purpose in going to Walden Pond was not to live cheaply nor to live dearly there, but to transact some private business with the fewest obstacles; to be hindered from accomplishing which for want of a little common sense, a little enterprise and business talent, appeared not so sad as foolish.

Henry David Thoreau

Three characteristics of the noble man's life: being virtuous, he is free from care; possessing knowledge, he is free from doubts; being courageous, he is free from fear.

Confucius

After realizing how caught up in the world of suffering he had become, Shantideva dedicated himself to his image of perfect freedom—bodhicitta, the mind of awakening. What does a mind of awakening look like in a world whose every aspect seems permeated with money? Is it possible for a mind of money to be a mind of awakening? How can that come about?

In my nearly thirty years of work with people around issues of money, I have watched the development and strengthening of three skill sets that enable people to come to a deeply visionary and generous relationship with money. I call them Knowledge, Understanding, and Vigor. Just one won't do; we need all three. And together they form the first three perfections leading to Shantideva's mind of awakening.

Like Shantideva, Confucius understood the necessity for developing all three together. Knowledge removes doubt, the ancient Chinese sage said, because we enjoy the confidence of knowing what we are doing. Virtue—or Understanding—eliminates care, because we are at peace in our own hearts. And courage—or Vigor—removes fear because we know we have the strength, persistence, and discipline to carry our journey through. Only when we have completed the three stages of adulthood are Vision and Aloha, which represent the fullness of Money Maturity, possible.

Christmas was coming, and my parents wanted to know what I was looking to find under the tree.

"You'll be in the school band next semester," my mother said. "Is there a particular instrument you want to play?"

For a moment I was stuck. I was nearly twelve, and the only musical instruments I knew by name were piano, drums, and violin. None of them interested me. Once, though, I had heard a boy playing a clarinet, and its high wild reedy tone sounded to me like the very voice of freedom. I didn't know its name, though.

"There's this long thin instrument you blow on with your mouth," I said to my mother.

"That must be a flute," she said.

"Sure!" I said, eager to pin a word to this unnamed reality. "It's a flute. That's what I want."

Come Christmas morning, an oblong box lay under the tree. I tore off the paper and ribbon and opened it eagerly. Inside was a thin, shiny metal tube in three sections.

"What's this?" I said, honestly wondering what it was.

"That's your flute," my father said.

"It doesn't look like a flute," I said. "A flute is black. It has different keys."

"You must be thinking of a piccolo," my mother said. "A piccolo is like a flute, only smaller. Sometimes they're black, I think."

"I guess I wanted a piccolo," I said. There was no hiding the disappointment in my voice.

"A piccolo is very much like a flute," my father explained. "Once you learn how to play the flute, you'll also be able to play the piccolo. Work with the flute now, and maybe someday you'll get a piccolo."

"Okay," I said, remembering that I shouldn't look a gift horse in the mouth. Inside, though, I knew I hadn't gotten what I wanted.

The gap between dream and reality became even clearer after the first school band practice. I saw what I'd wanted and I learned, belatedly, it was a clarinet. I told my mother as soon as I reached home that afternoon.

"That's a shame," she said. "It's too late to take your flute back for a clarinet. I wish you'd described it better in the first place."

Now I felt stupid as well as disappointed. "But, Mom," I whined, "a clarinet's what I wanted, not a flute!"

My mother turned on me. I expected her eyes to be angry, but instead they softened into pools of sadness.

"Be happy with the flute, George," she said. "It's been twelve years since I got a new dress."

In that moment, childish ways were put behind me and the world of adulthood opened.

On the path to Money Maturity, adulthood comprises three stages. Knowledge revolves on learning the specific, pragmatic, and intellectual skills needed to handle money effectively. Understanding concerns the heart; here we find ways to transform suffering around money. In Vigor we develop the energy to actualize ourselves in the world, to make our dreams real.

In that difficult moment with my mother over the flute that should have been a clarinet, I was encountering all three. My own lack of Knowledge had bound me into a confusion over flute and clarinet. Had I known the difference between the two instruments, I would have asked for the right gift to begin with. But sometimes, as I discovered, life isn't like that. We don't know, and we discover our ignorance painfully.

The emotional side of my mother's statement was equally important. I had no idea that my parents went without. After all, they treated me generously. I got a new pair of jeans every year and several shirts and presents always piled deep under the Christmas tree. I knew that my parents' priority was ensuring each of us boys the best possible education, but I had no idea they were going without in order to save up tuition money against the time when they would have three sons in college simultaneously. In the sadness I saw in my mother's eyes, I knew what their effort meant and what, literally, it was costing her.

Suddenly I had been knocked out of the self-centered perceptions of a child into the larger empathic world of adulthood. My mother was teaching me about Understanding, showing me what it means to come to emotional terms with our lives and accept them for what they are, without blame or resentment.

My mother also gave me a lesson in Vigor. She was working hard and sacrificing greatly in order to achieve a goal central to her life's meaning. Seeing that, I knew there was a much larger world with much more significant import than the flute I had or the clarinet I wanted. I knew that someday I too would work hard and sacrifice greatly for something that mattered deeply to me.

I was discovering that life's richness and meaning comes from mastering skills, recognizing but containing one's own sadness, and sacrificing something of the moment to gain an even more precious goal. In these lessons in what I later came to know as Knowledge, Understanding, and Vigor, I was learning about becoming an adult.

FINDING OUR ENTERPRISE

In adulthood we must turn inside, like Shantideva, to discover our inner purpose and strengthen our Understanding. Resentment and blame, however, pull us outward; they prompt us to look for a culprit, a devil, a miscreant in the exterior world, someone to point to as the cause of all our woe and suffering. Self-pity seems to look inward, yet in fact it traps sadness in a thought structure that holds tight and thereby defeats us. Adulthood takes an opposite route, where, like Shantideva, we look inside ourselves and take responsibility for our own lives by developing skills that create a different outer world for us by creating a different inner person. These skills involve virtue and learning, patience, endeavor, vision, selflessness, and generosity. Taking on the tasks of adulthood around money means developing these skills.

Miriam, a teacher who had attended one of my Money Maturity seminars, came in to see me a few years ago in the midst of a difficult divorce. At first it seemed she wanted my help in preparing the financial side of her legal arguments. She dwelt on her attorney's strategies, and she discussed the financial arguments she feared her husband would make. Before long the subject of the conversation shifted to Miriam's home life and her daughter's fast-approaching thirteenth birthday. I wondered where she was going with all this.

Miriam complained that as the one breadwinner in the home she was having trouble making ends meet. She didn't know if she could afford the mortgage. She never ate out and at home every meal came from a can. She felt she was letting all kinds of financial things go, creating one money mess after another because of her own ignorance of budgeting, saving, and investing. The messes bothered her most. Miriam feared that she was leaving a legacy of financial chaos to her daughter—the same legacy her own mother had left for her.

What had begun as a purely factual conversation became intensely emotional, a transformation made obvious by Miriam's quivering upper lip, her obvious sweating and shifting in her chair, and the way she wrung her hands. This emotion peaked on the subject of the daughter's thirteenth birthday. The child looked forward greatly to this birthday, considering it her passage into adulthood, and Miriam had planned an elaborate surprise party to celebrate the event. Now Miriam was afraid that, in her reduced circumstances, she couldn't afford any kind of party at all. She felt overwhelmed by shame.

How do we become adults around money? I could see Miriam was asking this very question for her daughter, and for herself as well. Despite thirty-five years of life, a good job, a house, and a mortgage, Miriam had no idea what made for a healthy relationship with money. She did know, though, that she didn't have such a relationship—a refreshing honesty I wished I encountered more often. She recognized too that she was caught up in suffering, and she was willing to do whatever she had to in order to get out of it.

Miriam needed a helping hand, which was why she had come to me. I offered her one, by suggesting that her concern about creating repeated messes was a belief system she was clinging to. It was her Innocence.

"No, George," she said, shaking her head, "it's a fact. Just look at my life."

"I am looking at your life. What I see is a woman who holds a professional job, owns a house, handles a mortgage, is raising her daughter responsibly, and has the good sense to hire professionals to help her through her divorce," I responded. "All this is evidence of anything but a mess."

Together, Miriam and I looked at the real adulthood issues in her life. She did need to learn more about budgeting, saving, and investing so that she could meet present demands, despite the uncertainty of the divorce, and still help her daughter into the future. Also, Miriam's experience of herself as a maker of financial messes kept her emotionally distraught and undercut her ability to accomplish what she was capable of. Over time, as we continued to work together, she came to experience more ease around money and to discover more vitality as she gave up her old image of herself.

The immediate issue Miriam faced, one more urgently pressing than the divorce, was her daughter's birthday. How could she honor the birthday, be a good mother, and teach her child how to be mature around money? It felt like another mess looming. I suggested a few ideas. For one, in regard to Money Maturity, the daughter was old enough to be aware of her mother's relationship to money. As Miriam worked on her own sense of peace and responsibility in regard to her financial life, and as she adopted a healthy Vigor around it, her daughter would pick this up. As for the birthday party, perhaps Miriam could handle it in a similar way.

"Why," I asked Miriam, "do you think that lavishing money on your daughter with a fancy party is a good way to express your love for her? Is it really the best way to celebrate her passage? I'm really impressed that you want your daughter to learn about money. It seems to me that throwing an expensive bash would fly in the face of that lesson and undercut what you're trying to do."

"Maybe so, George. But I still want to celebrate her birthday. It's important for both of us," Miriam said.

"Of course it is. I suspect, though, that if you give it some thought, you can come up with a rite of passage that is more personal and allows greater intimacy between you. It's important too to acknowledge that the financial situation you're in now is okay, there's nothing wrong with it. Perhaps there's a way for you to express your generosity somehow other than partying."

All this got Miriam thinking. The next time I saw her, after her daughter had turned thirteen, she told me how she had taken her and two of her friends camping in the Adirondacks. The time was filled with laughter, warm and joyful. "Much better than a party," Miriam said.

Years later, when Miriam was reflecting on all the time she and I had spent together helping her develop adult skills around money, she said to me, "I thought I was learning about money, but really I was learning about myself."

In achieving Money Maturity, we develop the inner potentialities of which money is only a by-product. Passing through the three stages of adulthood is a necessary step on the road to becoming a complete human being, someone who is whole, fulfilled, free, even happy. In working through these three stages, we are dealing directly with the factors that figure into happiness: Knowledge, which expands our reach into the world; Understanding, which softens hard edges and enables us to connect more deeply with others; and Vigor, which enriches us beyond money by polishing each moment with creativity and accomplishment.

On the path to Money Maturity, Knowledge, Understanding, and Vigor need to develop mutually and simultaneously. To enter adulthood, we have to acquire the basic skills in each area to work through our dysfunctional places. This is where we do the digging, the plowing, and the healing. We create life within ourselves and vitality around us through dedication and hard work.

If we truly wish to achieve Money Maturity, there's no escaping the demands of adulthood, of going beyond resentment, blame, and self-pity to discover our own deepest selves. Henry David Thoreau recognized this as he headed off for the woods surrounding Walden Pond. He had made an appointment with himself that he was resolved to keep, no matter how hard it proved to be. He knew that if he failed to do this work, his life would seem foolish and meaningless. He called this inner work his enterprise and business.

Our souls too are enterprises waiting to be launched. Acquiring Knowledge, Understanding, and Vigor provides the skills, insight, and energy we need to achieve the success Thoreau sought—namely, Money Maturity.

THREE STAGES, ONE CHALLENGE

I discovered some of this reality for myself when I first began to explore the connection between money and freedom. One day while I was still working as a tax accountant, I was struck suddenly by the fact that many of my clients appeared stuck in their lives, going round and round like bald tires slipping in snow. People of my own age who had grown up in the idealism of the 1960s were losing their commitment to values as they aged, grayed, and became suburban clichés. It disturbed me that social and economic pressures shrank many individuals' lives and robbed them of the dream that freedom was possible. Freedom, I was convinced, should be the primary goal of our lives, the objective toward which all our energies move. Why did everybody focus on retirement? Shouldn't we be concerned with achieving freedom long before we start thinking about front porches and rocking chairs?

The work I was doing inside myself centered on freedom. In the back of my mind a fantasy lived. Someday I would sell my tax business and move to Bali, there to live on a pauper's income and devote all my time to writing and painting. I would be a latter-day Paul Gauguin, the one-time stockbroker who gave it all up for art amid the lush colors of the South Seas. Like Gauguin, I longed for freedom within myself. And I wanted to help other people achieve the same freedom.

One night I sat down with a pencil and a pad of paper and tried to figure out how the money skills I had developed in accounting and tax preparation could be devoted to freeing people from the drudgery and pettiness of their lives. I never went to bed that night. I scratched out ideas until the sun came up, and in that early light I realized I had my answer. There was a strategy by which people might, with discipline and focus, achieve financial freedom much sooner than they ever thought possible.

After numerous refinements, I called it "How you might retire in twelve years by saving 12 percent a year." It was basically straightforward, and many of the details appear in chapters 6 and 11. By committing to a simple lifestyle upon retirement, saving assiduously, making ample use of IRAs and other retirement plans, and investing the money through no-load mutual funds in the asset categories that offered the highest rates of return over the past twenty to fifty years, even people on ordinary incomes could potentially accumulate a nest egg big enough to finance freedom.

When I began presenting this strategy to seminar audiences, the reception was enthusiastic. I thought I had solved the freedom problem simply by applying a specialized intellectual skill. The size of the audiences I drew again and again and again told me I was having an effect. That impression grew when, as the years passed, former students would stop me on the street to tell me how much good I had done them. Once, in fact, when I was flying to California and just about to dive into one of those tiny, cold airline salads somewhere over Kansas, the man next to me said, "You changed my life."

"What?" I responded, not sure I heard him correctly or that he was talking to me.

"You changed my life," he said again. "I retired because of you. I thought I would probably work till I was sixty-five, another twenty years or so at the dead-end job I had. Then I took your course. Within two years I had cut my expenses and was living on my investments. I've gone back to work since then, but I only do what I want when I want."

Still, wonderful as this story and others like it were, a fly marred the ointment. A number of clients in my financial-planning practice looked to be perfect for the twelve-years-at-12-percent approach, and they signed on. A number succeeded admirably. Remarkably, though, a surprising number were soon sabotaging their financial plans. Some of them couldn't imagine a positive life goal with enough substance and depth to keep them motivated from month to month, year to year. With no real objective, they fell off the wagon and back into their old ways with money. The most frustrating clients were the chronic over-spenders. Some of these people never met a credit card they didn't charge up to the limit. Others had come into large amounts of money through inheritance or divorce and were doing their best to burn through the wealth and spend themselves back into poverty.

Clearly Knowledge alone—the twelve-years-at-12-percent strategy—wasn't enough. Some of the saboteurs lacked insight into their own emotional issues around money. Others, particularly those who had depended on someone else for income, had no discipline or focus. An unlucky few came up short on both counts. If I was to succeed with these clients and help them win a chance at freedom, I needed to provide the Understanding they were missing and show them how to develop the Vigor they needed. Even more important, I had to determine where all this dysfunctionality came from by seeing deeply into the Innocence and Pain each client brought into our relationship and working from compassion to nudge them toward awareness.

I was doing the same work on myself. While I had some Knowledge, I was emotionally ragged. Despite my growing business success, I felt angry at making my living by doing taxes, which often bored me. Vigor also presented an issue for me. I resisted a vigorous life, just as most of us do. When I finished with my workday, I retreated from the world and lost myself in television and fantasy. These "entertainments" sucked away energy I could have devoted to claiming my place in the world through meaningful activities. As I plumbed these feelings and beliefs, I dredged up Pain that was long hidden and faced up to Innocent beliefs formed in my childhood, such as the notion that work was negative, hard, and draining.

One morning a client called with a complicated tax question. As soon as I hung up the phone, I jumped out of my chair and dived into my tax library on the trail of the answer. Suddenly I became conscious of myself, of what appeared to be incongruous. I didn't like tax research; it was boring, dry work. Yet here I was, answering my client's request with enthusiasm and energy. I looked down inside myself, seeking the wellspring for this seemingly incongruous action. Maturing as I did during the 1960s, I had accepted the notion that energy for moneymaking work arose only from greed or fear. It surprised me to discover what I found in myself at that moment: I was acting out of generosity and kindness. And I got there not by dropping out and taking a tramp steamer to Bali but by engaging the demands of adulthood.

Money Maturity, I was discovering, develops only in individuals who have realized adulthood through cultivating the skills of Knowledge, Understanding, and Vigor. Such individuals go beyond the simple notion of comfortable retirement to achieve a deeper sense of who they are, making themselves better people in the process.

And it all begins with Knowledge.

chapter 5

KNOWLEDGE I: MONEY'S VIRTUE

When the wise person has opportunity for gain, his care is that it be right.

Confucius

. . . it is remarkable what a change of temper a fixed income will bring about. No force in the world can take from me my five hundred pounds. Food, house and clothing are mine for ever. Therefore do not merely labor and effort cease, but also hatred and bitterness. I need not hate any man; he cannot hurt me. I need not flatter any man; he has nothing to give me . . . Even allowing a generous margin for symbolism, five hundred a year stands for the power to contemplate.

Virginia Woolf

The lesson Mahealani Sapolu had to learn was taught to her by the ocean that surrounds her home island of Oahu.

"When Ricky first told me about the bill collector harassing him and I realized I was pregnant, I acted almost like this whole mess didn't exist," she said. "It was the same thing I'd done that had gotten me into debt. I hoped if I looked the other way and didn't notice for long enough, everything bad would just go away."

It didn't, though. Her belly was growing and the debt hung over Ricky, herself, and their coming baby like a piano waiting to fall from a third-story balcony. Slowly Mahealani realized that she had to take matters into her own hands.

Late one afternoon, she wandered down to the beach, deep in thought. A storm offshore pushed the sea into swells that curled into wild foam, ran up the beach, and flooded back. For a long while, Mahealani sat and watched the water's endless, eternal rhythm.

"The water came up, then it went down. Up and down, it was the same amount of water. If the wave was really big, a lot of water rushed out. If it was a small wave, a small amount of water went back. What came in was what went out," she said.

"I was running my life just the opposite. I was putting out more money than I was bringing in. My sea was draining away, and it was taking me with it. Ricky and I were going under week by week, month by month. It didn't have to be much each time, but it was adding up steadily, until all those little numbers made one big number. I was beginning to see how we'd gotten $20,000 in debt without really realizing it was happening."

"I know a way out," Ricky suggested. "We declare bankruptcy. That erases all our debts. Then we can start over."

Mahealani thought about it for a moment, then slowly shook her head. "No way," she said. "We gotta do this on our own, every penny of it. I'd never feel right running away from this thing."

Acting with great ceremony, Mahealani gathered the credit cards from her purse and Ricky's wallet and cut them in half, one by one.

"Now it's just you and me," she said to her husband.

"But we're still not bringing in enough money each month," Ricky said.

"I know," she said. "That's the next piece."

Mahealani used the months before the baby's birth to find a job with a supermarket chain as a courtesy clerk. She put most of the money she earned against the debt she and Ricky owed, and her job benefits included health insurance for her growing family.

Even though holding down regular employment with an infant at home was difficult, Mahealani returned to work three months after her daughter, Pualani, was born. One of her sisters, who had three children of her own, lived nearby. She was happy to take care of Pualani during the day in return for groceries, fish, and meat Mahealani bought at her employee's discount.

"Some of my family disapproved. They said I should be home taking care of Pualani myself, and I really wanted to be with her too, but I just shook my head," Mahealani told me. "I needed to make the money to get us out of this hole once and for all. If I didn't do that, what kind of a life would I be giving Pualani?"

One of Derrick King's responsibilities as director of marketing was working with the marketing communications agencies his company retained to promote its personal computer products. After one agency the company had long relied on went out of business, Derrick faced the task of finding a new firm to handle the company's trade show exhibitions.

"It was a very important selection," he explained. "The technology business moves so fast that you have to seize the high ground and hold it. Trade shows can be critical because, if you make a big splash with a really effective presentation of new products, you can vault yourself into number one almost overnight. I needed an agency that would give us that kind of substantial impact. We were getting ready to roll out a new line of high-end workstations, and I wanted to come on like gangbusters."

Derrick talked to over a dozen Silicon Valley high-tech agencies, culled out the firms he determined were wrong for the account, and narrowed his list to three candidates he wanted to interview in depth. At their next regular meeting, the company's vice president of sales and marketing—and Derrick's boss—asked him which firms had made the cut. Derrick listed his choices.

"What about _____?" The vice president named an agency.

"I wasn't impressed," Derrick said. "They don't have the vision and creativity we need. And they were the weakest of all the agencies in terms of their system for following up sales leads after trade shows."

The vice president pinched his lower lip between thumb and forefinger. "I've heard good things about them," he said. "Put them back on the short list. Let's take a second look."

Derrick was stunned. Never before had the vice president interfered with his decision process and overruled him. Still, he figured it would make no difference in the end. Once the sample presentations were made and the candidate agencies were compared side by side, the one the vice president was interested in would look even worse.

That proved to be exactly the case. The three companies Derrick had picked presented trade show marketing ideas so brilliant it was difficult to choose among them. The fourth company, the one the vice president had added to the short list, was nowhere near as strong. Yet, throughout the presentation, the vice president fawned on the account executive who made the presentation. She was bright and highly professional. Still, the creative people backing her lacked the kind of blazing insight the company needed to attract strong consumer interest.

After the presentations were over, Derrick turned to the vice president and said with a smile, "I'll bet I know what you're thinking." He was sure his boss would choose among the top three.

"We'll go with _____," he said, again naming the firm he had shown an interest in.

"You must be kidding," Derrick said, his anger building. "They were outclassed. Any one of the other three is an obviously better choice. I'm not at all sure those people know what they're doing."

The vice president raised his left eyebrow. It was a signal that his decision was not to be questioned. "That's what I want. We go with them."

Derrick knew that, if he wanted to keep his job, it was time to shut his mouth.

After work, he went out for a glass of wine with his counterpart on the sales side, who was a close friend and confidant. Derrick told him the whole story.

"What I can't figure out is why he would choose that particular agency when the others were obviously so much better," he finished.

"Don't you see it?" his friend said.

"See what?"

"I swear, King, you are such a straight arrow. I'll spell it out for you," the other said. "You know the account executive who made the presentation?"

"Sure. She's smart. It's the creative people behind her who aren't up to par."

"It doesn't matter. What matters is the vice president's been having an affair with her for the past year. He chose that agency because he wants her near him. He's dallying at work, and his wife still doesn't have a clue."

It took Derrick long pondering to decide what about this revelation bothered him most. It wasn't the sexuality of the relationship, he determined, or even the shock of encountering infidelity so close by. He considered adultery wrong, but he knew it wasn't his job to trumpet a certain kind of marital morality at work. It was his job as a senior manager, however, to enhance the company's value for stockholders and to ensure that his fellow employees labored under the best possible conditions for success. Suddenly Derrick was being required to support an important decision that could harm the company by lessening its sales edge in a highly competitive marketplace. Instead of doing what was best for the company and everyone with a financial stake in it—including himself—he was expected to support his boss's romantic life on the side.

To make matters worse, his own career was at stake. If the company's sales slipped because a less-than-competent agency had been selected, Derrick's reputation as an effective manager would be tarnished.

Derrick faced another reality. If he protested, the vice president would fire him without batting an eye.

"I need that job," he said to me. "It pays me very well. I don't like admitting it in a way, but the money is important to me. I want to be able to put my boys through any college they get admitted to, no matter how high the tuition. If I just quit in moral outrage and take my chances, it might be months until I hook up with another company. Then I can't be sure I'll make the money I need to keep socking it away for my boys' college.

He paused. "And then there's Alexandria."

"How so?" I was unsure what he meant.

"If I'm not scoring big on salary, I'm not sure she'll stay. I can tell she's unhappy even though she won't spell it out for me. She's hardly worked at all, and I suspect she's afraid to launch out on her own because of the financial consequences. But if I'm not making major money, she could figure what the hell, nothing's holding me here, I might as well leave now. Unless I want to watch my life unravel, I'm stuck right where I am."

"You've been talking about everybody else's needs: your coworkers', your kids', your boss's, Alexandria's, your stockholders'. The question this all brings up for me is: What does freedom mean for Derrick King?" I said.

"Freedom?" Derrick asked.

"That's right, freedom. Freedom is what financial planning is all about."

When I first started working with Susanna Swartz to determine what she really wanted—and how she could use her money to create the life she sought—the saying about the needle and the haystack held true with a vengeance. As soon as I saw the glimmer of metal somewhere down below, Susanna tossed more hay on the pile to conceal the needle and keep me looking. I was hunting for the little shiny bit inside her that revealed the true Susanna, but she was determined to hide it from view. She could recite a long list of the world's outrages, particularly on the environmental front—slash-and-burn agribusiness destroying the Amazonian and Indonesian rain forests, the heavy industrial pollution attributed to *maquiladora* factories along the United States–Mexico border, overfishing on the Grand Banks, acid rain, the ever-lengthening list of endangered species—but she let little of herself out in the process.

"Why does what's happening on the Grand Banks, the Amazon, or the *maquiladoras* bother you so much?" I asked.

"Because it's wrong!" she countered. "It's simply criminal that people should treat workers or the environment like that, particularly when it's just to make themselves rich."

"Granted. Still, how are you connected personally to any of these issues?"

"I don't have to be connected," she said. "I only have to know it's wrong."

Underneath Susanna's involvement in environmental causes, I suspected, lay an unexplored reservoir of guilt at having been born into a wealthy family. One of the things I've noticed in my work with inheritors is that at least a significant number of them feel like victims to money. Often they come from families in which money was experienced as a stand-in for love. Their response to this predicament is to feel rage, as if they were wronged by money forces much more powerful than they are. Thus they come to feel like victims. The strongest of these inheritors rise above their feelings to do noble and loving things with their money. But for many the response ranges from oblivion and magical thinking to resentment and blame. This is a problem we're likely to see more of. As America gets richer, more and more of us or our children will inherit money.

Susanna's case was typical. She hadn't asked for privilege; it had merely come to her as an unearned providence of birth. Yet she felt a victim of that wealth—first at the hands of her father and brothers, then of her larcenous ex-husband. As a victim, she took up the causes of the environment as a fellow victim. As we discussed her concerns, focusing on the *maquiladoras*, she brought up not only the lax environmental rules governing these industries but also their reputation for underpaying and misusing their workers, mostly young Mexican women.

"Tell me what it is about the situation of a woman working in a *maquiladora* that most bothers you?" I asked.

"No matter how hard she tries, she can't have the same dreams I do," Susanna answered. "Say she'd love to buy a big old house and fix it up. She'll never have the money to do it."

Susanna's own cramped surroundings came to my mind. "Is fixing up a house something you'd like to do?"

"Of course not. It's just a hypothetical idea I tossed out. I could have said something else just as easily."

"What, for example?"

She looked stumped. "I can't think of anything else right now. The house just seemed like a good example at the time. Let's go on. You were saying—"

I thought I saw the needle glint again through the hay. "If you were going to fix up a house, what kind would it be?"

"I don't want to fix up a house, George," she insisted.

"I know you feel that way, Susanna, but humor me for a moment. We've been looking at the purposes of your life, what gives it meaning. I've got an idea. Before we get together again next week, I would like you to write down the kind of house you might want and how you'd fix it up—not because this is something you're actually planning to do, but because imagining a wonderful home may tell us something about the deeper goals in your life."

She nodded, unconvinced. When she returned to my office a week later, the first thing she said was "I still think this is a stupid idea." Then without a moment's pause she launched into a detailed description of a huge old Victorian she had spotted in the nearby town of Winchester— three stories, resplendent cupolas, stained-glass windows, even a dance floor to accommodate those truly spectacular parties. Just from the way Susanna described it, I could see she loved even the thought of such a house.

"Say you owned this house," I suggested. "How would you fix it up?"

"Not that this is anything I'd ever want to do, mind you," she began. "This house needs work—even structural repair, particularly to the roof—but even more important it needs the touch of a designer who understands the esthetics of vintage Victorians." She went on for the next quarter of an hour about interior and exterior painting, stained-glass restoration, carpets, replastering, wallpaper, and the like. She was thorough, detailed, passionate.

When she finished, I said, "You want a house like this. "

"No, I don't," Susanna answered.

"When you talk about it, you seem so involved, so animated. It's as if something is flowing from the core of you out into this room."

She paused before she said, "I could never let myself have a house like that. Then everybody would know about my money. I have more integrity than that."

I smiled. "They already know you have money. The truth has this way of getting around. And how does having a large house undermine your integrity? Integrity comes from a Latin word meaning wholeness. How are you being less whole by admitting to yourself what you want? It seems to me that integrity begins in facing the question of who you are as a whole person. That includes your own needs, wants, and goals."

Her voice became like that of a little girl asking her father for candy. "So I can want the house?" she said. "It's okay?"

"You can want the house. It's okay."

The first inklings of adulthood, and of Knowledge about money, come in small experiences of freedom, integrity, and a job well done.

I met Thomas when I was out looking for items to furnish my house. He made his living importing furniture from Asia, and his store was an establishment that celebrated the art and sensibility of furniture. After Thomas and I got to know each other better, I took him on as a client. The prospect of working with him delighted me. As it turned out, Thomas was as astute and successful a businessman as he was a connoisseur of furniture.

One day over lunch, I asked him if any family experience had shown him what it took to run a successful business.

"Not really," he said. "I think actually I learned more about business from my paper route. It was my first taste of moneymaking, and it fascinated me in many ways."

"Tell me about it," I said. "Did you live in a city?"

He smiled. "No, that polished Atlanta accent you hear now is something I acquired later, when I was learning the furniture business, before I bought the place I run now. Anyway, I grew up in this small town called Dublin, Georgia, and my brother had the paper route before me. Even before I inherited it, I collected for him. While he worked his way down the street, folding newspapers and flinging them onto front steps, I followed behind, ringing doorbells and telling each customer what he or she owed. Some people smiled, others growled and grouched. A few, some of them smilers, some of them growlers, always added a tip to their bill, whether my brother was doing a good job or not. The tip had to do with who they were as people, not with whether my brother was keeping the paper dry when it rained or closing the front gate to make sure the dog didn't get out. That surprised me.

"Other things surprised me too," Thomas continued. "When I

showed up on the front porch and asked for money—completely unaware of what it means to be a bill collector—I had a front-row seat on people's lives. I saw laughing, crying. I heard arguments, screamed curses, the silence that means a room has just filled with rage. I saw happiness too, these wonderful private smiles. And somehow money had something to do with it all.

"I learned even more about money's connection to human character when I started delivering as well as collecting. As most of us do with most jobs, I resisted the work somewhat. Getting up early on Saturday for the one morning delivery a week was tough during the winter. Even in the South, it can be cold before the sun comes up. Yet every afternoon when I went out to deliver was an adventure, always an adventure. I'd bump into different people, have to contend with various kinds of weather, sometimes even encounter a raccoon or a fox come in from the country to forage in the yards and fields of our village. I felt connected to the world, engaged.

"And the money I made thrilled me. I liked the feeling of coming away from my collecting rounds with pockets full of folded bills and jingling coins. It felt good to count the take, pay the monthly bill from the newspaper publishing company, and sock the profit in my bank account, some for saving until later and some for spending now. The money I spent bought things that felt forbidden, even risqué, like candy, Superman comics, and rock-and-roll records. That was my first taste of individuality and freedom."

Thomas sipped his coffee. "You know," he said, with an air of reflection, "there's a way that experience was the biggest adventure of my life. I've traveled all over East Asia on business, but those afternoons as a kid out on my own opened my eyes to the world. I didn't know all the people I delivered to, some of them were strangers, yet I learned how to pick up on the kind of people they were. I found myself curious about them, I wondered what their lives were like, what excited and interested them. When I found out, I used that information to guide my interactions with them, to make things lively and interesting. I still use these skills. Whether I'm working with an illiterate carpenter in Bali who builds bureaus for me or an educated young couple from Waltham who are furnishing a house, I pay attention to who the person is, what he or she likes.

"The basic things I learned about money then I relearn every day now. It's about freedom, honest work, and human character. If you want to be good at business, you have to understand that the real issue is the integrity at the root of human relationships."

The paper route taught Thomas the two layers of Knowledge about money, the one deep and the other practical. The first, and deep, layer of Knowledge is that money speaks of human character. This aspect of Knowledge came to him in understanding the difference between the tippers and the grouches, in experiencing the satisfaction of a job well done, and in tasting freedom in the small things he bought himself with his earnings. The second, and practical, layer of Knowledge lay in learning and developing the skills he needed to handle money well—collecting, bill-paying, budgeting, and saving.

The two layers of money Knowledge are woven tightly together. Only if we master money's practical side can we engage fully in its human lessons, and only if we perceive money's depths can we apply practical financial skills in ways that enrich our lives rather than detract from them. Without this deep level of Knowledge, our lives around money will be filled with conflicts and problems.

Practical Knowledge—the day-to-day skills needed to make our way through the world of money—is the topic of the chapters 6 and 11. This chapter concerns deep Knowledge—the understanding that freedom, integrity, and moral order exist in the world of money.

THE FREEDOM AND INTEGRITY IN MONEY

A common agnostic way of looking at money is to see it as neither good nor bad. In this view, money is neutral, a practical convenience and no more, a kind of blank screen onto which we project our feelings and belief systems, often with tragic or sad consequences. By valuing rich people over poor people, we encourage a nation of thieves. Because our culture values money itself over maturity, we engender a society of liars. By rewarding talent over generosity, we support conflict rather than compassion. By believing in what can be measured over what defies measurement, we translate virtue into the countinghouse and lose the ability to recognize honesty, loyalty, and sincerity. Thus money comes to represent evil, corruption, dishonesty, and greed because we ourselves project these qualities into the world. They belong not to money itself but to the recesses of our souls. We recognize that the source of this projection lies in our childhood experiences and the habits of Innocence and Pain.

But this view fails to reach the real core of money. Money is much more than neutral. It represents a positive good for humankind. In its early days, money was stamped with divine images, for money itself was divine. The divinity of money has two aspects, which are ultimately the same: freedom and integrity.

To people all around the globe, money represents freedom from care, want, hunger, drudgery. And, in a subtle way, every financial interaction embodies integrity. As we exchange money from hand to hand, as we arrive at a mutually agreed-upon price, money stands for integrity—with each other, in relationship, and inside ourselves.

Consider for a moment a situation not unlike the early times when money was introduced. You're a farmer, and you grow corn. You have planted acres of cropland, and you're a good farmer, one who tends to his rows and fields lovingly. The weather has been beneficent this summer, and you know the harvest will be good. This corn-farming, though, is hard, wearing work. You look in the mirror at the end of the last day of harvest, and the sight of yourself in the glass is something to behold—torn jeans, bedraggled shirt, a baseball cap that's more holes than hat.

"I know what I'll do," you say. "I'll take a bunch of my corn and go see George. He makes good clothes. I'll trade him corn for clothes."

Next day you fill a wagon with heaps of the golden harvest, and you head the mule down to my farm. Sure enough, you find me working at my sewing machine, stitching a pair of canvas pants tough enough to stand up to the rigors of farm work.

"I want a pair of pants like that, George," you say. "Let's trade my corn for your trousers."

"Nope," I say, pointing in the direction of the barn, where the granaries are overflowing with corn from my own bumper crop. "It doesn't make sense for me to trade for something I already have in abundance."

You push back the ragged remains of the baseball hat and scratch your head. "I guess you're right," you say. "But I still need a new set of clothes."

Without money we are at an impasse, though. The one exchange we would like to make—new clothes in return for something valuable—is impossible.

Introduce money into the equation, and everything changes. Now you can haul your crop to the local grain wholesaler and sell it for money. Then it's a simple matter to come to me and give me money for clothes. You sell your corn for money, you use the money to buy my clothes, and we're both satisfied.

The invention of money came from a profound understanding of the nature of human relationships, and it revolutionized our social life. Barter based on immediate needs limited the kinds of exchanges—essentially, acts of giving and receiving—possible at any given moment. Money widened the realm of giving and receiving; it fostered new relationships between individuals and added to the human capacity for freedom. With money, an infinity of gifts could be given and an infinity received. In a way, money was the original Internet. Money created a new, limitless world, one rooted in our sense of fairness and reciprocity with one another, a world similar to what we think of as paradise or the habitation of the divine. The stamping of ancient coins with the images of gods and goddesses signaled the insight that money was a divine gift, that it facilitated the deepest understanding of all the religious teachings—intimacy with the Godhead, with each other, and with ourselves. This tradition continues today, in the words "In God we trust" and the symbolic imagery displayed on U.S. bills and coins. Even now we acknowledge money as a gift from God.

Although the world at large and the financial realm contain their share of Pain, money embodies hopes and dreams, the stuff from which freedom is made. Money is the wine that brings out the divinity within ourselves and our community, the breath that keeps it alive. Many of the great religious traditions believe that observing the breath in a state of meditation helps us find our way to freedom and the underlying nature of reality. Likewise, observing our relationship to money helps us find our way to the spiritual realms of Vision and Aloha.

Knowledge gives us this understanding. We come to see, for example, that the center of all money interactions is the giving and receiving of gifts. Some mornings, when I buy *The Wall Street Journal* or *The New York Times* at a local newsstand, I am overwhelmed by the grandeur and generosity of what has entered my life. I put down less than a dollar, a tiny amount of money, and into my hands comes the creative product of hundreds of gifted people who devote themselves to finding out what is happening in the world and recording it in excellent prose. In return for a bit of money, I am gifted with useful information and the pleasure of reading. A miracle has graced my life.

Or think about an orange in the grocery store in winter, a piece of fruit that was picked in a grove in Florida or Chile or Israel and shows up only a couple of days later right around the corner. Count all the hands that have touched that orange to bring it thousands of miles and present it to you, fresh and juicy. Consider the new paperback edition of *Lord Jim* you just bought as the mingled effort of a now-dead Polish-speaking writer who lived in England, a publishing company in New York City, a printing press in Singapore, and the bookstore in your neighborhood or on your computer. Attend to the wonderful car you have an eye on, and think of the thousands of engineers, designers, steel and auto workers, transportation specialists, marketing consultants, and other hardworking people whose labor has put that vehicle on the showroom floor for you to admire and perhaps one day drive.

Once the Knowledge that all economic interactions comprise gift-giving becomes part of consciousness, we develop gratitude for everything we receive. Giving money becomes one way of showing gratitude. Every time we buy a newspaper or an orange or a Joseph Conrad novel or a new car, we say thank you to the person who sold it to us and to all the people whose labor has made this gift possible.

INTEGRITY WHERE WE LEAST EXPECT IT

Money turns on balance and fairness, right conduct, the exchange of gifts between individuals. At the core of each financial exchange lies integrity.

Most people have little or no trouble seeing the connection

between money and freedom. In popular parlance, we say that someone who has sufficient resources to live without working is "financially independent," a person "free" to do what he or she wants. Yet the notion that money contains an inherent integrity is shocking, the kind of idea against which we throw up our hands and bristle: "That can't be!" Commonly we think of money as immoral—a funding source for evil—or amoral—lacking any inherent quality of right or wrong. Yet money contains within itself both great good and the power to do great good, for ourselves and our communities. Money insists upon fair exchange as a way of resolving disputes and satisfying needs that rest in a place of balance between all the people producing a certain good and all the people who want that same good. Money requires integrity in relationship. Coming to this Knowledge against the backdrop of Innocence and Pain can be difficult indeed. Yet it is a step we must make in order to come to Money Maturity.

Some years ago, at a seminar I was giving, I stated my belief that markets demand integrity and that money works fairly, by balancing supply and demand in the way that generally works best for all of us. This statement sparked a woman in the audience, who fairly shuddered in outrage.

"What about price gouging?" she demanded, righteousness flaring her eyes. "What about corporate profits?"

As she spoke, I suspected that she had gone through some searing personal experience with money. But it was less her own experience than the general outrages of corporate America that fired her anger.

"What price gouging are you referring to?" I asked, wanting to find out more. "And what's wrong with corporate profits?"

"I'll give you an example," she said. "Check out the prices in the natural and health foods stores. I mean, they're just appalling. Compare a can of soup or a bag of apples there with the same product at Kroger or A&P. It's such a rip-off. People need organic and natural products in place of the poisoned food in the chain stores, but we have to pay these inflated prices to get them. That stinks. It's just another way of stealing from us."

This argument revealed a person who felt enslaved by economic forces and considered herself anything but free. And she believed the financial world lacked a moral order apart from criminal dedication to picking her pocket.

"There's another way to think about this and see the role of money," I answered. "Natural and health foods represent an emerging market. The people who are developing it have to pioneer everything, from growing the food to processing and marketing it. This kind of entrepreneurial task takes a commitment of enormous resources, energy, money, and time. No one will go to such trouble and risk unless they can win a substantial reward from the effort. The price reflects that reality. So, instead of the resentment you feel at the prices, you could experience joy that this kind of food—the very thing you want—is now available."

She wasn't convinced. "They are still making too much, I'm just positive."

"Okay," I said, "assume the profits are excessive, that there's a big gap between the actual costs of production and the price being charged. Now you're presented with an entrepreneurial opportunity instead of an occasion for draining away your energy through resentment and blame."

"I don't understand," she said.

"It's simple. You, or you and some of your friends, make a marketing arrangement with organic growers to buy their crop, then you resell at a price that undercuts the other natural produce on the market but still gives you enough profit to succeed financially. People will buy from you because you're charging less. You'll benefit, your buyers will benefit, and your competitors will have to drop their price if they want to stay in business."

"You mean, go into the grocery business myself?"

"Why not? If what you say is true, it would make good financial sense. Money makes it possible."

That was precisely what surprised this woman, and so many countless others in our society. Money creates a moral order that rewards us for our skill in delivering useful resources to other human beings. The exchange that brings me the newspaper, the fresh orange, or a classic novel embodies a relationship of integrity between buyer and seller. The degree of ease or tension between the amount supplied and the amount demanded determines price. Price in turn guides society in allocating resources most efficiently. Here, as in other ways, money creates an automatic integrity of relationship in the exchange between human beings.

In essence, this woman's resistance to the notion of money's natural ethics and her resentment at the price of organic produce sprang from ignorance—a lack of Knowledge. She, like many others, had never imagined economic forces erecting a moral order that rewards our effort and creativity in meeting other people's needs. Had she mastered the practical level of Knowledge, she would have had the skills to compete with the natural foods retailers she accused of overcharging. Yet as long as she lacked the deep, moral layer of Knowledge, as long as she viewed money and the people who handle it as evil, she couldn't even begin to get to work.

Money is intricately entwined in the critical and difficult issue of morality in society. There's no question that dark and troubled people as well as large impersonal institutions act in harmful ways around money. The important questions concern the way we handle that Knowledge: How does it color our daily money exchanges and our attitudes toward both money itself and our fellow human beings? Does the Pain of these experiences cloud our view of reality, or does it stimulate our movement toward mature behavior?

Unless we come to terms with the ethical issues around money and the moral questions confronting communities, our economic and political system will disintegrate and we ourselves will fail as persons. These issues, particularly the connection between money and social evil, merit a close look.

READING THE NEWS AND FACING THE CHALLENGES

As a news junkie who reads three papers a day, I am an unending believer in the free press as a source of up-to-date factual information and a champion against corruption and crime, a force that helps bring down the wicked and raise up the wronged. I delight in these virtues. Still, there is a problem here, not in what the press does but in how we read, listen to, or watch the news and how we interpret it.

Consider the language I just used to describe the press's worth.

Words like *wicked* and *wronged* spring from a point of view that sees the world in shades of victim and oppressor. This perspective spawns a language that, in our suffering, we relish hearing, a language that uses not the vocabulary of maturity, wholeness, or health but of resentment and blame. This language feeds those of us who feel miserable about how we have been treated around money by supporting our self-perception as victims. We project this sense of hurt victimization onto the whole of society and feel supported in the belief that our problems should be laid at the feet of someone else. Suddenly the world around us is dark, and we are allowed to escape responsibility for our own lives. When we see huge failures of integrity around us, it is easier to justify and ignore our own lapses of integrity.

Day-to-day challenges to integrity, from the big to the small, don't help us form a virtuous view of money either.

Recently I led a couple of discussion groups on the topic of integrity. Participants in both groups spoke of the lack of integrity mostly in terms of "they" and "them," as if the problem lay somewhere outside themselves, at some remove from their own being. It is commonplace for us to believe that we ourselves act morally, allowing a sense of right and wrong to guide our choices, while the rest of the world—including the financial realm—doesn't. In a December 13, 1996, *Wall Street Journal* opinion poll, 61 percent—or almost two out of three—Americans agreed with the statement that morality in America is "pretty bad and getting worse." Yet, asked to place themselves on a morality scale that ran from 1 (no morality at all) to 100 (completely moral), 89 percent of the respondents ranked themselves at 75 or above and 50 percent chose scores of 90 or above. The great majority of Americans pictured themselves as morally responsible individuals in a world that was anything but.

Rarely do people face up to the challenges to integrity in their own lives—even though, as my discussion groups showed, these challenges are all too commonplace. A teacher said that her principal and peers adhered to an unspoken agreement not to tell parents that their children might benefit from special education classes. The regulatory structure makes these classes ten to twenty times as expensive as mainstream education and draws away resources from other classrooms. The more special education students the school had, the poorer the education for everyone else, the angrier the community at large, and the greater the threat to the teachers' jobs. So special education stayed in the closet, even for the children it might have benefited.

Then there was the hotel employee who said his job required him to lie regularly. When people called for a one- or two-night reservation, he said the hotel was booked even if it wasn't. Since management wanted to hold rooms back for reservations of a week or longer, it was this man's job to turn short-term customers away via deception. Although he had spoken about the situation to his bosses and fellow workers, he couldn't get it changed. And the older he got, the more the lying bothered him.

Next came two women with similar stories about telling the truth and being denied health insurance as a result. One was a recovering alcoholic who had been sober for five years and was active in Alcoholics Anonymous. The other was turned away because of breast lumps, even though the tumors were benign and no woman in her family had ever suffered mammary gland cancer.

The story that disturbed me most—because it dealt with my former profession of accounting—came from a young consultant who had moved from being a stay-at-home mom into a successful business career after her husband's sudden death. Something her accountant said to her brought her to my class. She was about to make a trip to Dallas to see her brother when her accountant suggested that she write the trip off as a business expense.

"I'm going to see my brother," she answered. "That's not business. It's personal."

"You have customers in Dallas, don't you? Vendors?" the accountant asked.

"Sure."

"Then just say it's for business. The IRS will never catch it."

When she spoke to friends about this incident, they all applauded her high sense of ethics, but they acted as if she were at least a little daft for not taking advantage of the opportunity. Taxes are different, they said; doesn't everyone cheat, at least a little?

"But how do you *feel* about what the accountant suggested?" I asked.

"Lousy," she said.

"That tells you what you need to know. Your integrity is at stake."

I suggested that she look for a new accountant, interview likely candidates, and tell the group about the process when we met again the following week. She did just that and reported happily that she had brought in someone new. Then, during the group discussion, I happened to mention the obligation to report income in the year in which it is made. The consultant spoke up, clearly confused.

"I'm making excellent money this year, but I doubt I'll do as well next year," she said. "I asked the accountants I interviewed what to do about this. They all said I should hold all the checks I receive in December and deposit them in January, so I can report them next year when my tax rate will be lower."

I was appalled. Holding income back isn't simply unethical. It's illegal—and all three accountants had blithely recommended that the consultant break the law. For a whole day after I heard this tale, I was depressed by the remarkable ease with which these professionals were recommending illegal conduct.

Yet the consultant took an extraordinary action. She went back and confronted each of the three accountants. She told them that because of their illegal advice she would not work with them. She even threatened to report each one to their local professional organization.

She had a point, one that reaches right to the core of integrity. People who violate integrity are impossible to work with. If they are willing to lie and cheat and encourage me to do the same, I can count on the same deceptive behavior if we ever come into conflict. If there is no integrity now, there will be none then.

In situations like this one or the dilemma Derrick King faced, we need to insist on our own integrity, challenge others around the violation, or report violators to the appropriate authorities. Corruption cuts at the root of our way of life. As soon as we come to believe that the system has no moral center, we ourselves start to cheat, and we assume that everyone else is doing it too. We have moved away from money's nature into a place where we fall prey to greed for our advantage. Because we no longer value our own integrity, this greed allows us to tarnish everyone else's integrity, in the way that Derrick's boss was trying to undermine Derrick. We may have all the practical Knowledge in the world, but if we fail to develop and protect our integrity—as Mahealani Sapolu asserted fiercely to her husband when he suggested bankruptcy—we will never find freedom.

Part of Knowledge is understanding that, without integrity at the root of our economic exchanges, society will collapse, our relationships will be tainted, and we ourselves will fail as persons. A market system works only with moral foundations. Without integrity there is no confidence in fairness of prices. Markets become free-for-all anarchies driven by corruption, special deals, and special interests. In time the entire system comes down—precisely what happened to the corrupt right-wing dictatorships of Latin America and the equally corrupt left-wing dictatorships of Russia and Eastern Europe.

Unless we understand money's virtue, entering the realm of practical Knowledge is like wandering into the valley of darkness and wrapping ourselves in a cloak of evil we will never take off. Fearing that this cloak is all there is, some of us refuse to learn money's practical side. But the cloak of evil is our projection onto the whole world of money, a projection of our painful financial experiences and our own failures to maintain integrity when it is challenged and of an endless stream of news reports that capture the significant but little bits of daily evil.

A THOUSAND ACTS OF KINDNESS

Right about now, our most cynical side has a way of popping up and making a suggestion to the rest of our inner being. "Here's what we're going to do. We get everybody else to act with integrity around money. That gives us a special opportunity to be devious without anyone knowing. We'll get away with murder—well, grand theft anyway—so we'll get richer and richer and all those Goody Two-shoes won't even notice."

Integrity, however, doesn't work this way. What is healthy for our communities is profoundly helpful for our inner selves as well.

In practical economics, supply and demand must balance. That means that my needs as consumer and your needs as producer must come up equal for economic exchange to take place. Balance is internal as well. It involves perceiving the role of integrity and right conduct in all our money interactions. If we take something that is not ours, for example, we harm our balance by creating a shaking sense of both the world and our own integrity. This is why Confucius writes that it is fine for a wise person to gain—provided that the gain is right. And it is even more why he said that while an enlightened or knowledgeable person is free from doubt, a virtuous person is free from anxiety.

There is a saying I repeat often to myself: "It takes a thousand acts of kindness to undo one unkind deed." When we violate the integrity of money by acting wrongly in the economic realm—by being crabby, pinched, or dishonest in our financial dealings—we do such harm to our deep selves that it can take years of atonement to regain an uncompromised integrity. The effects of wrongdoing are profound. They harm us spiritually and psychologically, and they have a damaging effect on the way we do business.

Every time we cheat or lie in the arena of money, we send our souls an unconscious message: " I am a liar, I am a cheat." Then, when we make a move toward mature behavior, this message gets in the way. We project lying or cheating onto others or acknowledge it in ourselves. It blocks us from effective action and robs us of Money Maturity.

I saw this happen dramatically in the case of Ralph, a man I met socially who later became a client of mine. His engineering-consulting business soared after summer floods, and suddenly his expertise was in great demand. In one year he made more than he had in the prior six—a credit to his Vigor and hard work. Still, he didn't really understand the nature of money, and he soon fell under the sway of a "financial advisor" whose skills were dubious but whose politics mirrored Ralph's strongly antigovernment view of the world. The advisor convinced Ralph that he now had so much money he could give half of it away and still have enough to retire. Ralph did just that. He divided half his accumulated earnings among a number of charitable groups he believed in. Then, following his advisor's counsel, he sunk the remaining half into an investment vehicle that paid the advisor a huge commission and gave Ralph no flexibility—if he wanted out, he had to pay a large surrender fee. Still, Ralph thought he was doing just wonderfully until the IRS presented him with a whopping bill for his big year. Ralph was as honest a man as you could ever hope to meet, but he believed that every penny given to the federal government was wasted. A tax preparer recommended by his financial advisor and described as aggressive convinced Ralph to claim a long list of inappropriate deductions. He did just as the putative expert said, and Ralph's tax bill dropped—until an audit a couple of years later left him owing penalties and interest as well as the original tax obligation. Believing that he had come into the beneficence he deserved—and the government didn't—Ralph blinded himself to the advisor's incompetence and the tax man's illegalities.

Ralph's story offers a powerful look at key issues surrounding the inherent integrity of money. I think of it myself whenever I am tempted, in even the smallest way, to take advantage of a situation to my benefit and someone else's detriment, even if the someone else is a giant corporation, a government bureaucracy, or a slick, thoroughly unlikable salesperson.

Ralph was a man of remarkable honesty, and his generosity was extraordinary. I learned much from him about being a better person, and I liked being around him, partly in the hope that some of the goodness he cultivated in himself would rub off on me.

Yet Ralph's integrity was flawed by one critical crack: He hated to share the fruits of his labor with the government. He saw only bad in government, failing to perceive the positive benefit of roads, schools, environmental protection, democratic freedoms, and the like. This led him to choose his financial and tax advisors more on the basis of shared political vision than integrity. For this he suffered. His transgression harmed his ability to handle money with clarity. He lost a major portion of his banner year's earnings because he failed to follow the integrity money insists upon.

There is more to this than a simple morality tale or spiritual tit-for-tat—the what-goes-around-comes-around notion that if we act badly, bad will get us. The wound I have observed time after time is more basic and fundamental. When we violate money's integrity, we inscribe within ourselves the infallible knowledge that we ourselves are untrustworthy, deceptive, and self-aggrandizing. The next time we deal with money, we look into the eyes of the person on the other side of the transaction, and we say to ourselves "Down inside me someplace, I know I'm a lying selfish cheat I'd never trust. If I'm this bad, you must be too." As a result, we act suspiciously, skeptically, blinded wholly or partly to the transaction going on in front of us. Like Ralph we make bad decisions. We may even lose money, throw away opportunities, or destroy relationships—with spouses, partners, and children as well as business or professional associates. And it all happens because we failed to pay attention to money's essential integrity and to behave in the way it demands.

The flip side holds true as well. When we assert our own integrity —as Mahealani Sapolu did in facing her debt or as the consultant did in confronting the fast-and-loose accountants—we are asserting our right to pursue freedom through money. Holding true to ourselves makes us ready to take on the rewarding roles of adulthood within an economic community.

A perfect example of this came from a client of mine. Barbara worked in the accounting department of a midsize manufacturing company, a position she had held for years. She had never been happy in the job, however. When I saw her at our regular quarterly meetings, she always sang the same old song: This or that person was getting away with cutting corners at work, her boss didn't really care about the company, the company wasn't fair to its employees, it was sloppy about its environmental responsibilities, and so forth and so forth.

One day, as she launched into another chorus of this refrain, I said, "My experience has been that when I complain a lot about other people's integrity, I'm usually lacking some integrity myself. Any chance that's true for you too?"

Barbara sat up straight. "Well, I hadn't thought about that," she said. "Am I failing in integrity because I complain about the company but I keep on working there?"

"The issue needn't be so drastic," I said. "Sometimes I can uncover the right action by looking first at the smallest ways I'm missing the boat."

"Oh," Barbara said. Then she brought up something we'd talked about before. "Of course, I still avoid learning new things at work. When new programs, procedures, and systems are introduced, I drag my feet. I complain. Mostly I grumble to myself. I know it makes my boss's life more difficult, but I think he probably doesn't really know how little I'm learning. And when it comes to things I don't absolutely, positively have to learn to keep my job, I figure, why bother? I just let it slide."

"If I were you, I'd take a look at my integrity right there," I said.

Barbara did just that. Over the next year, she committed herself to looking at every action and attitude at work, even the small ones. She developed an intention to be direct and honest and to act with integrity in every aspect of her work. Her sense of freedom and happiness on the job increased, and she became genuinely interested in learning new skills. Eventually her boss noticed these changes, and Barbara's income grew as well.

GREEK GOLD AND FREEDOM

Aware of the importance of balance and integrity in regard to money, the ancient Greeks told a myth that shows what happens when things get out of whack. The story concerns Midas, king of a city in Macedonia, who was known all over the ancient world for his craven love of wealth. After Midas did a favor for Dionysius, the god asked him how he wished to be rewarded. Midas replied, "Pray grant that all I touch be turned into gold." Dionysius gave the king exactly what he asked for. At first, as he turned shrubs, flowers, furniture, and even the palace walls to gold, Midas loved his new power. Then he sat down to a meal—only to watch the bread, meat, and wine turn to metal as he touched them. Soon Midas was dying of hunger and thirst, and he begged Dionysius to release him from what had become the curse of the golden touch. The god told him to wash in a sacred river, and after Midas had done so, the curse left him.

In dealing with money and learning about it, we fear that we will become Midas, who finds not vitality and an infinity of possibilities in his gold touch but a slow, wrenching death. Everything Midas touches becomes money, but he cannot feed himself. Wealthy beyond counting, he is dead to the world, a man hungry and thirsty for the most basic needs of body and soul. Utterly lacking integrity of spirit, Midas mistakes greed for freedom.

If we maintain integrity in our wandering through this world, we can escape the Midas trap. As we work toward our own maturity, money comes to represent a far-flung freedom flowing from an integrity rooted deeply in ourselves. Knowledge begins in understanding that all of life is about freedom and that our relationship with money is a way of cultivating freedom—not of engaging in senseless accumulation, as Midas did. In Knowledge we pay attention to fields of information, bytes, pixels, and data on everything from savings percentages to fifty-year rates of return on specific classes of investments. Yet in every moment we hold to the deep knowing that it's really about freedom.

Virginia Woolf, the famous British writer who is quoted at the beginning of this chapter, explored this idea in *A Room of One's Own*. The key to women discovering their own literary voices, Woolf wrote, is having the financial wherewithal to afford the space and time to write. Woolf was arguing from her own experience. Having received an inheritance of £500 a year for life, she could devote herself to novels and essays without worrying where her next meal was coming from or becoming dependent on a husband for support. She was free to write as and what she wished. "Five hundred a year," she wrote truly, "stands for the power to contemplate."

Money makes the dreams and aspirations of our lives possible; it brings them within our reach. Without sufficient money, we simply cannot do what we want to do—whether that means writing novels, building a thriving business that makes the world a better place, or spending more time with our children as they grow up. The notion that we can be free internally and not free financially is absurd, simply a further expression of the notion that soul work and money work exist in two separate and distinct realms. They are in fact woven together within the undivided space of our own beings.

WHERE FREEDOM AND INTEGRITY ENTWINE

Knowledge is a step toward freedom—not merely in a practical, pay-the-bills way, but in a fashion that arises from within our souls. Knowledge breaks the taboo surrounding money by tearing away the veil of ignorance and letting the light in. It starts us on the long climb toward awakening and out of the suffering cycle of Pain and Innocence.

Knowledge begins in the understanding that it is our birthright to be free, that a path to freedom can be found and followed. Otherwise, what is the purpose of mastering money? We must first understand what freedom means for us, what the central purposes of our lives are, and how we intend to accomplish them.

Freedom is like the soul. Without it we are nothing. Lived in its presence, life becomes transformed. Often, when the topic of money comes up in ordinary conversation, people talk about retirement, or buying a bigger house or car or sending the kids to college. All these things do represent aspects of freedom, but there is more. Our first obligation in this world is to discover the circumstances in which our souls flourish. This the truest and deepest meaning of freedom—living under the conditions that make us most truly ourselves.

Once we understand freedom this way, we can escape the crazy compulsion for more that propels the rat race. Midas is the classic embodiment of this insanity. When Midas asked Dionysius for the touch of gold, he already had more wealth than he could consume in a multitude of lifetimes. Yet because he little understood his own purposes in this life, he confused more with better and asked for the god's gift—which soon turned into a curse. Had Midas been in a more truthful relationship with his own soul, he would have also been in a better relationship with money. He would have understood what he needed and known when to say "I have what I require. Now my soul may fly free."

As we follow our own dreams of freedom and understand their deepest and most spiritual implications, we discover that integrity and freedom overlap. In a most profound way, they are one and the same thing. On the surface, Derrick King's struggle feels like a choice between freedom and integrity. His boss's behavior trapped him in a difficult moral dilemma, yet the question wasn't only ethical. His financial needs, specifically his children's education and the fate of his marriage, played into it as well. Derrick realized he was free to act as he thought he should only if he had the financial freedom to follow his conscience. My task as Derrick's financial advisor was to try to help him find a way of bringing his conflicting meanings for freedom and integrity together.

Mahealani Sapolu intuited the deeper truth that freedom and integrity are the same thing. Looking through the darkness of her indebtedness and her family's compromised well-being, she spied freedom. It wasn't enough for her to say that money is a white man's invention she would have nothing to do with. She needed to clean up her financial act in order to discover her own spiritual health and integrity.

For Susanna Swartz, integrity could be found only in reaching for freedom—a material freedom she had denied herself out of resentment and guilt. But this freedom was not that of Midas glorying in his ubiquitous gold. Rather, she was breaking the bonds of childhood and allowing her soul to speak without fear of censure—by her father or brothers, her former husband, her own inner voice, or the community disapproval she projected outward.

For each of us, establishing the ground of freedom and integrity in money gives meaning to the acquisition of practical money skills—the topic of the next chapter. For each of us, this meaning is a gathering of maturity.

TRY THIS: OBSERVING MORAL CONDUCT

All spiritual traditions promote the cultivation of virtue as a path to freedom. In many Buddhist traditions one must perfect *sila*, or moral conduct, before one is taught contemplative or wisdom practices. The Buddha's core teaching contains a specific disciplined way to freedom, or Nirvana, called the Eightfold Path. Three of the path's eight elements involve virtuous conduct: right speech, right action, and right livelihood. Each of them is worth looking at in our financial lives.

Consider the example of Shantideva. Once he recognized the suffering he was embedded in, his first two actions were to dedicate his mind to freedom and to vow not to act wrongly again. A dedication to freedom in our financial lives inspires us to pursue the practical Knowledge of money that will get us to freedom. A determination within ourselves to act with integrity clears away many of the cobwebs of Pain and Innocence that keep us from understanding the practical ways money works in the world.

Paying attention is a way of saying that the deepest parts of our souls count. For the next week, practice a considered awareness of the way you approach every interaction turning on money. Adopt the attitude of meditation, a quiet, kind observing of each moment. Watch the moral issues—the questions of freedom and integrity—that arise, for instance, when you open a checkbook to pay bills, reach into your pocket for parking meter change, or purchase groceries. Attend closely to your emotional responses. Watch also your yearnings for money. Notice whether they are in truth longings for integrity and freedom.

These questions can serve as a guide:

When do you handle money with kindness and moral integrity? When do you find yourself compromising those virtues? Can you notice the actual moments and the Pain and Innocence that trap you at those times? See if you can identify the downside personal and financial consequences of acting unvirtuously.

When you make a purchase, does gratitude at the gift you have received fill you? Or do you find yourself consumed with resentment at having paid too much, being taken for a ride, or seeing yourself as the victim of financial forces? If you find yourself without gratitude, pause and notice what you're receiving. See if you can first appreciate what you're getting and then find gratitude for it. Notice the difference internally between feeling gratitude and feeling resentment. What potential financial consequences can you imagine from changing your attitudes toward money from resentment to gratitude?

When you pay another person for his or her services—in business, home, or elsewhere—do you feel guilty because you aren't paying them enough? Or do you feel fear of being taken and paying them too much? Or is your response a simple gratitude?

When you contemplate money, do you see the promise of freedom it holds? Can you notice the freedom that the coins in your pocket and the bills in your wallet represent?

TRY THIS: YOUR LIFE IN MONEY— DEEP KNOWLEDGE

The next step in your financial autobiography is to determine your understanding of freedom and integrity around money by looking at your life. You can use these questions to guide your thinking and self-discovery:

Consider all the people who have taught you—consciously and unconsciously—about money: parents, schoolteachers, coaches, relatives who were wealthy or poor, and so forth. What lessons did you learn from each of them about freedom and integrity? Be detailed and specific.

Consider all the figures you have admired, both living and dead—writers, artists, politicians, athletes, business leaders, physicians, and healers, inventors—anyone whose life has struck you as admirable, important, and worthy of emulation. What lessons did you learn from them about freedom and integrity? Again, be detailed and specific.

When you dine out with friends and the check arrives at the table, do you pay your fair share? If the drinks have been left off the bill, would you say anything about it? Does it matter one way or the other? Do integrity issues arise for you in such a setting?

Do you feel that dealing with money intrudes on the real purpose of your life? What is that purpose? Does your conflict with money involve some sacrifice of integrity? Do you feel as if you are giving up a piece of yourself in exchange for the dollar? List all the ways this happens. Then choose a few of them and vow to act differently in the future.

Do you cheat around money? Steal? Claim things that are not yours? List all the ways you do these things—say, at work, on tax returns, on loan and insurance applications, at check-out counters. Consider what would happen if you changed your behavior.

chapter 6

KNOWLEDGE II: PLANNING, PROPS, AND PRACTICALITIES

The Props assist the House
Until the House is built
And then the Props withdraw
And adequate, erect,
The House support itself
And cease to recollect
The Auger and the Carpenter —
Just such a retrospect
Hath the perfected Life—
A past of Plank and Nail
And slowness—then the Scaffolds drop
Affirming it a Soul.

Emily Dickinson

Greed is inevitable in the absence of an inner aim.

Jacob Needleman

Juggling a job and a baby at home, Mahealani discovered she had inherited much of her father's persistence and doggedness. She worked as many hours as the grocery store manager would allow her, and every moment at home she spent caring for Pualani, fixing meals, washing clothes, and cleaning. Hers was a life at hard labor.

"It feels pretty much like it's worth it," she told me. "Every two weeks I get that paycheck. When I put my money together with what Ricky is bringing home, we're still not making a lot, but it's better than it used to be."

Yet even with two incomes, Ricky and she were barely paying down the debt that hung over them.

"It seems like there's always something," she said. "I pay the rent, and then there's the utilities, and we have to eat, and it's nice to take in a movie on Saturdays, and the baby's starting to wear shoes and you know what that costs. Practically everything that comes in goes out, and there's just about nothing left."

"How much do you need to live on per month?" I asked. "What's the minimum you need to get by?"

Mahealani's face went blank. "I really don't know," she shrugged.

"Really?"

"Really," she said. "I never even thought about figuring it out."

"I'll give you a piece of advice," I said. "Until you do, you won't even begin to get out from under that debt. You need to know how much you're bringing in, what you have to pay out in necessary bills, and how much of what's left over you can apply to the debt."

"Is that a budget?" she asked.

"It is indeed."

"Okay," she said.

Working with her usual persistence, Mahealani toted up every penny going in and out of her house over the next two months. She put all the family's expenses in one column, penciled her income and Ricky's into another, added both columns, and subtracted total expenses from total income. Less than $100 remained.

"At this rate, we'll still be paying that debt off when we're old, gray, and nearly dead," she said. "But I figured out something in going through this exercise. If Ricky and I can lower our expenses, we'll have more money to pay off the debt. And maybe we can even find a way to cut the cost on the debt too. That way more of the dollars we pay on it will whittle it down, instead of just being sucked up by finance charges."

Mahealani insisted that Ricky pack his own lunch every day rather than pick up a hamburger and fries at a fast food joint, and she cut their entertainment expenses to one movie a month. Ricky grumbled, but he went along. And he developed a new respect for her savvy when she talked a finance company into consolidating their credit card balances with a single loan at 11 percent interest rather than the 18 percent they had been paying.

"But, you know, I'd like to be doing more than just working to get out of debt," Mahealani said.

"What do you mean?" I asked.

"I'm punching a clock to make so much per hour. That's all. I'd like to be spending my time doing something more worthwhile."

"What have you done in your life that made you feel worthwhile?" I asked.

She thought for a moment. "When I was pregnant, I had this feeling of being right in the middle of life. Sometimes I felt like all the power of the universe was moving through my body out into the world. I still feel it sometimes when I'm playing with Pualani. I realize I made her, she's a piece of me. I'd love to have a way of living that gave me that feeling of being in the middle of life again, of creating something vital."

"That's something we should look at more closely," I said. "It's important to get a sense of where you are going, not just in negative terms like getting out of debt, but in a positive way, like taking steps toward making your life what you want it to be."

⌐⌐⌐

"So you've told me you have three primary goals in your life," I said to Derrick King. "The first one is to ensure your children the best education they can absorb and you can afford."

Derrick nodded. "That's paramount."

"A second goal is to keep your marriage together. Is that right?"

Derrick nodded.

"And the third thing you'd like to do is to provide yourself with enough financial freedom that you wouldn't have to cover up your boss's romantic life on the side just to protect your job and salary," I said.

Again he nodded.

"There's something else I've wondered about. I keep asking myself: What does freedom mean to you? You've expressed all your goals as if they were negative, as if they were pushing your nose down to the grindstone. What does freedom actually look like to you? I keep wondering too about the time you spent in the Peace Corps after college—do you still have an interest in that kind of experience, for instance?" I said.

"Those two years were a long time ago, it was just a youthful fantasy," Derrick said, his hand waving dismissively. "I have much more important things to think about. Look, George, I feel like I'm caught between the devil and the deep blue sea. I have to make a big salary to afford my boys' college and to keep my wife happy at home. That means I have to keep the job, even if I'm uncomfortable with what I must do to protect it. It looks impossible."

"It probably is, at least the way you've framed it," I agreed. "Why do you have to send your boys back East for college?"

"Eastern schools are best," he said.

"Why do you think so?" I asked.

"Everybody agrees," he answered.

"But why do *you* think so?" I persisted. "I'm pushing for a reason that's personal, that belongs to you and you alone. If we really look at what is motivating you about your sons' future, we may find some other way of accomplishing the goal you're after yet lessen the financial conflict you feel.

"For example, if your deepest goal for them is a top-notch education, you have less expensive alternatives closer to home. If you don't want to send them to USC since you went there, you could consider UC Berkeley or UCLA. If you want a small liberal arts school, you could think about Reed, even Stanford. The tuition is high, but it's practically around the corner from you, so you'd save on transportation and perhaps even living expenses. The point is that by determining what you're really after, you may be able to shift your financial goals to give yourself more freedom around your job situation."

Then I asked, "What does Alexandria think about all of this?"

"I haven't involved her," he said. "In our family it has always been my responsibility to make the major money decisions. After all, I make the money. It's up to me to decide how to spend it, and it's up to her to run the house and be there for the boys. This is the way we've always done it." Derrick paused. "Recently, though, she's been letting me know she doesn't like it this way."

Derrick mused in silence for a few moments. "Maybe you're right about the college education issue," he said, in a voice both resisting and accepting. "If I can get some more flexibility, maybe I could start thinking about Alexandria."

———

"I agree. I've done my penance," Susanna Swartz concluded. "I'd like to start living a real life again—not in this dump, but in a house, a big house, a Victorian. How much can I afford?"

I named a figure I knew she could spend without compromising her ability to live the rest of her life on what she had and still pass a large legacy on to her children and to charitable causes. She nodded. I had further thoughts.

"Here's how we'll do it," I continued, launching into a broad outline of my financial plan for her. "Together we should figure your monthly and annual budget. We'll keep those amounts of cash in the money market and a short-term bond fund. We take the remainder of your assets, outside of your family stock, and invest it in a mix of mutual funds, some of them index funds and others actively managed. I'd like to put a significant portion of your money in small-cap value mutual funds in order to give your portfolio some real growth potential. The remainder I'd divide among high-quality corporate bond funds, a large-cap value index fund, an international—"

"Stop, George," Susanna interrupted me. "Listening to that stuff makes my head hurt."

"But you need to know," I countered. "This is your money I'm talking about."

"It sure is. But I don't really want to know the details of what you're doing with it. I just want to know if you're listening to me and if I can trust you."

"And that's it?" I asked.

"The details of money management put me off. I have no interest in them, and I'm not about to twist my head around to learn all that gobbledygook about money. That's your job. I'll tell you what I want, and I expect you to figure out a way to do it. You have those initials after your name because you've put in the time to learn all about money. When it comes to finances, you're a certified smart guy, which is precisely what I'm not. I'm paying you so I can use your brains instead of mine.

"I'll tell you what I want, and you make it happen. Spare me the details."

I thought for a moment about what she had said. "The bottom line is you want to know I'm listening to you and giving you good advice you can trust."

"Exactly," she said.

Between a part-time nursing job for a health maintenance organization and a second part-time job as a self-employed health-care marketing specialist, Esther made good money. She was smart, energetic, and motivated, yet she didn't really know what to do with the money she made. She came from a poor Cape Cod fisherman's family where nobody had a penny extra. Now Esther, the first person in her family to attend college, was surprised to find herself earning more than she needed. She sent money back to her folks, and she saved. When I met her, she had $36,000 stashed in a bank savings account earning only a few percentage points of interest a year.

"At least it's safe," she said to me.

Beyond that, money baffled Esther. Whenever she tried to think or read about financial planning or investing, or whenever she talked to a stock or insurance broker, she felt diminished by money and overwhelmed by the complexities of it.

"I'm smart enough," she once told me, "but money's one thing I just don't get. I can earn it, I can save it. But beyond that, I don't know what to do with it."

Esther came to my twelve-years-at-12-percent class in order to learn enough about money to avoid becoming a mark for the investment sharks who make their money preying on the untutored. This is precisely why I gave the class—to show people how to take on money themselves, all the way from finding their sense of purpose to under-standing how to invest. Esther loved it. She realized quickly she had known all along what she wanted: a little house on the edge of the Berkshires in the Connecticut River valley and the ability to travel more. She was eager to learn from other cultures how they handled health issues and to share with them what she knew. Like many peo-ple, she had always felt her ideals were beyond her grasp. The course offered her hope, and enough information about money that she could begin to chart and follow her own course.

Esther dedicated herself to saving a steady 20 percent of her income, depositing the funds on the first of every month to a discount brokerage account to buy no-load mutual funds. When she had a windfall, she contributed extra. She saved more than I proposed, but she invested less aggressively than I recommended. Still, twelve years later, she has the cottage in the Berkshires, $400,000 in mutual funds, a lifestyle simple enough to allow her to retire. And she enjoys a love of her work in both nursing and marketing.

"The great thing, George, is I can do what I want," she said. "I'm not constrained by money. I take long weekends throughout the sum-mer and a month to travel in the winter. But I love my job, so why should I quit? Retirement wasn't what I got from your course and from working with you. What I got was peace of mind around money—just by creating a discipline and following it, by having a goal worth pursuing and putting my energy toward it. I think both the emptiness and the kind of longing I felt earlier in my life are gone because of the work I've done around money. With the sense of secu-rity I have now, I feel my work can be filled with play for me, some-thing I can enjoy for itself. And I do."

This chapter, together with chapter 11, provides you with the same skills I taught to Esther over a decade ago. How you approach them and what you do with them is up to you. Ideally, you too will discover the same sense of freedom and peace she has.

WHERE KNOWLEDGE BEGINS

Wisdom concerns not only the farthest reaches of our imagination but also the most prosaic details of everyday existence. To become masters of the profound in money's realm, we must first understand the practical.

A lack of Knowledge can get us into trouble, not only with money but also with the rest of our lives as well. You can see this in Susanna Swartz's story. Her lack of Knowledge about money contributed to the loss of a sizable portion of her inheritance. Recovering from that loss meant facing the issue of her own ignorance, if only through the medium of working with a financial advisor she could trust. At the other end of the wealth scale, Mahealani Sapolu faced Knowledge issues around budgeting, overspending, and indebtedness. For her, the simple, practical act of penciling out a budget was a first wavering step toward freedom.

Knowing money alone is nowhere near enough. Yet unless we know money, we can never become who we most wish to be.

THE ELEMENTS OF FINANCIAL PLANNING

The practical aspects of money are connected to the spiritual well-springs of our souls through financial planning. This process is so powerful, so grounding, so affirming of who we most truly are and choose to be that often it can cure the Pain of childhood just by awakening us to the facts of financial life.

The process reminds me of the Emily Dickinson poem quoted at the beginning of this chapter. Financial planning provides the props that support the house we are building—which is the depth of our lives. When we finish, the props can be withdrawn and we may behold what we have built—our own souls, free and full.

Most of us, though, have a somewhat less lofty view of the process. When I ask a seminar class to define financial planning, most of the participants respond with an answer that mentions something about investing. They're right, but only partly. Investing is a means to an end, and financial planning begins with determining the ends. Only when we know where we are headed can we decide the means—that is, the process of saving and investing—needed to get us there.

The two pillars on which the financial planning equation is built look like this:

THE FINANCIAL PLANNING PROCESS

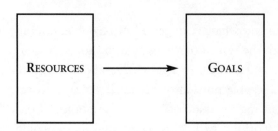

Goals drive financial planning. If you were to sit down with me and say "George, I want you to do a financial plan for me," I couldn't even begin until I know what your goals are. Without understanding the future you desire, I have no idea whether, for example, to put most of your funds into the money market or to invest them very aggressively in the stock market.

More important than deciding these tactical considerations, however, goals connect our surfaces to our souls. They spell out our dreams of freedom in practical dollars-and-cents terms. This dream of freedom charges financial planning with energy and direction.

When I first begin goal work with new clients, I want them to give me the most profound, the deepest, the biggest goals they can think of. If they want to build a corporation bigger than Microsoft, I want to know it. If they want to finish medical school, then move to Africa to take up where Dr. Schweitzer left off, I want to know it. If they want to write the great American novel, I want to know that. To become who we most truly are, we must be free first to dream, then to translate that dream into the practicalities that might allow it to be accomplished. Only then, working from a competent level of Knowledge, should we consider compromises as we attach dollar signs—reality's most potently sobering symbol—to the dream. Right there, where dream and dollar cross, the surface and the soul connect.

The resources included in financial planning cover what accountants call assets—real estate, cash on hand, stocks, bonds, mutual funds, trusts, inheritances, and the like. They also contain inner resources like dependability, timeliness, energy, dedication, discretion, enthusiasm, optimism, persistence, honesty, the ability to earn income, and the capacity to save.

Mahealani Sapolu had practically nothing in the way of assets when I first met her. She rented her little house, and she and Ricky lived from paycheck to paycheck, so there was no extra money around. Yet she had significant inner resources, which she came to appreciate as she committed herself to getting out of debt—a clear focus on her central purpose, high energy, and enough determination to make a pit bull sit up and take notice. Such inner resources are more important than many of us realize.

A recent study by University of Chicago economist Susan Mayer shows just how important they can be. A liberal Democrat appalled by the debate over welfare reform and a former single mother who remembered all too well her own hard times, Mayer wanted to find out how big a role the amount of money in a poor household played in helping children escape poverty. Mayer discovered that money was less important than the personality characteristics parents modeled for their children, particularly the ones employers value, such as diligence, honesty, skills, good health habits, and reliability. Children born to parents with these attributes tended to do well in life even when family income was low.

The attributes Mayer studied are what I call inner resources. As a financial planner, I find that it is often difficult to identify clients' inner resources and even more difficult to strengthen them. Yet all inner resources share one element in common—they ask us to sacrifice something of the moment for the benefit of others or for a larger, more distant goal. Our capacity to save is our greatest inner resource around money. Without this ability to put money aside, to say no to the present in order to say yes to the future, financial planning is likely to be chaotic and unrewarding.

Like goals, resources start off as qualities that seem to exist independently of money, then we put a value on them in dollar terms—associating, for example, our ability to make or save with an amount of money. Add in the assets with an obvious cash value, such as real estate and mutual funds, deduct debts and other obligations, and we have a realistic assessment of what we have to work with to make our dreams real.

Once we understand goals and assess resources, we can implement an investment strategy. Three key and highly interrelated variables are involved in developing a strategy: time, rate of return, and risk.

To understand how these three elements work together, let's take a simple example. Right now you have $500 in your pocket, and you've laid your heart's desire on a slick road bike that costs $550. Your goal is the bicycle with the $550 price tag, and your resources are the $500 you have saved. If you want to wait no more than a year to get the bike, you know you have to come up with $50 more over the next twelve months. Fifty dollars is 10 percent of $500. Therefore, the annual rate of return you need on your $500 savings is 10 percent.

If you put your $500 in a bank account at the current rate of 2 percent annual interest, you'll have $510 at the end of the year, more than you have now but still well short of your $550 goal. At a 2 percent rate of return, it will take you nearly five years to reach $550. But, since 10 percent is close to the average return of the stock market over many decades, you probably would do better to invest the money in the stock market for a one-year period.

The word *probably* introduces risk to the picture. Many of us think of risk as the chance that we will lose everything we have invested. That can happen, of course, as it did to individual companies in the great stock market crash of 1929 or the savings and loan debacle of the 1980s. Technically, however, risk is nowhere near so catastrophic. Risk is simply the degree of uncertainty attached to an expected rate of return; it is a measure of volatility. Investing your $500 into a bank account carries almost no risk. Barring an asteroid impact on Earth, the total financial default of the U.S. government, or some other highly unlikely catastrophe, you'll make that 2 percent in a year. The risk is nearly zero.

Assume, though, that you're impatient and you want your bike in six months, not the five years you'll have to wait at a nearly risk-free 2 percent annually. You're going to have to earn 10 percent in only six months, which means an annual rate of return of approximately 20 percent. Investments are available that offer prospects of 20 percent per year or even more. There's a catch, though—increased risk. Volatile stocks in high-growth sectors, small-company stocks, and venture-capital investments can post extremely high returns, for example, but they can also lose money.

Generally, the higher the anticipated rate of return on an investment, the higher the degree of uncertainty about that return.

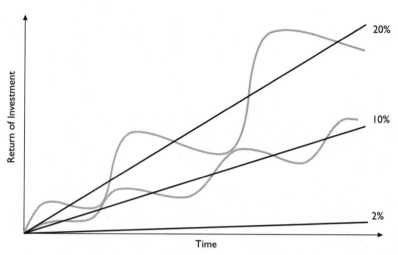

Asset classes with higher returns over time also exhibit higher volatility

As we will explore in depth later in chapter 11, the relationship between return and risk isn't absolute. Still, it's close enough most of the time to use as a reality check. If, for example, a so-called investment advisor approaches you with a deal he says is guaranteed to make 100 percent in six months with absolutely no risk, you can be sure he is a liar, a criminal, a lunatic, or all of the above. Put your money somewhere else.

In launching a financial-planning process, it is as important to understand our relationship to risk as it is to determine goals and assess resources. To translate resources into goals, we need to become very clear how much risk we are willing to take and understand the degree of risk our investments entail, then commit ourselves to sticking with the program we initiate. Virtually all mistakes in investing occur not because we choose the wrong investments but because we fail to understand our own volatile relationship with risk. If we don't come to terms with our emotional responses to risk, we will fail as investors—and our goals will remain unfulfilled.

The investor who fails to understand his or her relationship to risk—and loses as a result—often follows a classic pattern of investment behavior.

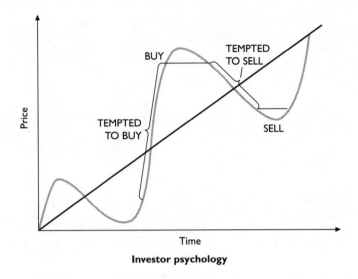

Investor psychology

As the stock market heads up, you hear from friends how well their stocks are doing and how much money they're making. They encourage you to buy stocks as well, to share in this increasing prosperity. But you remember those family stories about Grandad, how he sank it all in railroad stock right before the crash of 1929 and lost every penny. "No way," you say, "I'm not that big a fool." Still, the market continues to rise, higher and higher. Your friends buy yachts, trade in the Chevy for a Lexus, barbecue T-bones instead of veggie burgers, move out of that modest working-class bungalow into the classiest neighborhood in town. You're still not convinced. In your heart of hearts you call them fools, but you also envy their newfound fortunes.

Then you pick up your newsmagazine of choice, and the front cover screams "BOOM!" The country is growing like July corn in Iowa, there's no recession even remotely in sight, unending prosperity is the wave of the future, the lead article proclaims. Now you change your mind. You realize you're not Grandad, your friends must be right, and certainly the magazine is. You call a broker and put all your money down.

You couldn't have done it at a worse time. Ironically, the market is most dangerous right when it seems the safest, the time when everyone agrees "If you have money, buy stocks." Since everyone who is even minimally inclined to get into stocks has already done so, no supply of outside money remains to keep pushing prices up. So it's not surprising when you call your financially savvy friends to tell them your good news about finally getting into the stock market, and they say, "Really? The market looks awfully high right now. I'm starting to sell." They're not the only ones. As more and more people sell, prices begin to drop. You're not worried, though. After all, the market was still going up when you bought in, so you've made a little money already, even if some of your original gains have evaporated. But as prices fall past the point where you entered and you realize you're losing part of your original investment, an edge of panic sets in. The market continues to fall, and you keep losing. You think about selling, but you say to yourself "No, I don't want to be a loser," and you hold on, clinging to an Innocent belief despite the Pain you are feeling. You dig in your heels, suffering every moment, until the market has come down a total of 35 to 40 percent—the average bottom of all bear, or falling, markets in this century. You're sure you've had enough when your newsmagazine of choice declares "DEPRESSION!" on the cover. That does it. You're ready to abandon your goal of retiring to write the great American novel and put the kids through the Sorbonne. You tell your broker to sell—and yourself that Grandad had it right all along. You take what remains of your savings and sock it in the bank, where it's safe and sound—and the returns are too anemic for you ever to regain the ground you have lost. Surely the market will once again go up, yet you'll be standing on the sidelines and the opportunity you might have had will be forever lost.

Most of us get burned in precisely this way—buying high and selling low on emotional waves—because we fail to understand our own response to risk. A number of recent studies demonstrate how average investors achieve lower returns than either the mutual funds or the stock markets they invest in. This seeming contradiction occurs because most investors operate just the way I have described—entering the market in periods of euphoria, when risk (of loss as opposed to volatility) is actually greatest, and selling in a panic close to or at the bottom, when risk is in fact lowest and opportunity greatest. Unless you come to terms with your own emotional responses to risk, you too will fail as an individual investor in exactly the same way.

Each of us has many options in regard to risk. To start with, we can reduce risk by reducing our goals—deciding to buy a cheaper bike or live a simpler lifestyle in retirement, thus lowering the rate of return required from investments. We can also reduce investment risk by working harder and saving more or by lengthening the time we are willing to wait for our goals to be achieved. If we simply can't stomach volatility, we can lower the risk of the investments themselves to our comfort point by putting more money in insured certificates of deposit and Treasury bills. We also can come to terms with our emotional relationship to money by strengthening our grasp of Knowledge and Understanding and learning to invest intelligently, acting in a clear and unshaken manner despite the unending volatility of markets. Or we can hire a trained professional investment advisor who constructs a portfolio that matches our risk-return profile and keeps us from falling into the usual traps of investor psychology—exactly the option Susanna Swartz chose with me, and one we will discuss in more detail in chapter 11.

To sum up, financial planning concerns employing resources to reach goals. Adding the element of time—how long do you want to spend amassing the resources needed to reach the goals?—determines the discipline and control you must set for yourself, the rate of return you need, and the risk you must assume. Each of these elements bears a closer look.

GOALS: WHO, WHAT, WHERE WE WANT TO BE

Unless we aspire to be a saint like Francis of Assisi, we each live a life of compromises, as the yearnings of the soul yield before the demands of day-to-day life. In my own life I have held to a commitment of making sure that, no matter what necessity forces me to do, I make my spiritual needs the deepest goal in my life. This isn't to say that my soul's concerns always win. They don't. But I always am sure that I make a place for them, however small, both in the present moment and in future visions of myself. Even when pressures are most intense, I remind myself that my spirit is the prize toward which I am moving. At the same time, I have searched the world of money to find a secure foothold from which I can develop internally as I choose—and not as financial necessity dictates—and act externally upon the world as I intend. Slowly I have come to realize that working with money is in fact the spiritual journey, that the path I am following within myself and the work I am doing in the financial world are in fact one and the same spiritual quest.

For all of us, the purpose of goal work is to resolve the apparent conflict between life and money and to decide where each of us needs to be. We have to locate the source of our own integrity, determine what the dream of freedom means to us, and decide how to move toward it. This is hard, demanding work. But if we fail to explore and articulate our goals, we will not so much lead our lives as find ourselves trapped in a hell of confusion, frustration, and purposeless acquisition.

In chapter 2 I told the story of the young woman client who at first was unable to articulate any real goal for herself, largely because she had built her life on an Innocent belief that she could never have what she really wanted. Once she faced this idea down and freed herself from it, she developed her dream of running an alternative health clinic and actually brought the project into reality much sooner than she had ever thought possible. A number of other clients I have worked with offer additional illustrations of the crucial relationship linking goal work to spiritual and financial well-being.

THE PHYSICIAN, THE BUSINESSWOMAN, AND THE ATTORNEY

A MOTHER WITHIN. When I first met Elaine, M.D., she impressed me with her seeming clarity. She told me flat out, "I want $1 million. That's what I'm after." Her answer wasn't particularly unusual; when I first ask clients their goals, they often name the $1 million figure. Yet, for someone with such a definite and clearly defined financial objective, she was going about it in exactly the wrong way. She worked long weeks as a family practitioner in an inner-city clinic, where she earned but a fraction of what she could have taken in as a specialist in an upscale practice.

"Why are you working such long hours for much lower pay than you could get elsewhere when your goal in life is to make $1 million?" I asked. "It must be grueling."

"I'm doing what really matters," she said. "I didn't endure the medical school grind so I could cure acne in the rich and famous. I wanted to make a difference. Where I'm working is where medicine faces the biggest health-care challenges of all."

"When would you like to have the $1 million?"

"As soon as possible. That's why I'm here."

Suspecting that she was concealing her own deepest goals from herself, I led Elaine through the goal-work exercises described later in this chapter. She was focused and in command until she said something about having children, and I could see her eyes soften. Moments later tears welled up in her eyes and spilled down her cheeks. Clearly, something deep in her was coming out. Elaine's tears signaled the shock of recognizing the emergence of well-hidden personal truth.

"You know," she said, "I want $1 million because that's what it'll take to afford the baby I want."

She and I explored her story more deeply. It came out that just a year earlier she had ended a live-in relationship with a very well-to-do man who owned a big house, loved to talk money, and convinced her that having a child bore a price tag of at least $1 million. Focused exclusively on the demands of her medical work and awed by her lover's financial skills, Elaine assumed he knew what he was talking about. When the relationship ended—but her desire for a child continued unabated—she threw herself into her work, regularly putting in sixty to seventy hours a week, and saved assiduously, trying to amass the money she thought would allow her to have a baby.

Truth was, the former boyfriend had overestimated the cost of raising a child by a substantial margin. Once Elaine recognized that fact and understood how she had taken this man's values on as her own, she could see clearly what she needed to do next. Her real goal wasn't financial; her salary was more than adequate for having and raising a child. She wanted the personal gratification that a family would bring, and the $1 million goal was actually getting in the way. She could achieve what she wanted more by finding a partner who shared her interest in having a family and building a relationship than by working long hours to save $1 million. She decided to take the pressure off herself, cut back at work to forty-five hours a week, and develop a social life in which meeting a man of compatible interests was a possibility.

Three years later I happened to spot Elaine on a downtown street, arm in arm with a good-looking fellow, pushing a baby carriage. She wore a look of contentment. This was a woman who had found what she needed—not from money itself but from working through what her original financial goal represented to her.

CHANGING HORSES MIDSTREAM. Rosemary was young, well tailored, ambitious, and highly intelligent. She had gone into real estate sales in the Cambridge area at the end of the 1970s, just before Massachusetts home prices skyrocketed through the early to mid-1980s. A saleswoman with both high ambition and boundless energy, she developed a practiced eye for the right clients and the right properties. In five years she had saved close to $250,000 and showed no sign of slowing down. She attended my seminars and did the basic goal exercises I offer in them. Then she came to me as a financial-planning client.

"I'm absolutely clear about what I want," she said. "I want you to invest my savings the same way you manage your own. I'll make money the way I know best, by selling houses, and you'll make me more money the way you know best, by investing it."

"But what do you want to do with this money?" I asked. "I don't really know what your goals are. You need to understand that I manage my own money in a way that is far riskier than anything I offer my clients. I have confidence that in the long run the strategy will work. This is what I know, it's what I do. But I wouldn't dream of subjecting clients to the risk I take. They couldn't stand it."

"That's exactly why I want to invest with you," she said. "You know what you're doing. So do I."

Rosemary's powerful presence radiated certainty and determination. I took her demeanor to mean that she indeed knew what she wanted and that she was expressing her goals. I did then what I have rarely done since: I took her on as a client without further exploring her personal goals. I invested her as I invest myself, with an eye to the long term and a relatively high degree of risk. While there was every reason to believe that her holdings, like mine, would increase impressively over a period of years, in the shorter term they could drop if the stock market took one of its many downturns.

It surprised me a little when Rosemary called my office six months later and said, "I've made a change of plans."

"Oh," I said, a sense of foreboding building in me. "What are you planning?"

"I've decided to go back to school," she announced.

"There are some good evening business programs," I said.

"You don't understand," she countered. "I never finished college. I've decided to quit real estate altogether. I want to go back to school full time and major in social work. It'll take me three or four years, and I'll probably want to do a master's as well, which will take another two years. So I need to know from you—can I do it?"

My heart sank. I had invested Rosemary in the stock market on the assumption that she would be keeping her money in for a period of years, perhaps decades. Now she was returning only six months later and wanting to take it out. Had I known that to be the case when I first developed her investment plan, I would have put her mostly in T-bills, money-market funds, and short-term bonds, all investments that have little risk and are ideal for money that will be used in the next one to three years.

As I talked with her on the phone, a tide of emotions ran through me. It was clear that her sudden decision came from a place deep inside her. No doubt it flowed from some tender place I didn't know about. My ignorance made me angry—at her for keeping this side of herself from me and even more so at myself for not uncovering this hidden aspect of her in our financial-planning work together.

As it turned out, Rosemary was lucky. In the six months she had been invested, her assets had increased about 10 percent. But if our conversation had occurred just after the 1987 Black Monday stock market crash, she might not have been able to go back to school. The market went up again, but slowly, and it would have taken two years for Rosemary to get back to where she had begun.

Her story illustrates the need for thorough goal work as a way of understanding both short-term and long-term goals and choosing the investments that are right for each. The issue here, though, wasn't one of investment strategy but of understanding—by both me and Rosemary—what she was after, and when.

THE MAN WHO WOULD BE APARTMENT KING. I

worked with Richard only long enough to know I didn't want to work with him anymore. An attorney by profession, Richard had an income of $50,000 a year and no savings to speak of. He refused to do any goal work with me. He told me all he wanted was to make $1 million or more from nothing in three years or less.

"It can't be done safely," I said. "But why do you want so much so fast? What do you have in mind to do with the money? What are you really after?"

He looked at me oddly—the way I imagine Vince Lombardi would have glared at anyone who questioned the value of winning at all costs. "The money's what I'm after," he said. "The million *is* the goal."

When I told him again that the odds against making so much money in only three years created an unacceptably high degree of risk, he shook his head in disapproval.

"Cut this prudence crap," he said. "You just watch me, George. I'll do you a favor by showing you how it's done."

Even though Richard never became my client, he and I moved in overlapping social circles and I heard from time to time how he was getting along. At first he seemed to be succeeding, at least in money terms. Somehow, using his legal skills and powers of persuasion, he bought an apartment building for $300,000. He put no money of his own down and borrowed the entire purchase price. Over the next two months he converted the building to condominiums, sold the units to their current tenants, or evicted them to sell to new buyers. Richard left a wake of angry people behind him as he posted a $300,000 profit and promptly sunk all the money into a larger building. Remarkably, within a year and a half he had a net worth of more than $1 million, all of it in real estate.

"What would you do now if you were me?" he asked me at a mutual friend's birthday party.

"You have to diversify. You need to put a portion of your holdings into other forms of investment, like stocks and bonds," I said. "As it stands, you have all your eggs in one basket. You're very vulnerable."

"Still preaching prudence, eh, George?" he said. "Maybe you're right. But something tells me I've got one more big score to make. Watch me prove you wrong yet again."

He sold the building he owned and rolled his profit into an even larger apartment building with a huge mortgage. Then his luck changed. The New England real estate market peaked a couple of months later, then crashed like a piano off a cliff. Property values sank about 20 percent, consuming the profit Richard had made up till then. He lost his apartment building to foreclosure and returned to square one, with nothing to show for his three-year foray into real estate.

Richard's story reminds me very much of the truth of philosopher Jacob Needleman's reflection that "Without an inner aim, greed is inevitable." If we do not know where we are headed, there is no central purpose to ground us, to hold us firmly to life's reality. Richard lacked scruples, morals, and any future vision of himself as something more than wealthy. Without integrity and a dream of freedom, he was locked in the eternal hell of acquisition. No flames burned his body, but he was always after more, too divorced from his inner being to know what was enough or when he had reached it.

THREE STEPS TOWARD GOAL-SETTING

In working with clients and seminar participants over the years, I've encountered two distinct personal pathologies around goals.

The first is an inability to express them, sometimes even to admit goals into consciousness and recognize them for what they are. The young woman who ended up creating an alternative health clinic was a classic example, as was Susanna Swartz. Because of beliefs formed in her Innocence, Susanna was unwilling to say—even to herself—that she deeply wanted to buy and fix up a big Victorian house.

The second pathology concerns the inability to execute a strategy leading to the goals one wants to achieve. Hamlet, Shakespeare's reluctant hero, is the prototypical victim of this particular pathology, in which an individual knows what he or she wants to do yet cannot find the resources within the self to take action. This is a problem of energy, or Vigor, which we will discuss in chapter 8.

As we begin with this part of the work, it is important to understand the differences between fantasies, goals, and Vision—the sixth stage in Money Maturity and the focus of chapter 9. Fantasies constitute plans for wild escape, like running off to Tahiti or assuming voluntary self-exile among the literati of Paris's Left Bank. Fantasies are emotional responses to Pain, unrealistic dreams that return us to Innocence and, rather than activating our desire to master Knowledge, Understanding, and Vigor, leave us in dreamland, blame, or resentment. Somehow fantasies remain unachievable, outside our grasp. They are the sorts of things we would do if the lottery comes up with our numbers, an unknown rich uncle dies and leaves us a couple of million, or Steven Spielberg pays an absolute bundle for the movie script we haven't yet written.

Goals, by contrast, can be accomplished. They have a practical, achievable flavor, the sort of objective that can actually be reached within a single lifetime. They are also powerfully motivating, pushing us toward Knowledge, Understanding, and Vigor. Goals may include Vision—that is, they may reach beyond the needs of ourselves to encompass the welfare and benefit of a community.

I remember some years ago listening to a TV talk show where Ted Turner, a captain of the media industry and the prime mover behind the visionary CNN, said that his father taught him that the only goals worth having seem too grand to accomplish. Psychologists I know would disagree, calling such goals delusional and evidence of a narcissistic disorder, but Turner's perspective has great value. Most of us, I am convinced, sell ourselves short and set our goals too low. I never cease to be amazed at the extraordinary talents of practically everyone I meet. Each of us embodies skills, knowledge, intuitions, and sensitivities that are special, unique, and distinguishing. So often, though, we hold ourselves back from what we could be, achieve little of what we might, settle for small dreams or no dreams at all, and bury our greatest talents in the mud. It is here, in the undreamed dreams, that we wallow in the "quiet desperation" Henry David Thoreau named as the core of most people's lives.

For years now, in both my private practice and public seminars, I have used the three exercises that follow to help people recognize, identify, and clarify their goals. Dream as grandly as you can; reach for more than you think possible. Pull the special parts of you up out of the mud, polish them off, and make them a part of your life again.

Make a record of your work through these exercises in the spaces provided here or in the notebook or computer file you've created for the end-of-chapter material. You will find that the exercises build one upon another and that your insight into yourself will deepen as you progress through them. You may even find that you want to do them now and then again in a few months or a year. Indeed, I often come back to all three once or twice a year. Whenever I find myself in a crisis that is shaking up how I think about the elements of my life or when I am feeling down and defeated, ready to abandon the very projects or people that only shortly before had given my life meaning, I do these exercises as a way of sorting out and deciding what to do next. The exercises told me when to move from the city to the country, when to buy a house, how to balance the world of work and money with that of spirit, play, and family. They even suggested to me that it was time to start this book.

Big Bucks, and Then . . .

This exercise is a set of three scenarios to be worked through in order. The first one, called "plenty of money," is playful and fun as well as revealing. Here's the question to consider: "You may not be as wealthy as Bill Gates or the Sultan of Brunei, but you do have all the money you need, now and in the future. What will you do with it? From this moment forward, how will you live your life?"

As you write your answer, let yourself dream. This part of the exercise has nothing to do with realism. Run loose, without tether or rein. Give yourself the right to have, do, or be anything that comes to mind. Only when you have completed this part of the exercise in the space that follows should you go on to part two.

This second segment is called "just a few years left." You've just come back from a visit to a doctor who has discovered from your lab reports that you have only five to ten years to live. In a way you're lucky. This particular disease has no manifestations, so you won't feel sick. The bad part is that you will have no warning about the moment of your death. It will simply come upon you in an unpredictable instant, sudden and final.

Let the emotional import of the situation sink in, then address yourself to this interwoven question: "Knowing death is waiting for you sooner than you expected, how will you change your life? And what will you do in the uncertain but substantial period you have remaining?" Again, spend time with this question and let the full answer emerge from you. And don't go to the next part until you've finished here.

Now you are ready for the last step, named "twenty-four hours to go." Again you've gone to the doctor, but this time you learn you'll be dead within twenty-four hours. The question isn't what you would do with the little time you have. Instead, ask yourself, "What feelings am I experiencing? What regrets, what longings, what deep and now-unfulfilled dreams? What do I wish I had completed, been, had, done in this life that is just about to end?" As with the other two parts of this exercise, write your answers with the greatest honesty and candor you can summon.

Knowledge II: Planning, Props, and Practicalities

These three sets of questions move you deeper into yourself with each step. Typically, "plenty of money" reveals material desires—a bigger house, a Lexus, summers on the Riviera or among the Greek islands. Often, though, the answer also begins to reveal hidden desires and unfulfilled longings. "Just a few years left" pulls away more of the disguise—except, I have found, for those with young children, whose attention tends to go entirely to their offspring and reveals few of their personal dreams. For most other people, "just a few years left" removes some of the material trappings of "plenty of money" and uncovers areas of vulnerability that are deeper and closer to the core and that demand to be resolved, not swept under the rug.

"Twenty-four hours to go" cuts deepest of all, opening the bedrock of the self. Suddenly it becomes clear which issues in life are superficial and which are central. Sometimes this exercise delivers a major surprise, a longing or a wish hidden away so completely that it has never before surfaced, not simply to a financial advisor but often to oneself.

A couple of examples from my financial-planning practice show more about how this set of exercises works in uncovering our deepest goals. The first was an unmarried professional woman in early middle age who had come to me for advice in handling her growing retirement savings accounts. On the plenty-of-money question, she stated a desire to become self-employed as a way of adding flexibility to her career. She also wanted to own houses on both Atlantic and Pacific coasts, write a book, and speak well and confidently in public. "Just a few years left" brought up a number of personal issues. My client wanted to spend more time with her niece, particularly interested in a backcountry trek to the foot of Mount Everest in Nepal. She still wanted a flexible career, but she was also interested in cutting back to three workdays a week. With "twenty-four hours to go," her issues were only two, both deeply personal. She regretted that she had never learned to speak in her own voice with full authority. This was, of course, a repeat of the interest in public speaking that had emerged in the plenty-of-money exercise, but she restated it in a personal way that pointed toward the Vigor stage of Money Maturity. And she felt great remorse that she had yet to meet the love of her life. This regret was clearly related to her earlier interest in the Nepal trek with her niece, but it applied to a more intimate and deeply personal level of her being.

In terms of my working with this woman, the exercise made me aware of two concerns. I needed to be conscious of the places where her relationship with her career and the making of money might get in the way of her profound desire for more personal authority and a major love interest. At the same time, though, I paid special attention to the ways money might be employed to help her realize the goals of developing her voice and presence and using that skill to broaden her opportunities for meeting someone with whom she might develop a long-term relationship.

The second example shows again how well the three steps in this exercise peel back the levels of desire in an individual and reveal his or her core. This client, a man I had known socially for almost ten years, came to me out of a sense of overwhelming frustration with a life that required a complicated frenzy to make ends meet and left little opportunity for peace. A poet who is well known for his ability to perform his own verse and the work of other writers, he had been making a good living by using his performance skills to train people from corporations, nonprofits, and government agencies in effective ways of communicating. With "plenty of money," he said he wanted a new, bigger house, but otherwise he would continue to do everything he was already doing—a curious answer, in that he had owned up to a powerful frustration with his fast-paced lifestyle. The just-a-few-years-left exercise changed everything, revealing a part of this man I had not seen before. He said, without hesitation and with intense passion, that he wanted to devote his life to something permanent, like acting in movies made by independent producers. "Twenty-four hours to go" uncovered a powerful longing. He said that although he was successful as both an artist and a trainer, he felt lonely in his work and unrecognized for his skills and accomplishments.

That last and deepest unfolding gave me something important to work with. I knew the issue wasn't based in his primary relationship; he had a good marriage. Nor was it based on public recognition, for which also he did not lack. Clearly, the need was for something more intimate than workplace accolades. I shared with him that one of the most valuable efforts in my life has been a search for mentors—people, often older, who exhibit great goodness and virtue and with whom I can spend time. My client, by contrast, had spent much of his life mentoring others, but he had never enjoyed such a relationship for himself. Healing this wound by developing the resources needed to find mentors and nourishing those relationships became a central focus of his financial plan.

I also encouraged him to move some of his professional energy toward acting in independent films, which he had revealed in "just a few years left." He discovered that his goal was not so much a less frenetic and more peaceful life as much as one that let him connect with the full range of his creativity and gave him the ability to deepen the connections he began making with mentors.

BEYOND DEATH AND TAXES

This second exercise is a kind of tic-tac-toe game that separates desires from obligations and demands. It begins by drawing a grid, like this:

	Got to	Should	Like to
Have			
Do			
Be			

The next step is to fill in the cells. Into the "got-to" column, put all the things that, from the level of your heart or soul, you simply must do lest your life lack or lose meaning. "Have" refers to possessions, "do" covers accomplishments and activities, and "be" covers states of existence.

The same distinctions apply to the "should" column, which covers areas where you feel an obligation to do, have, or be. In the "like to" column, put the fluff and extras, like a month's vacation in Tahiti, the mansion on Lake Tahoe, or the Mercedes with onboard navigational electronics. Before going on to the next paragraph, get a pen and fill in the exercise.

Now that you've completed the exercise, what does it reveal? Typically, issues of career, family, and home appear in the "got-to" column. Travel, special vacations, and second homes in resort locales usually occupy the "like-to" column. The "should" column fills up with practical issues as well as obligations, often toward parents and sometimes toward children. It is not unusual for money issues to appear in the "should" column, such as budgets, paying bills and debts, completing tax returns. Items in this column often entail a judgment or criticism of oneself.

Sometimes people fill in nothing but the "got-to" column. I saw this most dramatically in a woman who participated in one of my seminars. She put everything—or, more precisely, the best of everything, from the fastest Pentium computer to a BMW, a big-screen TV, elegant leather couches, and a restaurant-size refrigerator—in the "got-to" column. She had been raised in grinding poverty, and now, as an adult who made a very good living, she focused exclusively on acquiring the objects she envied in other people's lives. Obviously, her life was out of balance.

When the "got-to" column takes over like this, everything in one's life feels important. If you find yourself in this situation, assume that much of your list needs to move to "should" and "like to." Go through your list item by item and move the ones it seems right to relocate.

The "should" column can be highly revealing. For example, it often includes projects that drain away resources at the expense of the more profoundly fulfilling activities in the "got-to" column. The woman mentioned in chapter 1—who worked a demanding, exhausting job and simultaneously cared for her terminally ill sister—is an example. She felt so strongly obligated to attend to her sister's all-consuming needs that she had nothing left over to realize her own personal goals. In such cases, I try to find out how much time and energy the client is devoting to "should" demands, then I play devil's advocate in an attempt to help him or her understand the cost of this misdirected effort. Even ten minutes a week spent on a "should" can drain valuable energy from the fulfillment of life goals. There's a significant psychological and spiritual difference between "*got* to visit Uncle Joe in the nursing home" and "*should* visit Uncle Joe in the nursing home." When we arrive at Vision and Aloha, doing good deeds for others becomes a central activity of our lives. But we can't leap there by a simple act of the will, skipping over the adult stages of Knowledge, Understanding, and Vigor. If we cannot realize our own life goals, then we can never give freely and completely to others. Instead, our lives will be saddled with resentment and blame. Typically, these negative emotions already taint any generous gestures listed in the "should" column. Drop them until they make their way into the "got-to" column. In the meantime, focus on doing what needs to be done to realize your dreams. As you fulfill your goals, you will find that Vision and Aloha flow naturally from you.

Usually, too, as clients age and their childhood issues resolve, parents tend to move from the "should" to the "got-to" column. The ancient need for kinship in the face of death's inevitability becomes stronger as time helps resolve the emotional leftovers of childhood. As we mature, we learn the kind of adult relationship we want with our parents. This new desired connection, the one arising in our own maturity, appears under "got to" rather than "should," which is the provenance of a more childlike attitude.

When money appears in the "should" column, I've learned that I need to be particularly careful as a financial planner. The draining quality of the "should" column often comes from old messages that originated with our parents, not ourselves, and are not spoken in our own unique voice. Thus they rob energy from what is ours in origin, which is expressed in the "got-to" column. Psychologically, people who mix money with parental issues project images of their mothers and fathers onto me, and they draw me into conflicts that have nothing to do with me but are rooted instead in their psychological histories. The money issues in this column are judgment voices speaking in new guise. I find I have to let people who mix financial and parental issues understand how supportive I am of them and how different I am from their parents around money. This gives them the room to sort out emotional questions fraught with child-parent, Innocence-Pain issues by working through Knowledge, Understanding, and Vigor.

Exactly this situation arose with Susanna Swartz, who had been trivialized around money by her father and brothers. One day she exploded at me and my staff over not being informed about an incidental change in her account statement. I realized this wasn't about the account statement. Rather, it was a replay of her childhood experiences of trivialization. Empathizing with her, I made the connection between her current feelings and her childhood clear enough that she could hear me when I gently but firmly told her that outbursts directed at my staff were inappropriate and unacceptable.

Once a seminar participant wrote only one item on the entire grid: "Got to understand my own death." A healthy vigorous physician, he was doing a great deal of hospice work, which had led him to contemplate the meaning of his life in a profound way. Another participant tore up the paper in disgust and anger when she realized that everything she wrote dealt with her gifts and service to others. Lacking any goals that pertained only to herself, she was struggling to define who she was and to speak with a personal authority freed from her unending sense of responsibility to others. Yet another individual, a young man who was a highly successful entrepreneur, had only one entry, this in the "like-to" category: "leave a legacy of a thousand years." Then there was the man with but one "got to": "go out of my way to do at least one kind act every day." Both these latter two people displayed the generosity and selflessness that are the building blocks of Aloha and Vision.

It's possible that you already have, are, or do practically everything listed in your "got-to" column. If so, consider yourself fortunate and shift your focus to what appears in "like to." Little stress needs to be put on budgeting, saving, or investment performance. Life—as well as financial planning—is that much easier all the way around.

TIME FLIES

This exercise creates a matrix that links goals to time and creates priorities among your goals. Turn a sheet of paper lengthwise. Across the top write a series of columns representing time frames stretching from one week to a lifetime. Down the side of the paper put the categories you find most important, starting with such areas as career, health, family, relationship, community, creativity, and spirit, then adding any others that are meaningful and important to you. The resulting matrix looks like this:

	1 week	1 month	6 months	1 year	3 years	5 years	10 years	20 years	life
career									
family									
relationship									
health									
community									
creativity									
spirit									
your category									
your category									
your category									
your category									

The next step is to fill in the cells, following your own intuitive process. Start with the first box that appeals to you. Fill in your goal for that time frame and category and label the box with a 1. Go to the next box that appeals to you—which may be anywhere on the matrix—and label it 2 after you've filled it in. Continue this process, numbering each box in order.

It has been my experience that this order reveals the priority we place on the goals in our lives. Usually the first boxes represent either our most important objectives, the ones that speak to us from a place of calling or longing, or they are the goals we can accomplish easily and are likely to earn attention and effort. I focus the financial-planning process on about the first ten goals.

The other important aspect of this exercise is the time frame. You'll remember from our discussion of the basics of financial planning that time is an essential element in making investment decisions. Knowing how far out into the future we need to plan allows us to compute a necessary rate of return and choose the best investment vehicles.

Sometimes, too, time tells about more than money. The doctor who had entered only the understanding of his own death in the prior exercise actually added two additional time frames to the matrix: life of the planet and life of the universe. This was most definitely a man who thought in the long term. At the end of the exercise, he asked, "How do you go about figuring out short-term goals? I've filled in everything from five years to the end of the universe, but for the life of me I can't figure out how to map out the next five years."

His wife answered, "Don't worry, honey. I've got the next five years down to the last detail. It's from there on out that had me baffled."

CLEARING THE SAVINGS HURDLE

In every one of the goal-setting exercises, we face a basic fact of life: What we do today affects what we can choose to do tomorrow. Except for people born extraordinarily wealthy, this reality forces us to deal with saving. To have the resources to fulfill our dreams at a chosen time in the future, we need to set money aside now.

Whenever I tell a seminar that saving is the key to building toward goals and dreams, the groans swell into a chorus of objection: "My God, George, it takes two of us to earn enough just to make ends meet," "Have you seen the cost of college tuition these days?" and "Everybody knows the poor working stiff has been slipping backward for years now." People have even told me that they wouldn't save because it supports the military-industrial complex—apparently believing, in a stroke of blinding naïveté, that somehow consuming doesn't.

The real issue here is less the substantive content of the objections—which are largely erroneous, based on bad or incomplete data—than the strong emotional issues that lie behind them. The block to saving is the cycle of suffering, the alternation of Pain and Innocence that keeps us locked in a hurtful place: the fantasy of an easier life and the hurt that arises when we can't quite get there. We are eager for information—actually, more Innocence—that supports our Pain. We want the newspaper and the television to tell everyone how badly we are suffering so somebody in power will take notice and fix our hurt. If news stories imply that our Pain is someone else's fault, or if that's just the way things are, we can remain in Innocence. Not only need we not do anything about the situation; we are powerless to fix it.

Shuffling between Innocence and Pain in the dance of suffering, we read what we need to believe to keep things just as they are. And we are particularly vulnerable to bad news. Richard Thaler, an economist at the University of Chicago, has shown that people are more than twice as sensitive to losing a certain amount of money as they are to gaining a similar amount.

Personal income is a case in point. Again and again I've heard seminar participants tell me that income in this country has been going down steadily, so that people now have less money in their pockets than they used to—and, therefore, can't be expected to save. That's just plain wrong. Most of these notions come from newspaper reports that misinterpret the income effects of changing family size, ignore the growing self-employment sector, and assume that people at the bottom of the ladder stay there forever—when most of them actually move up over time. The truth of the matter is real personal disposable income—that's the amount of money after taxes available to the average individual and adjusted for inflation—has risen by nearly 30 percent in just fifteen years. Like all the excuses summoned against saving, this one doesn't hold up.

The block against saving stands out even more prominently when the savings habits of Americans are compared to those of people in other countries. Citizens of the member nations of the European Union save 10 percent to 15 percent of their incomes a year, and the savings rate in Japan runs higher, well into the teens. Chile, one of the fastest-growing and strongest economies in Latin America, boasts a savings rate of 29 percent—which means Chileans invest almost one escudo for every three they bring home. As monumental as this savings rate may seem, however, it is dwarfed by the efforts of the emerging economies of Asia, such as Malaysia, Singapore, China, and South Korea, which save in the 30 to 55 percent range.

In the United States we save less than 5 percent, the lowest rate of any industrialized country. The Chinese put away ten times what we do. When people complain to me that we are simply incapable of saving, I wonder how it can be that impoverished China can save ten times more personal income than the United States, which is the richest nation on Earth.

Without savings, there can be no investment, and without investment, there can be no growth. This basic economic relationship holds true for both individuals and nations.

Part of the commonplace American block against saving can be resolved by deepening Knowledge. Learning more about the importance of saving in realizing our personal dreams of freedom can contribute to developing motivation and to seeing how discipline can lead to fulfillment. Accurate information regarding the high rates of return possible for investors and the power of compounding is crucial, topics we will cover in depth in chapter 11. However, there remains an important emotional component to the resistance to saving, one that can be resolved only by working through the Understanding stage—which is the topic of the next chapter.

In the meantime, it is of benefit to understand the profound and powerful value of saving, to see it as a practice that deepens our lives not only financially but also spiritually.

All the great spiritual traditions emphasize the need to develop a consciousness of personal responsibility. This pursuit begins with eliminating clutter from our lives so we can see into them with clarity. This is known as the path of renunciation. It is practiced, for example, by Muslims during Ramadan, Jews on Yom Kippur, and Christians during Lent. It was the spirit of renunciation that led the Buddha to the search for the ending of suffering and Shantideva to the mind of awakening. Renunciation pares life down to its basic elements so that the individuals following the practice can see clearly, without distraction, into their own souls.

In the world of money, a dedication to saving is the path of renunciation. When we save, we push away instant gratification—a kind of distraction into the immediate—for a deeper sense of the whole of our lives. We understand that more lies ahead, that we have things we must do before death takes us. We are looking into ourselves. We are steeping ourselves in the Knowledge of living with the integrity that leads to freedom.

KNOWLEDGE'S NUTS AND BOLTS:
A GUIDE TO THE TOOLBOX

Up till now, this chapter has dealt with the timeless issues of Knowledge, such as freedom and integrity, goal-setting, the elements of financial planning, and saving as a spiritual practice. Except for understanding the nature of Knowledge itself, the rest of this stage on the path to Money Maturity is time-bound. Sound investment advice varies from one place and period to another. What looked wise and prudent as an investment strategy in 1800 is very different from what wears the mantle of wisdom and prudence today.

Additionally, the specific aspects of Knowledge are massive in detail. Practical Knowledge is the subject of hundreds of books, thousands of issues of countless periodicals, hundreds of television shows, and scores upon scores of university degree programs from coast to coast. Mastering this much information is a gargantuan task.

Instead of burying you under an avalanche of financial information, I want to point out in the following pages the elements of Knowledge that you, working either on your own or with a financial advisor, will need to master in order to develop and implement a financial plan designed to reach your goals. Chapter 11 discusses each of these areas in greater detail. As we go through the basics, I will tell you which pages in chapter 11 to turn to for further information about the areas where you discover you need to know more. If you are a novice in this area, I encourage you to read chapter 11 in depth, studying carefully each section that applies to you. Alternatively, if you are already adept at Knowledge, you may want to skim this section, taking only what you need.

ASSESSING RESOURCES

A realistic financial plan begins with listing your strengths and weakness around money. Essentially, you are making an inventory of the areas where your Knowledge is adequate and those other areas where it is deficient. Start the list with the inner resources and virtues we have already discussed. Next, move on to your relative mastery of the specifics of practical Knowledge such as taxes, investments, budgeting, estate planning, insurance, retirement planning, and economic theory. Assess both your current state of Knowledge and your willingness and interest in accumulating Knowledge on each topic. Wherever you come up short—that is, where you know less than you need to and/or you are uninterested or unwilling to learn what is required—you'll need help in order to reach Money Maturity and realize your life goals. Knowledge includes both knowing money and knowing where you don't want to know more—the areas where professional assistance in money matters is your preferred choice. Only you can decide where that boundary lies.

The following checklist can help you complete this assessment. For more on inner resources, see the discussion beginning on page 316.

		current state of development	willingness/interest in developing further
virtues	diligence		
	honesty		
	skills		
	good health habits		
	reliability		
	other		
money competencies	taxes		
	investments		
	estate planning		
	budgeting		
	insurance		
	retirement planning		
	economic theory		

The second step is calculating your net worth, which represents your resources stated in dollar terms. The basic calculation is simple. You total your assets and your liabilities, then subtract the liabilities from the assets. The remainder is your net worth. Detailed assets and liabilities checklists and further information appear in chapter 11, beginning on page 318.

There's more reason to calculating net worth than brushing up your arithmetic skills. Net worth and the return it is earning allow you to determine how close you are to realizing your life goals. For the sake of example, let's assume that you have a net worth of $250,000 held in savings and checking accounts and earning an overall annual rate of return of 2 percent. If you want to live on this money, you have a yearly income of $5,000 before taxes and inflation to work with—not exactly a princely existence, particularly after inflation of 2 percent annually eats all your gains away and Uncle Sam takes some more. You're actually losing money. But if you are invested in the stock market, where the average historical annual rate of return is 11 percent, your average pre-inflation, pretax gain would be $27,500, a substantially higher sum that offers more possibilities for a free if Spartan way of living. Obviously, your actual return will vary with stock market conditions, dropping in the event of a crash like 1929 or a decline combined with high inflation like the 1973–1974 period and rising in strong bull (that is, rising) markets. The fundamental point remains, however: Your net worth and its total return indicate how close—or how far—you are to living out your dreams.

How do you determine how close you are? A more complete discussion of using net worth to determine the amount of income you can draw from your assets begins on page 319.

BUDGETS: SETTING LIMITS

Unless you are so fabulously wealthy that your supply of money is boundless, the next step entails knowing how to live—and save, if you are building your net worth—within your means. Overspending will delay the fulfillment of your goals or eat away at the net worth that is supporting you. Several times a year I meet with people who come to realize they can retire just by paring their budget and investing their net worth more efficiently. Chapter 11's section on budgets, which begins on page 320, shows you how to construct both realistic and bare-bones budgets. It also addresses three areas where many people spend too much—taxes, insurance, and credit card debt—and where Knowledge skills can greatly increase saving and net worth.

INVESTMENTS: GROWING YOUR MONEY

Once you clearly comprehend your resources, including net worth, and you have assessed your ability to live within a budget and save money, you are ready to move on to investing. Knowledge allows you to create an investment program that matches volatility and return to your needs, dreams, and psychological comfort with different levels of risk.

Before you begin choosing appropriate investments, three specific details of Knowledge need to be dealt with. The first concerns what is known as total rate of return and its importance in understanding investment performance.

The second has to do with perceiving the effect of different rates of return on the growth of your assets and net worth. This understanding is much more than theoretical. If, for example, you invest in assets with the highest rates of return—in the neighborhood of 20 percent annually—rather than the lowest—perhaps 2 to 2.5 percent per year—for ten to twenty years, you could end with five to twenty-five times as much money. Over the past half-century, different categories of investments have delivered substantially different rates of return that need to figure into your investment choices—for example, Treasury bills (4.7 percent), gold (5.1 percent), art (8.5 percent), real estate (including rent, 7.1 to 10 percent), and stocks (12.6 to 19.8 percent).

Third, you need to comprehend how powerfully the compounding of different rates of return over periods of years affects the growth of your savings. When an asset's annual return is reinvested in the same asset rather than taken out and spent, the money grows dramatically.

Let's pause for a moment and consider how powerfully these principles of investing affect building the resources you need to dedicate yourself to your life's purpose. For the sake of example, you've figured you need resources well into the six figures and you are willing to wait as long as fifteen years. You already have $20,000 saved and you figure you could contribute $2,000 per year to an IRA. How much money could you accumulate? (For the purpose of this exercise, we are ignoring the uncertain effects of inflation or taxes). If you put it all in the bank at 2 percent, you would accumulate a total of $61,000, most of that from your $30,000 contribution to your IRA over 15 years. If you invested in gold and received its historical return of 5.1 percent, you would accumulate $85,000. In rental real estate at 9 percent, you would have $131,000. If your blue-chip stocks returned 12.6 percent, you would be worth over $196,000. In small-cap value stocks at their historical rate of 19.8 percent, you would be worth $442,000.

Very few people know about small-cap value stocks or about the other high-return asset categories described in chapter 11. Clearly, learning about different asset categories, rates of return, and the power of compounding will have a powerful impact on the successful accomplishment of your dreams. To find out more about these three aspects of investing, read the section of chapter 11 that begins on page 329.

With return comes risk—the next topic of major importance. Attractive though the stock market's 12 to 20 percent annual rate of return may be, all of us at some time fear that Newton's law of gravity has a way of bringing Wall Street back to Earth—what goes up must also come down. Risk and return are in fact related. Each of us has to determine how much risk we are willing to bear in the hope that a desired return will be realized. There's a wisecrack in the financial planning community: Either you eat well or you sleep well. Eating well takes money, and that means accepting some degree of risk. But risk can bring anxiety of the sort that wakes you up at night.

Two issues are involved in understanding risk. The first is pure Knowledge: knowing how volatile, or risky, different classes of investments are, such as stocks versus bonds or money market funds. This topic is discussed in detail beginning on page 334.

The second issue is your own psychological makeup and emotional reaction to reversals of fortune. The stock market, for example, has a long history of high returns. Still, if you invest in the stock market, you can expect on average to lose money one year out of every four, an experience that can prove nerve-racking. Sometimes, too, the market takes a fast and frightening dive. This happened most powerfully during the 1987 crash when the stock market shed 38 percent of its aggregate value in only two and a half months. Such experiences can be wrenching, and you need to assess your own willingness to ride the rollercoaster versus strolling the flat and narrow.

If you decide to take even some risk and invest a portion of your savings in high-returning stocks, you face the question of deciding which stocks to buy—big companies or small, established or entrepreneurial, domestic or foreign, low tech or high tech. A good general guide to stock selection comes from the only theory of stock market behavior to win the Nobel Prize. The theory, developed by three well-known economists, proposes that the best strategy for maximizing return and minimizing risk is to buy a representative selection of stocks and hold them for a long time, despite periods of fear or apparent market peaks. A further theory, developed by two economists, one at the University of Chicago and the other now at Yale, suggests that buying certain categories of stock can both boost returns significantly—into the heady realm of 18 percent per year over a twenty-nine-year period, and nearly 20 percent annually over a seventy-year time frame—and reduce risk. These two fascinating theories, and a discussion of four other even higher-returning equity categories, are given attention beginning on page 338.

In investing, as in many other areas of life, the old dictum warning against putting all your eggs in one basket holds true. A number of specific time-tested principles on risk reduction allow us to mix different categories of assets with high rates of return and high risk and achieve a total portfolio with both high return and considerably reduced risk. These principles, which include taking advantage of the opportunities in international stock markets, are explained in chapter 11 from page 344 on.

Investing includes its own form of budgeting. In the same way that cutting household expenses increases net worth, reducing investment fees and taxes can boost total return significantly. Page 350 tells more about how to do this and gives some tips on how to construct a mutual fund portfolio.

Even if you know what you want to invest in, you have to figure out how to invest. Once upon a time not so long ago, the only person to turn to with your savings or inheritance was a stockbroker. Most brokers worked with large national firms that advertised extensively in print and on TV and radio. Unfortunately, many brokers offered only a narrow expertise focused on the investment vehicles their firms marketed. Also, since brokers made their livings from commissions on the investments they sold, many investors distrusted their advice because of the conflict of interest this compensation arrangement created. They considered every conversation about a new investment just another sales pitch. How could you trust a broker to give you straight advice when you knew that he or she was tempted to steer you toward investments that paid a big commission rather than the ones that best met your goals?

This conflict prompted the rise of a new profession, the one we now know as financial planning. Financial planners are more broadly educated in money issues than are brokers, and they undergo a rigorous certification process. In addition to knowing about investments, financial planners are competent in taxes, insurance, retirement and estate planning, employee benefits, and budgeting. Additionally, more and more financial planners work on a fee-only basis rather than on commission from investment sales, a compensation arrangement that helps resolve the conflict of interest plaguing brokers.

At the same time, the explosive expansion of the mutual fund industry has given every individual investor a way of entering the stock market with the help of professional money management and the added advantage of risk reduction. Now even small investors have choices beyond the old nationwide-brokerage monopoly: Invest in no-load (that is, no-commission) mutual funds on their own, or work through a financial planner. Chapter 11, beginning on page 350, provides more information about choosing a financial planner, the advantages of mutual fund investing, and what has become known as the consumer movement in the financial services industry.

THE FINAL EVANESCENCE OF KNOWLEDGE

The story goes that the Mullah Nazrudin was asleep and dreaming when a hand reached out of nowhere and dropped a gold coin in front of him. Again and again the hand let coins fall until they numbered nine. Just as the hand was coming forth with a tenth coin, it began to fade. Before the last piece of gold fell, the hand completely disappeared. "No, no! I want ten!" Nazrudin shouted, so loudly that he wakened himself and sat up in bed. The ever-subtle mullah lay back down, pulled the pillow over his eyes, and said softly, "Okay, okay. I'll take nine."

The areas of Knowledge we have just discussed—rates of return, risk levels, various kinds of investments, financial advisory fees—all sound specific, detailed, and precise. In fact, much of Knowledge is like the mullah's vanishing gold, a realm of fading relative truths, ideas that work for a time and then lose their validity. The history of science teaches this lesson. Ptolemy gave way to Copernicus, who gave way to Galileo, who gave way to Newton, who gave way to Einstein, who in time will yield to a new vision of the cosmos. Chapter 11's specific advice is the one section of this book that ten or twenty years from now will seem at least vaguely out of date. Even as I am writing this, academic theories as well as social, political and economic forces are shifting the very ideas and asset categories I have discussed, pushing them in new and unknown directions. In a hundred years chapter 11 may appear laughably wrong-headed.

Knowledge is not wisdom, which remains deeply truthful despite the passage of time. Knowledge is impermanent; it changes, drifts away, fades, like fog or smoke. You might wonder why you should learn something transient. Considering impermanence to be one of three basic characteristics of existence, the Buddha taught that seeing a moment of impermanence with absolute clarity would lead to nirvana. The danger of Knowledge is not its impermanence but our inclination to cling to what we know as if it were absolute. You will remember the exercise from chapter 1, where I asked you to attempt to hold on to a thought or belief and you discovered how difficult that is. Often Knowledge is like that, essentially Innocent, perhaps even naive, evaporating like Nazrudin's vanishing hand and its glimmering gold coin.

Economic theories can do exactly the same. For instance, a number of very bright writers and financial thinkers feel strongly that the powerful stock market returns of the past are a fluke, that the future holds only miserly promise. Some argue, for example, that the real worldwide gain on stocks in this century has been much lower than what the U.S. stock market has returned. After all, the American market is a survivor left standing among the fallen. Other major markets that existed in the nineteenth and early to mid twentieth centuries were wiped out completely—by the advent of communist governments in Russia and China and of the Nazis in Germany, for instance, and by the Great Depression and World War II in the rest of Western Europe. Investors who had all their money in those markets lost everything. If such losses are factored against the returns in the U.S. stock market, on balance the gains are much more modest than the 11 percent yearly average commonly used as a benchmark.

Other financial analysts argue that the current valuation levels of the U.S. stock market are far too high to be sustainable and that it will take decades of mediocre performance to get back to reality. These experts are joined by others who say that high returns are delivered only by high risk. Since the dramatic collapse of communism has lowered the risk of nuclear holocaust, and since the extraordinary worldwide growth of both democracy and capital markets has lowered risk to companies, returns will drop by a corresponding amount.

Perhaps that is true, and perhaps it isn't. The only truth is that we don't really know what will happen.

Likewise, we don't fully understand why some types of assets do better than others. There is a logic to the higher returns stocks offer over bonds and real estate. Stocks represent ownership in the most creative aspect of the economy, namely its ability to devise and produce new products and solutions. By contrast, bonds stand for debt, money lent to productive capacity, while real estate houses that capacity. Neither bonds nor real estate provides the ownership in the economy's ability to produce that stocks do. Since they stand at a farther remove from the source of production, they return less. That much makes sense.

Yet when we look at the average returns of different stock categories, the differences among them are much harder to explain. Do the newest economic theories, which posit markedly higher returns from certain categories of stocks, pertain simply to historical flukes with no bearing on the future, or do they give us a deep insight into the complicated way we actually measure risk against return?

Still, some trends from the past do take on the appearance of important truths that apply to the future. Perhaps the greatest lesson of this century comes from the clear evidence that market economies like our own are vastly more dynamic than controlled economies. The dramatic collapse of the right-wing totalitarian systems of South America and the left-wing totalitarian systems of Russia and Eastern Europe in the late 1980s and early 1990s, as well as the financial troubles affecting the controlled economies of Asia in the 1990s, underscores this Knowledge.

The history of Western capitalism demonstrates how dramatically creative a market economy can be.

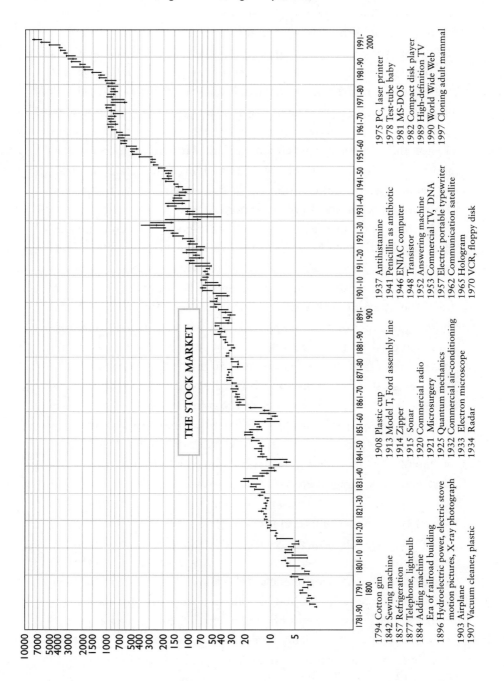

THE STOCK MARKET

1794 Cotton gin
1842 Sewing machine
1857 Refrigeration
1877 Telephone, lightbulb
1884 Adding machine
     Era of railroad building
1896 Hydroelectric power, electric stove
     motion pictures, X-ray photograph
1903 Airplane
1907 Vacuum cleaner, plastic

1908 Plastic cup
1913 Model T, Ford assembly line
1914 Zipper
1915 Sonar
1920 Commercial radio
1921 Microsurgery
1925 Quantum mechanics
1932 Commercial air-conditioning
1933 Electron microscope
1934 Radar

1937 Antihistamine
1941 Penicillin as antibiotic
1946 ENIAC computer
1948 Transistor
1952 Answering machine
1953 Commercial TV, DNA
1957 Electric portable typewriter
1962 Communication satellite
1965 Hologram
1970 VCR, floppy disk

1975 PC, laser printer
1978 Test-tube baby
1981 MS-DOS
1982 Compact disk player
1989 High-definition TV
1990 World Wide Web
1997 Cloning adult mammal

In a couple of hundred years, we've leapt from the cotton gin to the CD player and the cloning of Dolly the sheep, and we have seen life expectancies double. In ordinary middle-class America we live lives whose comfort and luxury would prompt the envy of medieval kings, barons, and earls. The free flow of money, like water seeking to find its level, can discover the places where we humans most want change and growth and where change and growth are indeed possible. We are eager to pay for products and ideas that make our lives better. Because of markets, money in free flow tends to find where those products and ideas are being born.

In contrast to the skepticism I have described, some economic theories suggest that we haven't seen anything yet, that all the growth characterizing the world's economy in the past two centuries is just a warmup for a mushrooming expansion the likes of which has never been seen. According to these models, we are entering a period of even more rapid expansion. In the past, growth has been subject to limitations imposed by the increasing costs of finding new capital, labor, and raw materials. But as the raw materials we use become more and more the stuff of the mind—which is the ultimate source of the computer and the other technologies of the information age—and as we come to rely on new, virtually unlimited sources of raw materials through the expanding, futuristic fields of biotechnology and nanotechnology—which develop valuable commercial products from common items like water, bacteria, and air—the old constraints hold us back less and less. Both costs and the limits of production fall, while profits and the possibilities of growth rise.

For all this, the deeper lessons economics teaches us have to do with humility and hubris. Events have a way of bringing even the sharpest and most adept financial professionals to their knees. When the stock market crashed in 1987, the fall in prices surprised many money experts as surely as a blitzing linebacker blindsiding a quarterback. For all their Knowledge, practically no one in the financial-services industry had seen it coming. The complexity and immensity of financial Knowledge in the modern world is such that no one individual can master it all. Even the best and most studious of us at some moment realize we have been brought to Earth, humbled by the limits of what we know.

Apart from the drama of big-time market reversals, even the day-to-day-workings of financial markets constantly remind us how little we really understand. For example, although we have an idea why stocks do better than bonds and real estate over the long run, we have no idea which asset category will do best over a shorter time frame, nor do we have a notion of exactly how they will fare over the next ten years. Probabilities are one thing, certainty quite another.

Hubris is the opposite of humility, a blinding pride in our own power that can combine disastrously with the lemminglike behavior of investors stampeding toward the latest hot new trend. This leads to an overdevelopment of the capacity to produce goods in the hottest areas, which, when the hot trend cools, can be followed by recession or depression. Overdevelopment happens inevitably as markets, in their tendency to allocate resources efficiently, direct money to the places that seem most profitable. This is a problem particularly where investors receive inadequate information about underlying investments. Eventually, too much money ends up in one place and capacity is overdeveloped. If companies in an overdeveloped economy want to avoid going broke, they lower their prices, hoping to sell whatever they can in an effort to forestall financial disaster. The fall in prices produces deflation and fierce price competition, which can result in corporate bankruptcies and raise the specter of depression. This is precisely what befell the East and Southeast Asian economies during the crisis beginning in the summer of 1997, a crisis that has since spread to Russia and Latin America and threatens the whole world. Faced with a capacity to produce that outstripped the world's ability to consume, these economies saw prices for goods fall to levels that wouldn't pay for the investment in plant, equipment, and materials it took to manufacture them.

Deflation can be more dangerous than inflation. In the U.S. economy, deflation has always preceded or accompanied the depressions we've experienced. The change to an information-based economy, however, may decrease this danger, both because the investment in plant and equipment is much less and because the intellectual aspect of contemporary products gives us more flexibility to adapt and change. It also helps that our economy is becoming more and more self-employed, entrepreneurial, and service-oriented, which adds to its flexibility and adaptability.

Frankly, I am bullish on the future of the United States. For all the growth we have seen, I feel that we will see even more. Yet I could be terribly wrong. In the end, no one calls the future; the crystal ball is a feature of fairy tales, not economic analysis. We can know only that the world changes, sometimes as fast as the swish of a horse's tail, and that our Knowledge must be as dynamic as the world itself is. Above all else, we must hold firm to a clear comprehension of our purpose, the goals we explored early on in this chapter. The facts making up Knowledge may shift, yet the structure of Knowledge as a stage on the way to Money Maturity remains the same. It is always the function of Knowledge to identify our goals, assess our resources, and choose a path that leads from resources to goals. The path we travel may shift, but the task of seeing where we are going and staying the course on the road to wisdom—heading now uphill, now down, now over the mountains, now along the river toward the bright meadows beyond— remains ever the same.

TRY THIS: YOUR LIFE IN MONEY— PRACTICAL KNOWLEDGE

The next step in your financial autobiography is to record your current understanding of the practical aspects of Knowledge. You can use these questions to guide your thinking and self-discovery:

When you are presented with an opportunity to learn more about money, are you interested? Or do you resist, hold back, and push it away?

Do you have a clear vision of your goals? If you answer no, how do you intend to create and maintain a vision of your future?

How clear are you about the time frame needed for accomplishing your goals?

How well do you understand the path you are taking to accomplish your goals?

How have your vision and your understanding of the path you are following changed over time? Be specific.

How have your resources, both inner and outer, changed over time? How will they change in the future? Be specific.

What is your present financial status? Do you know your net worth?

What is your monthly income? What are your assets? What are your liabilities?

Do you stand to inherit money? How much? How complete is your knowledge in this area?

Have you made a budget? Do you adhere to it?

If you know your Knowledge is weak in a specific area, do you seek professional help? If not, why do you hesitate? What stands between you and access to the kind of expertise that could help you clarify and accomplish your goals sooner than you may be able to do on your own?

Are you saving enough to meet your goals? If not, what steps will you take, and over what time frame, to boost your saving up to an adequate level?

chapter 7:

UNDERSTANDING: THE DEEP HEART'S CORE

*Do you have the patience to wait
till your mud settles and the water is clear?
Can you remain unmoving
till the right action arises by itself?*

Lao-tzu

*What looks like
fire is a great relief to be inside.*

Rumi

Being on a budget proved harder for Mahealani Sapolu than she had thought it would. She expected to find it difficult to say no to herself. What she didn't expect were the feelings the experience roused in her.

"One day last week, on my lunch hour, I was wandering through this discount store in the shopping center where I work. I didn't really intend to buy anything. I was just killing a few minutes before I had to punch back in," she said.

"Then I spotted this blouse. It was raw silk, and it was beautiful, this fuchsia color I just adore. It'd been marked down, too. They'd lopped almost $30 off the price, it was a really good deal. I mean, I really wanted this blouse."

"What did that want feel like?" I asked.

Mahealani thought for a moment. "It was like a shiver went through me. In the same moment I felt hot and cold, all at once and all over. My palms got sweaty and I was breathing faster. It was a rush. Like chugging a cold beer on a hot day. Like thinking about great sex."

"So what'd you do?" I asked.

"Nothing really. I opened my purse to get a credit card to buy it and then I realized I don't have any credit cards anymore. So I walked away." Mahealani's voice darkened. "Probably somebody else has bought it by now. I'm sure it's gone."

When I am working with someone who has been a chronic over-spender, I try to help that individual see into the feelings surrounding both spending and restraint, to open the heart at the core of his or her personal issues around money. Often knowing how these feelings feel helps us tolerate them when they're about to do us harm. As our under-standing of them develops, we learn how to transform them into some-thing rich and life-changing.

"You feel sad, don't you?" I said, naming the obvious.

She nodded.

"Can you say why?"

It took a while for the words to form. When they did, they rang clear and true.

"All my life I've never had enough," Mahealani said. "When I was growing up, I knew what it felt like not to have enough to eat, to wear hand-me-downs and clothes from the Goodwill, to lie to the teachers at school because I didn't want to admit sometimes we didn't have money for pencils and paper. I knew what it was like to have the *haoles* look at me and say 'She'll never amount to anything. She's just a lazy Hawaiian.' We were always on the short end of the stick, my family and me. I vowed to myself I wasn't going to live like that when I grew up. One way I've tried to make it different is to give myself what I want, to spend money on a whim. It's a way of filling up that hole in me. And when I can't do it—like now, because of this budget we're on—I feel like I'm abandoning myself. One time, when I was really little, my mother lost me for a little while in a crowd. I feel the same way now, like my mother's left me behind, when I can't spend money I want to spend."

"Have you ever thought about going into that hole inside you and seeing what's in there?" I asked.

Mahealani looked at me as if I had just opened the front door to the insane asylum and stepped inside.

"You must be out of your mind, George," she said, with the sweet firmness of a woman who was both courteous and strong-willed. "It's dark in there. It's like a nightmare. It's no place I want to go."

"I can understand your fear," I said. "But I'll tell you something. This place you're afraid of and the feelings it contains are the real source of your own strength and power. Believe it or not, that's the most profound and spiritual part of you."

Later, Derrick King had to admit he had seen it coming, but he had been looking the other way, ignoring the obvious. He thought he had time. He believed—because he dared not believe otherwise—that major life changes like the breakup of a family transmit numerous early warning signals, evolve slowly over months and years, unwind in gradual stages that allow you to step in at any point and say "Stop. Let's talk about this before it goes any further. We still have time."

Only Derrick didn't have time. He came home late from work one day, and a particularly grueling day at that, to find a note from his wife pinned to the refrigerator with a chili pepper magnet. In a few lines of pencil on blue-lined paper, Alexandria announced she had left him and taken the two boys with her.

That first evening, Derrick acted as if little had happened, as if he were writing the classic text on denial. He popped a frozen quiche Lorraine into the microwave, assembled a green salad, poured a glass of chardonnay, and settled into his dinner. The house did seem oddly quiet, he had to admit to himself. He didn't have to search through the rooms to know he was all alone; the peculiar, unusual silence told him that. But he kept saying to himself "She'll be back. She'll bring the boys home. This is just a temporary thing, I'm sure. I'll bet she comes back before the night's out."

The night passed, morning came, and still Derrick's wife and sons had not returned. He convinced himself it would take a little more time. He went to work as usual, put in his usual long day, and said not a word about his domestic situation to any of his coworkers.

A full three days passed before what had happened finally hit him in the middle of the night. Cold raw terror bolted through him.

"I woke up all of a sudden, sweating everywhere, with a feeling like I had been stabbed clear through," he told me. "There was no way I was going to sleep that night. I went downstairs and I paced around the house, this big empty house. I realized she really had left me, it was over, I had lost my family before I had even known it was possible. I wandered into the kitchen and I noticed the time on the clock on top of the stove. It was three o'clock in the morning. Then I remembered this line from F. Scott Fitzgerald, this novel I'd had to read years ago in some English class, where he said in the dark night of the soul it's always 3 A.M. Now I knew exactly what he meant."

The following weeks and months of Derrick's life seemed a daily deepening exploration of Fitzgerald's observation on the darkness of depression. As Derrick admitted the reality of his situation and his denial crumbled, he felt as if he were falling into a bottomless pit of despond. Alexandria had indeed left him, with no intention of ever returning or trying to patch up a marriage she now saw as a vampire sucking her life away. She told him she wanted a divorce. In but the blink of an eye, Derrick had been transformed from a man in seeming command of his destiny to a victim of forces clearly outside his control.

"From the way I was raised I had this idea that if you played it straight and worked hard, things would go your way and your family would love you," Derrick said. "It sure didn't work out that way. Alexandria didn't notice what I was doing, how I was working hard for her and the boys as well as for me. I didn't know that a thing like this could make you feel so pissed off, so hurt way down inside."

"Maybe that's the terrible point of all this, to help you see into the Innocent beliefs that have structured your life," I said. "You're having to explore feelings you didn't think you'd ever have to investigate. Now circumstances are such that you simply can't escape them."

"No fooling," Derrick said. "And this thing could cost me a bundle. Unless I can talk Alexandria into reconciling, I'm going to have to pay alimony and child support. We'll need to sell the house, and the real estate market's not doing well at the moment, so I'll lose money there. I feel like I'm being held upside down and all the change is being shaken out of my pockets."

"I have something for you to read," I said to Derrick. I handed him a sheet of paper on which "The Question," one of my favorite poems by Rumi, had been reprinted. "Rumi lived in the thirteenth century in what is now Afghanistan," I explained. "He was a Sufi mystic as well as a poet. He had this remarkable way of seeing what was subtle, profound, and essential in human experience."

Derrick eyed the poem like someone who thought it might bite. He scanned it once silently, then began to read it a second time, aloud.

One dervish to another, What was your vision of
    God's presence?
I haven't seen anything.
But for the sake of conversation, I'll tell you a story.

God's presence is there in front of me, a fire on the left,
a lovely stream on the right.
One group walks toward the fire, into the fire, another
toward the sweet flowing water.
No one knows which are blessed and which not.
Whoever walks into the fire appears suddenly in the stream.
A head goes under on the water's surface, that head
pokes out of the fire.

Most people guard against going into the fire,
and so end up in it.
Those who love the water of pleasure and make it their devotion
are cheated with this reversal.
The trickery goes further.
The voice of the fire tells the truth, saying I am not fire.
I am fountainhead. Come into me and don't mind the sparks.

If you are a friend of God, fire is your water.
You should wish to have a hundred thousand sets of mothwings,
so you could burn them away, one set a night.
The moth sees light and goes into fire. You should see fire
and go toward light. Fire is what of God is world-consuming.
Water, world-protecting.
Somehow each gives the appearance of the other. To these eyes
  you have now
what looks like water burns. What looks like
fire is a great relief to be inside.
You've seen a magician make a bowl of rice
seem a dish full of tiny, live worms.
Before an assembly with one breath he made the floor swarm
with scorpions that weren't there.
How much more amazing God's tricks.
Generation after generation lies down, defeated, they think,
but they're like a woman underneath a man, circling him.
One molecule-mote-second thinking of God's reversal of comfort
  and pain
is better than any attending ritual. That splinter
of intelligence is substance.
The fire and water themselves:
Accidental, done with mirrors.

"What's this mean?" Derrick said.

"There's a lot in the poem, and it's something we may want to come back to. Let's start with just this for now. Fire represents the feelings we want to run from, while water includes the easy feelings, the things we are comfortable with. Often only when we face our most difficult feelings do we discover who we really are."

"What's that have to do with me?"

"Painful and costly as this experience is for you, it's an opportunity for you to go into your fire, which represents some truth hidden deep inside you, rather than to simply wrap yourself in the water, which stands for your Innocent beliefs about family, work, love, and the place of money in your life. Fighting the fire is like fighting a part of yourself. The water seems more comfortable, soothing, the place to heal your wounds. It's not. Healing means walking into the fire, toward what is burning inside you."

Derrick wore a puzzled look. "But what's this poem and what you're saying have to do with money?" he asked.

"Everything," I answered.

<hr />

"When I think of money, particularly the way men talk about money, I get angry. Really angry. Deep down ticked off and ready to fight."

The decision to buy and renovate a large Victorian home had snapped some ancient chains inside Susanna Swartz. Her protective shield slipped off, at least at the corners, and much of what she had kept hidden about herself she now revealed in bits and pieces.

As she and I met to set up her financial plan, she told me more and more stories about what she had been through—a woman with money who felt abused by that same money. She let me in on her childhood, her marriage, even a few men she had been involved with in the aftermath of her contentious divorce. In some mysterious way she understood that the reason she was seeing me had more to do with the unfolding of those stories—particularly about the way her father continuously belittled her and her brothers parroted the same demeaning line—than it had to do with the details of money management.

"Some part of me came to believe them," she said. "I started thinking I was less than they were."

Although he appeared to value Susanna, her ex-husband behaved in much the same way, albeit more subtly. He praised Susanna for her intelligence and knowledge around art, history, and politics even as he was convincing her that he should handle all the day-to-day details of the family's financial life.

"Of course, I believed him, the rat," she said. "He was like my father with a courtesy transplant. He told me the same thing my father did, that I was financially stupid, only he did it in such a nice way that I thought he really had it all figured out. Then he said he'd take care of everything, so I didn't have to worry. All the while he was shifting a chunk of my money into his control. He must have planned it for years. I'd really like to get him for what he did."

"Get him? What would you do?" I asked.

"I had this fantasy about hiring a mafioso—you know, the kind of nasty guy who wears a corduroy hat and alligator shoes and talks in a husky voice. I'd like to have him do to my ex what those terrorists in Italy used to do—shoot him in the kneecaps, cripple him, not kill him but cause him a world of pain, make him hurt as bad as I do."

"You're angry," I said.

Susanna's face seethed. "You can be sure of that."

"I'm also sure that as long as you stay that way, you'll never achieve the clarity and ease you need to understand not just the financial side of things but the rest of your life as well," I said.

"Nonsense, George," Susanna said. "Look, my father, my brothers, my ex—they did mean and nasty things to me. They were the ones who worked their garbage on me, not vice versa. They deserve anything I want to do to them."

"Of course, what they did was wrong. I'm not debating that point," I said. "Still, the task you face at this point in your life is understanding your own feelings, the feelings that underlie the stories of these wrongs done to you. The one way for you to restore your sense of equilibrium and to heal the pain you feel is to acknowledge those fundamental emotions of anger and rage, enter them as your own, and discover what lies within them.

"You're living a life based on a reaction to your father. It's not your life but his. He dictates it through your anger; you're letting him call the shots. The only way for you to get hold of your own life and live it the way you wish is to heal the anger by acknowledging it and knowing it much more deeply than you do. Then you can dismiss your father from his position of power over you."

Susanna looked at me awhile without moving, then slowly nodded her head. "You may have a point."

Understanding is the most revolutionary teaching of all the Seven Stages. Because of its life-transforming nature, Understanding often takes us in directions and over distances we have never imagined possible. In Understanding we go back to the beginning, to contemplate Innocence and Pain again and resolve the cycle of suffering once and for all. Understanding stands at the center of the Seven Stages, the fourth chakra of seven, the place where the transforming action of the heart takes hold. In Understanding we resolve the dilemma of childhood by unraveling the knot of suffering, letting stories and identifications go, turning suffering into wisdom and truth. Such transformation is possible because Understanding gives us the capacity to enter, with grace and acceptance, the darkest areas of suffering. Its power can change a life, a transformation I have witnessed time and again.

Una was lurching through a divorce, which was going pretty much as the marriage had, only worse.

"For ten years we had handled our conflicts over money by ignoring the subject," she said. "There simply wasn't any communication. So when we got to talking about the property settlement, our nonexistent communication turned into total breakdown."

For two years Una and her husband tried to discuss their financial issues in person or in writing and only created a wider gap.

"Finally I began to practice letting go of stories and letting the feelings be, just the way you taught me," she said. "At first I observed how I clung to defensive patterns of thought involving the sense of fair and unfair or shameful patterns of thought about secrecy and protectiveness. But then I noticed the power of the feelings I held underneath these stories and beliefs, particularly the deep fear I had of losing my security."

Two experiences brought this home to Una. At the time she and her husband were still living together, albeit in separate parts of the house.

"One evening I was alone, sitting quietly in my room, when I heard a key fumbling at the front door, and the door opened and slammed shut. At the moment I heard my husband's key, a bolt of terror unlike anything I'd ever felt before straightened out my spine and raced like a streak of lightning up my back and out my head. I just watched the feeling and let my thoughts go, so I could let the experience in fully. My sadness over the divorce deepened after feeling that terror, but I knew this experience was different and more clarifying than stewing on all my thoughts about being taken advantage of."

The second experience happened within a few days.

"I was going to bed one evening, and I heard my husband fumbling about in the kitchen, making one of those damn, noisy midnight snacks of his. What I felt was rage, an anger so big I knew I could murder him. I let my violent thoughts go. I really wanted to feel the feelings. I'd never felt so angry before—no object, no thoughts, just pure anger. For some period of time, maybe two minutes, maybe twenty, I felt like I was being washed inside by some pure light. Go figure—anger, rage really, yet washed by light. These two experiences were a major turning point for me. Afterward I felt a deep sadness but also an accepting peace with our divorce."

A different approach to the settlement negotiations occurred to Una as she came out of these experiences. She chose to be cautious but open, creating a setting where the two of them could look at the financial data of the relationship and discuss their interests in each asset. Una had no idea where this approach would lead, but she sensed that for her it was an important step in facing her fear of losing financial security and in meeting each moment with clarity.

"It was amazing," she said. "After all the hassle and fighting and misdirection, we sat down and in two meetings of two hours each we settled it. We were in complete agreement about our decisions. During these meetings, when my fears and other feelings came up, I worked with them, by letting the stories go and the feelings be. In the end I felt such a sense of confidence and well-being."

THE DIFFERENCE UNDERSTANDING MAKES

Understanding delivers a type of financial freedom different from any other. It makes money itself, and all of its emotional consequences, a rich tapestry of growth and transformation. Innocence, Pain, and Knowledge have made us more adept with money, by teaching us to let go of old patterns and acquire skills. Understanding goes further. It changes our lives, so that we experience the richness of money even in the midst of—particularly in the midst of—the most difficult, painful experiences around money. In Understanding we allow ourselves to become vulnerable, troubled, confused, challenged—and, ultimately, awakened. Understanding is our first taste of awakening.

Understanding provides a newfound sense of engagement, excitement, even joy in the face of difficulty. Whenever I recognize that I am suffering during a money crisis and I realize I can practice Understanding instead of continuing to suffer, everything changes. What felt horrible before becomes instead the most amazing adventure. Understanding transforms our relationship to money's suffering in just this way.

Before we explore how the practice of Understanding actually works, a few more examples will demonstrate its life-changing power to transform us from the ground up.

Brian made his living by actively trading highly leveraged derivatives on Wall Street, a pursuit in which hesitating for even a moment could cost him and his clients a fortune. While he loved the thrill of what he was doing, he was terrified underneath at the danger he skated across every day. The practice of Understanding helped bring to him not only a greater sense of quiet but also measured confidence in the moments of decision. And when he blew it, he learned to accept his own fallibility.

"The most astounding thing for me," he said, "was paying attention to my feelings at critical decision times. I used to think I couldn't pay attention to one more thing, but now I see that was just a way of pushing a part of myself away. It doesn't interfere with my thinking process at all. In fact, I am calmer and clearer as a consequence of the practice of letting thoughts go and feelings be. Frankly, I do better as a trader too."

Joel had been downsized. When he saw the pink slip on his desk, his self-esteem evaporated.

"I thought about how you said in the seminar money is fair, and I begged to differ. In fact, I thought you were full of it," he told me. "I wanted to argue with you about your ideas and beliefs, about the unfairness of the goddamn system, but then I realized that just wasn't the point. The point was that I, Joel, had gotten a pink slip and I felt lousy about it. I knew what was important for me was to feel the feelings, and I did. There were lots of them—rage, terror, disappointment, and an immense despair."

That evening proved a turning point.

"It's funny, but I couldn't wait to get home as I drove in the evening traffic," Joel said. "My feelings were so intense. My thoughts were a jumble of memories of things that had been said, of what-if scenarios, of angers and fears and supplications. I was eager to get home because I knew this situation was handmade for the practice of Understanding.

"When I got home, I dropped everything in my living room and went out on the porch in the evening light. To me it was darkness. I dove into the feelings, completely letting all the scenarios and thoughts and stories go. I paced back and forth on the porch, eager for the feelings, primarily of anger and betrayal, eager to learn from them. And I did. I now see every difficulty that life throws at me as an extraordinary opportunity to deepen the experience of difficult emotion, so that these feelings become almost like friends."

Joel spent a long weekend working with his feelings, moving through them like a wordless drama unfolding act by act before him.

"Over time I came to realize what an extraordinary opportunity I was being given to reinvent myself in the corporate world. Sometimes this went slowly, because I had to revisit the feelings, particularly sadness and disappointment, many times over the next few months. But in another way, the process went amazingly fast, probably because I let myself feel my feelings fully. This time proved to be rich and yeasty."

Eventually Joel found a job, one that fit him better than any he had had before. Working with his feelings made it easier for him to Understand the patterns that landed him in unsatisfactory jobs in the past and to avoid following the same mistaken path.

Alison, a client of mine, had two small sons at home, and she had committed herself to caring for them full time for two more years. This was what she wanted, and her husband too. Yet she was plagued by messages of how important it was for her to be an independent woman. As a result, she was often a mess at home—forgetting responsibilities, sometimes feeling completely immobilized, full of guilt and shame at not making money.

As she learned Understanding and mastered the practice of letting thoughts go and feelings be, however, things changed. Life at home grew easier, less crazed.

"What I learned most from the practice was how to be at peace with myself," Alison said. "I could be with the boys in the middle of spilled milk and crying and me feeling like a wreck, and I could actually get into it. I let go of the stories telling me I was being a lousy parent and a dependent woman. I just felt the feelings, and learned I could be peaceful among them."

When the end of her stay-at-home time came, Alison discovered she felt little fear about the grind of looking for a job.

"If I could be at peace with my sons at home, looking for a job seemed like no big deal. I carried my experience of peace over into the work world and I found my life fuller, and richer, at home and on the job."

⟦⟧

Anthony, a partner in a big-name law firm, changed his legal practice to work that satisfied him more deeply personally and gave him more time with his family. He spoke of coming to a place of courage he'd never experienced before.

"Courage is what's really changed financially for me. I used to make my money decisions from a place of beliefs about what is true. The experience I had at your workshop was like an opening of the heart. It led me to truth itself, a place that has nothing to do with belief. It's something I never imagined before. I've found the place from which my financial decisions have to be made. That's what I learned from you."

⟦⟧

I will teach you three approaches to bringing this transformative power of Understanding to bear on your own life. The first is a meditation practice that you can apply in your daily life as well. This practice—of letting thoughts go and letting feelings be—forms the basis for learning the nature of suffering and the way to end suffering.

As we will see further on in this chapter, two other techniques are also useful, particularly valuable for people who have trouble identifying their feelings and are likely to feel stuck in Understanding. The first of these is seeking out mentors, and the second is actually living virtue from day to day.

HELL'S TRUTH

The work of Understanding starts in the very place where Dante begins his pursuit of paradise—in a dark and dangerous wood, blocked on his approach to heaven by three terrible beasts. The beasts in the opening of the *Inferno* are more than ill-tempered wild things. They represent incontinence, violence, and fraud. Their way is the swath avarice, wrath, and forgetfulness carve through the world, where money wields great power. Remarkably, when Dante turns away from the beasts to choose the one path open to him—entering hell in the company of the Roman epic poet Virgil—he encounters these very same sins and evils in the shadowy fires and learns their consequences. Time and again Dante stops in horror and fear at what he sees and turns to Virgil to ask if there isn't another way. Each time Virgil counsels the poet to maintain his strength in the presence of such powerful feelings and to remind him that the path to heaven lies in the careful observation of tumultuous feelings within himself and the disastrous external consequences of harmful actions. In essence, Dante will be saved only by encountering—with the full feeling of a human being and the deep observation of a poet—the forces of hell itself.

Wonderfully, the *Inferno* follows the same path as the poem by Rumi I shared with Derrick King. Just as in the *Inferno*, fire represents the difficult feelings we would just as soon run from. Water stands for the easy, the simple, the well known. In some manner, too, it symbolizes a willful ignorance. Rumi's water turns us away from ourselves. The fire calls us deeply into who we are.

"Most people guard against going into the fire," Rumi writes, pointing to the deeply human aversion to going down into our feelings, "and so end up in it." Paradoxically, avoiding that encounter with oneself turns up the heat and makes the difficult feelings all the more difficult. But the feelings we are trying to avoid are as old as we are. They have been with us since we were babies. They are part of what it is to be human, and in pushing them away we push away a portion of ourselves.

The fire turns out to be a comfort, the water a seduction into continuing pain. In certain rare moments, we understand this reversal of comfort and pain. The Buddha also viewed the observation of suffering as a path to freedom. Suffering along with impermanence (as discussed in chapter 6) and selflessness (which we will discuss in chapter 8) are in Buddhism the three basic characteristics of the human condition. The Buddha felt that if we could see one moment of suffering with absolute clarity, we would become free. Shantideva described this capacity to observe our suffering as the perfection, or *paramita*, of patience.

Understanding requires the strength needed to enter the fire, to take Virgil's hand and drop into hell, to encounter directly the dark night of the soul. As Dante, the Buddha, and Shantideva show us, allowing ourselves to be vulnerable enough to move into the fire to the very bottom of the inferno opens us to the discovery of freedom.

LEARNING THE PRACTICE

In the mid-1970s, deeply unhappy with doing tax returns for a living, I longed for a more meaningful life. Although it was easy for me to fall into blaming society and its many ills for my unhappiness, I possessed just enough clarity and honesty to suspect that I myself might be part of the problem. I was meditating, yet meditation alone wasn't enough. I needed help from others.

One day a new tax client walked in. She had a warm, supportive nature, and I soon found out she was a therapist. Suddenly and out of nowhere, like a geyser erupting from rock, I began unburdening myself of the painful feelings dammed up inside me. When, much to my surprise, I found myself telling my new client I wanted to go into counseling but had no money to pay for it, she told me she could put me in touch with a network of peer counselors. The idea was intriguing. The monthly charge was minimal, within even my meager budget, and there were many counselors to choose from. As part of the arrangement, a new person like myself was trained in counseling skills and paired with other new people to do reciprocal counseling.

Most people in the group worked with just one other counselor, but I was so eager to resolve the split I felt between spirit and money that I sought out help from many people. Soon I had as many as seven counselors to choose from. Each had his or her strengths, and I learned how to match the skills of particular individuals with the issues or feelings I was dealing with at any given time.

Then there came this particularly difficult week when dreaded tax season was fast approaching, my savings were practically gone, and my heart felt as far from money as I was from Shangri-la. I longed for some other way out than an endless stream of tax returns for what seemed an endless stream of years into the future. But no one seemed able to help. I had already seen practically every counselor on my list. Only one was still available: Lester, definitely the bottom of the barrel. He lacked empathy, and he always wanted to take my counseling session in a direction I didn't want to go. I had no real desire to call Lester, yet I was feeling inside myself such a powerful yearning for a truth free from money that I picked up the phone and called him.

When Lester appeared at my apartment, he set to work with me in his usual controlling manner. As soon as I tried to tell Lester something about the circumstances of my yearning, he told me to shut up.

"Just feel the feeling," he ordered.

I let the feeling flow for about thirty seconds. "You see, this split I experience—" I started off.

"Just feel it," he interrupted. "I don't want to hear about it."

I tried feeling the feeling for another thirty seconds, which seemed long enough. "Well," I began, "I have this powerful longing—"

"Shut up, Kinder, for God's sake," he demanded. "Close your mouth and feel the feeling."

We seesawed back and forth for nearly the whole hour. As the time passed, the feeling in me deepened. It began as a lump in my throat, then it was racing up the lines of my jaw and into the bones of my head like a scream, now it filled my eyes with the moisture of deep sadness. Finally it possessed my whole body as if I were a leaf in its wind. A wooziness took me over and I stayed with the yearning I felt, beyond thought. The white wall behind Lester began moving. Its color changed to pink, an undulating wall of pink, a sea of flesh on which I floated like a tropical island in paradise, until some force plucked me off this inviting warmth and dropped me flat onto something hard and cold.

So this was yearning! And I had *felt* it!

Suddenly I realized that the only time I could have experienced lying on a sea of flesh was in my own infancy, most likely soon after birth, as I was laid across my mother's belly. Whenever I encountered the hard cold surface of the world, a yearning for something like that same tropical sea of the soul rose in me.

At first I thought this experience itself was profound. Soon, though, I realized that the profundity lay not in the experience, which could never be repeated, but in the process, which could be endlessly repeated. It took me even longer to realize what I had learned from Lester: the structure of suffering itself and the way to end it.

The first aspect of the structure of suffering lay in the stories I was telling myself about the approach of tax season, my distance from Shangri-la, my precarious financial situation, and the unfairness of it all—a structure we can call Innocence. The next aspect was the "I, me, and mine" that kept clinging to the stories. Finally there were the feelings, in my case of yearning. Lester's repeated order to shut up and just feel was his way of saying "Let your stories go, including stories of yourself, and let your feelings be. Open to the experience of your emotions as they are. Don't try to figure them out by chattering away. Don't try to change them. Just pay attention. Notice them just as they are, and let the images that arise during the process go." Lester had given me a meditative process for which my years of spiritual practice had well prepared me—to contemplate a feeling in the body in the same way that I might focus on a simple prayer or the journey of my breath until I came to peace with it.

Just as Rumi says in his poem, the end of suffering was palpable. Entering the fire inevitably led to moments of transformation. I spent the following six years training as a counselor, devouring every psychological workshop I could find while building upon, deepening, and developing within myself this profoundly simple process I learned from my bottom-of-the-barrel counseling friend. Now I want to teach it to you.

LETTING THOUGHTS GO, LETTING FEELINGS BE

You know the situation all too well. The boss came to work in one of those moods. As soon as the first little thing went wrong, she was down your throat. You were ready for the attack, your defenses in position, and you met her anger with an anger of your own, until the conflict devolved into a shouting match. Then she backed off, at least for the moment, stomping off and slamming the door of her office so hard the glass rattled in its frame. You went back to work too, tapping at the computer keys and glaring at the screen but actually fuming inside, less writing the report due in the afternoon than plotting new and nasty ways of taking revenge.

Now it's hours later and you're driving home. The scene between you and the boss weighs on you. It is all you can think of. The boss's imperious, demanding nature, her niggling perfectionism, the way she picks at everything you do—it all fills you with rage. Your heart races, the blood pulses behind your breastbone and throbs in your throat, your fingers tighten around the steering wheel. Then you think of this morning's possible consequences on your life and career.

"My God," you say, "she could fire me. Now, that's all I need. Bills to pay, and me without a job. And I can just see the recommendation she'd give to the next place I went looking for work."

In an instant your anger changes to fear. Forget self-development and the spirituality of work. Forget too the righteousness of your anger against your boss's unreasonable demands and lousy management style. This is about survival. If you want to keep eating, you need that job.

By the time you reach home, you're planning to make it up to her. Chocolate? Flowers? An apology on linen paper with gold-leaf margin? No, all that's obsequious overkill, you decide. "I'll just be nice to her," you say to yourself, "act as if it's all in the past. Let bygones be bygones."

It has yet to be gone from your mind, though. The obsession continues; your mind races and your body churns all evening long. Through the night you can barely sleep, tossing and turning as you replay the morning's argument, worry over your fate, plan compensatory behavior, and wonder how long you can keep on living with a boss like that.

The problem in this situation isn't your boss. It is your own way of handling difficult emotions that arise in the world of money and elsewhere as well. And you are not alone in this. Practically all of us do exactly the same thing. Facing tough feelings like anger, anxiety, or despair, we lock on to the thoughts coupled to the feelings and lose our presence in the world. After such a struggle, you cannot work on the job, nor on the way home are you driving with anything more than a fraction of your being. The greatest portion of you is locked in a cycle of suffering, obsessing on thoughts tied into the knot binding Innocence to Pain.

Often it has amazed me how much more stupid we adults are around such emotional issues than a young child is with a hot stove. The first time the child touches the stove and pulls away with singed fingers, it has learned not to touch a stove again. We adults do just the opposite with our difficult feelings: We go back to the hot stove time and again, and always we come away with burned flesh. We keep thinking that a particular situation—this morning's fight with the boss or, say, a credit card bill that's three times larger than we expected—causes the feelings that obsess us. We focus on the issue and work wildly to correct it, by smoothing over the relationship with the boss or resolving to stop reaching for the plastic to pay for things glittery and frivolous. The resolution feels acceptable and rational, and we assume that everything has been taken care of. Yet the feeling remains within us, lurking underneath to seize on the next available set of circumstances, waiting to blister our fingers once more.

THE BASICS

Such suffering is so unbearable that we'll do anything we can to escape, avoid, and rid ourselves of our feelings. To blunt suffering's unbearability, we may turn to chocolate binges, refrigerator raids, television, sex, alcohol, drugs, gambling, or overspending. Recourse to any of these outlets keeps us dependent. They keep us from growing rich—both with the inner richness of maturity and the outer richness that comes from figuring out our goals and accomplishing them. Instead, we act as partial beings, locked into neurotic habits that perpetuate the very suffering we wish to resolve. We become a small child walking again and again to the same hot stove and laying our fingers down on the searing metal.

There is another way, one that leads to clarity and ease. Instead of looking at the immediate situation of our suffering and attempting to change it, as we might a television channel, we resolve once and for all to come to terms with these underlying emotions. This way is simple to state and powerful to do. It is a matter of letting thoughts go and letting feelings be. This practice is the central activity for the heart following its path to freedom.

The spiritual context of the practice is summarized perfectly in a poem from the *Tao Te Ching,* which legend says was written by the long-ago Chinese master Lao-tzu.

> *The ancient Masters were profound and subtle.*
> *Their wisdom was unfathomable.*
> *There is no way to describe it:*
> *all we can describe is their appearance.*
>
> *They were careful*
> *as someone crossing an iced-over stream.*
> *Alert as a warrior in enemy territory.*
> *Courteous as a guest.*
> *Fluid as melting ice.*
> *Shapable as a block of wood.*
> *Receptive as a valley.*
> *Clear as a glass of water.*
>
> *Do you have the patience to wait*
> *till your mud settles and the water is clear?*
> *Can you remain unmoving*
> *till the right action arises by itself?*
>
> *The Master doesn't seek fulfillment.*
> *Not seeking, not expecting,*
> *she is present, and can welcome all things.*

The practice of letting thoughts go and feelings be follows Lao-tzu's counsel; it focuses on being present and welcoming all things. And it accomplishes the work of Understanding. In this practice we learn to accept even our darkest and most difficult places—not by running away from them, trying to think them away, or trying to do something about them, but by entering them deeply. Like the Master in Lao-tzu's poem, we allow our mud to settle and our water to clear. Through the practice of letting thoughts go and feelings be, we learn to love ourselves, and even in our deepest woe we uncover a kindness to ourselves. Here we enter the old wounds, cease to judge ourselves with the special harshness self-judgment marshals, and forgive. That is, we recognize and accept our inadequacies, learn humility, heal the plaguing hatreds of self and others. Simple as the practice itself is, often it can transform a life.

THREE ATTITUDES OF PRACTICE

THE OBSERVER. The practice of letting thoughts go and feelings be begins with a meditation. Sit quietly with your eyes closed. As you become quiet and concentrated, watch for even the tiniest moments of suffering. Observe them closely to see how they are structured. Notice in particular how suffering reveals itself as uncomfortable feelings in the body. Attend to whether the feelings are linked to thoughts and stories by the clinging activity of identification, by "I, me, and mine." Whenever you notice that you are suffering, let the thoughts go. Focus entirely on your feelings, no matter how uncomfortable they appear, simply observing them as sensations. Pay attention to how "I, me, and mine" disappears. As you become peaceful again, return to the breath.

In your daily life make moments of suffering, particularly around money, the bell of awakening that calls you to this meditation whenever they arise. While learning to let your thoughts and identifications go, develop a deep and abiding interest in knowing all the feelings in your body, from the most obvious to the most subtle. Become sensitive to their slightest nuance. Observe particularly your vulnerability and fragility around money.

While this practice can be learned as an adjunct to meditation, it is not only a meditative technique. It can be used in any setting where difficult feelings arise.

The big fight with the boss serves as an example. Imagine yourself in the evening after getting home from work, when your body and mind are a riot of feelings. Almost as soon as you try to calm yourself and focus on the breath, the morning's scenes replay themselves in your memory. You attempt to return to your breath, but in a matter of seconds you are hearing the glass in the boss's door rattle and rethinking the ornate revenge you planned at the computer. Instead of going back to the breath, now you focus on the feelings of anger. You let go of thoughts; that is, you pay attention not to the scenes replaying in your head but to the anger manifesting itself in your body as churning stomach, racing heartbeat, and clenched fists. It doesn't matter that thoughts may continue to plague you. Continue to let them go, and, with a gentle firmness and without judgment, return to the feelings.

If you keep attempting to return to the breath in the face of feelings so strong and powerful that you are drawn to them instantly and continuously, you're just practicing how to repress feelings. But when you let the story go and focus on the feelings themselves, you are going right to the heart of the matter—a bundle of difficult emotions that have been with you since childhood, perhaps even since the time when you curled inside the womb. They are making themselves known through your body.

Since our culture emphasizes living in the mind over living in the body, many people, particularly men, find it difficult if not impossible to locate feelings physically. Pay particular attention to the upper half of the body, from the waist up—the pit of the belly, the chest, the shoulders and neck, the wrists or hands, the jaw. Feelings may manifest themselves as tightness, tension, tingling, even numbness. Pay attention to each feeling's temperature (hot or cold), softness or hardness, moving or stationary quality, and dimension. (Is it flat or three-dimensional? Does it have a shape? Is it like a point or a line?)

If you find it difficult to locate feelings, be patient with yourself. Sometimes it takes a while; I once worked with a college professor who spent two years trying before he could sense feelings in his body. You can help yourself heighten awareness of emotions by observing in everyday life the sensations that arise whenever anger, sadness, anxiety, envy, greed, or frustration is working on you. Slowly, over time and with continuing self-observation, you will discover the feelings, particularly if you are working simultaneously at letting thoughts go.

Letting go of thoughts separates the structure of suffering—the knot of identity binding Pain to Innocence—from the underlying feelings. It allows us to see the difference between thoughts and feelings, and it lays the groundwork for accepting those feelings, no matter how difficult they may appear. As we become more and more comfortable with the full spectrum of our feelings, we find that they stick less and less to our current dilemmas. They may well appear, but, as we continue the practice, they lose their power to immobilize us. Feelings become less daunting enemies than old friends, as comfortable and well fitting as an old pair of shoes. Once we genuinely experience this ungluing of thought and feelings, the practice happens almost automatically whenever suffering plagues us—and the steady transformation of money woes to money blessings has begun.

THE KINDLY MOTHER. Acting as a neutral observer of our feelings can seem impossible at times, particularly when we are struggling with powerful feelings, particularly anger, sadness, or fear. In this circumstance I often build the practice not on observation but on kindness. I imagine myself tending to each of my emotions with maternal kindness. In effect I am still observing the physical manifestations of my feelings, but I treat them the way a mother does when her child bursts into the house crying over a bee sting or a skinned knee. I bring that same maternal kindness to the feelings in my body, not to the circumstance I am in, so that I am still letting thoughts go and letting feelings be. This is easier than it may sound. I say things to myself like "It's all right, George," and "Everything will be okay," and "Don't worry, it's not your fault." Sometimes I imagine giving my feelings a hug, or I say "Ahh" to them, the way a mom comforts a child who just fell off a bicycle. Thoughts have a way of flitting in and out, almost instantaneously (remember the exercise in chapter 2), while feelings linger, giving me plenty of time to direct toward them all the kindness and compassion I can summon.

You might wonder how I can bring kindness toward a feeling as seemingly unkind as anger. Whether the anger is directed at myself or at someone else, I find that often it has arisen from some part of me that feels offended, hurt, or humiliated. I direct my kindness to the hurt rather than to the anger, for hurt is the root of the feeling.

I find the practice of kindness to be so powerful that I often follow it for months at a time, cultivating a mother's compassion toward every feeling in each moment of the day. This practice leaves me feeling forgiving and kindly toward almost everyone and every circumstance. It turns everything I encounter into medicine for the soul.

THE WARRIOR. Sometimes, rather than acting as an observer or a mother, I adopt the attitude of the warrior. The warrior stands tall; he or she faces the enemy completely, without apology, surrender, or retreat. I find this attitude particularly useful when difficult external circumstances threaten to overwhelm me with depression or despair.

Some years ago I faced too much all at once: On one and the same day, a difficult divorce became final and I found out my mother had terminal cancer. My mother lived less than five more months, and without my marriage, I was having to face up to a life that had become both emotionally impoverished and financially difficult. The double whammy of divorce and death ground me down into the deepest despair I had yet known. I was lucky enough to be living with a good friend who provided excellent support, and I also benefited from the people I knew at work. Yet just leaving work for a few minutes in the middle of the day to get a sandwich would drop me into despair. By the time I reached the street, I felt like a stone sinking in a sea without bottom.

The attitude of the warrior saved me. Whenever I left the safe confines of my shared apartment or my job, I reminded myself that I was about to sink. At the same time I formed a fierce determination to be completely alert and attentive to every second of that sinking. As Lao-tzu's poem counsels, I became "alert as a warrior in enemy territory." Instead of fighting the sinking or giving in to it, I resolved not to let the despair destroy my alertness. Rather than struggling against depression, I became totally curious about the experience of despair and determined to understand it by meeting every moment of the feelings on my own terms.

I now look back on this time as one of the most amazing emotional periods of my life. The practice of the warrior allowed me to live with the greatest burden of darkness I had yet faced—to, as Lao-tzu promises, "be present, and . . . welcome all things."

THE PRACTICE IN WORK AND RELATIONSHIP

The practice of letting thoughts go and feelings be leads us into Rumi's fire. We meet our shadows, becoming so acquainted with them that they no longer feel like anything other than ourselves. In the fire, darkness becomes light. Entering it we emerge in the water, now as clear as Lao-tzu's, our mud settled.

Mahealani Sapolu used the practice whenever the urge to reach for a credit card burned in her. Every encounter with the desire to spend taught her how to let go of the want she had cultivated in an impoverished childhood. In Derrick King's case, the practice showed him that his rational approach to solving problems without attention to underlying feelings simply didn't work. And Susanna Swartz was able to move away from anger toward the men who had hurt her and gradually adopt a new kindness toward her own previously unacceptable humiliation, an attitude that allowed her to make friends with her own fragility.

The practice is employed in any and every difficult, troubling, or painful experience around money. For example, if we are chronic overspenders like Mahealani or self-employed people who consistently charge less than the market will bear, the practice gives us a way of observing feelings as we sense the urge toward a spending binge rise or we write up a deeply discounted invoice. By getting to know the feelings behind the behavior and letting go of the thoughts formed in reaction to them, we will gradually find a way to stand our ground in these areas and stop sabotaging our financial plans for freedom. If we dedicate ourselves to these practices, our experiences become transformative.

Two more examples from my own life illustrate how the practice works and how it can help us open to Understanding.

THE CLIENT FROM HELL. Early on in my career as a financial planner and an asset manager, I gained a client who, on first glance, seemed a godsend. He was a smart, talented man who turned over to me the management of his considerable fortune. He also referred friends, family, and business associates. In perhaps a year, this one man and his network accounted for at least 50 percent of my business.

This proved, however, to be a decidedly mixed blessing. At first, I was so bowled over by this man's confidence in me and the large amount of money he brought me to work with that I paid little attention to his personality quirks and irritating behavior. The man was a boor—curt, loud, oafish, dismissive of any opinion and all feelings but his own, crude, oblivious. With each passing month, I found this harder to take. Yet I had to take it. Because I was locked into so many different relationships with him, hardly a day went past that I didn't see him personally in my office or talk to him two or three times on the phone.

At first I took a rational approach to the issue. I tried many things. I acted like my client's best friend, I rolled out the humor and good deeds, I started a few good-natured disagreements, I cajoled, I acted as if he didn't matter as much as he thought he did. Nothing worked. He stayed just the same, and the irritation remained.

Frustrated and already at work on the practice of letting thoughts go and feelings be, I decided to shift my focus from external circumstances to internal events. I was growing aware that Understanding requires patience, that often the lesson of patience is taught by the person we least expect. At the time I was reading about the Chinese invasion of Tibet and the remarkable way the Tibetans responded. Chinese soldiers have demolished monasteries and killed and tortured tens of thousands of monks and nuns, defaced and destroyed priceless ancient Buddhist scriptures and art, clear-cut the ancient Himalayan forests, and launched one campaign after another to destroy the Tibetan nationality and obliterate its language. Yet when the Dalai Lama, the Tibetan leader in exile, is asked what he thinks of the Chinese, he says, "They are my greatest teacher."

As bad as my client made me feel, no way was he as bad as the Chinese army, I told myself. And if the Dalai Lama had the wisdom to point to an archenemy as his greatest teacher, surely I could learn something from my hellish client.

I looked anew at how sad, angry, exasperated, anxious, and depressed I felt at different times with him, and I kept working at letting my thoughts go and letting the feelings be. Sometimes the practice frustrated me. I wanted to reach out and grab my client by the shoulders, and shout in his face, "Change, you fool!" He didn't, of course. Yet I persevered, remaining with the practice, observing daily the momentary sensations of difficult feelings I had never truly observed before.

It took years until something lifted in me. Much as my client continued to do things that annoyed me, my feelings deepened toward him. He came across to me as an old and dear friend. I think of him now, years later, as one of my greatest teachers, the man who taught me more than anyone else ever has about how to handle anger, frustration, annoyance, sadness, fright, and despair.

THE PRACTICE IN RELATIONSHIP. Money is a leading cause of pain in relationships and divorce in marriage, as Derrick King found to his painful surprise and I myself have discovered anew on more than one occasion. Invariably a struggle over money is about more than finances. It often concerns how we love and want to be loved and how we have been wounded around money in the past. The vulnerabilities, wounds, and Pain of each individual arise in unknown and uncontrollable ways that can tear a relationship or marriage apart by fastening on to stories, images, or "points" we insist on repeating endlessly, to the chagrin of ourselves or our partners. The practice can provide a method for getting at the feelings that underlie the conflict and helping both parties open to one another, deepening their Understanding of themselves and of each other.

Some years ago I had begun dating a woman I had known for a long while and with whom I remain a friend. One day, out of seeming nowhere, she burst into my apartment full of anger and rage over an issue of who owed whom how much money. I knew quickly that she was unaware of certain financial transactions and that she had misinterpreted a number of events in the prior month. It was clear too that each of us held different assumptions about money. The problem was, she was in such a lather, so beyond herself with anger and rage and the situations themselves so complex, that I saw no way I could unravel the stories on the spot—nor would she have let me. I faced a classic fight-or-flight situation. I didn't want to fight back by raising my voice in a screaming match. My friend was so angry that I thought she might start throwing lamps, dishes, or books and break up my apartment. Flight wouldn't work either. Running from the conflict, by refusing to pay attention to her concerns, could torpedo the relationship. What to do?

Suddenly I had an idea: Why not the practice? Instead of either fighting or fleeing, I sat down and paid attention to my feelings. I let my body language communicate to my friend that I was listening to her continuing rage, yet in fact I knew she would repeat herself so often and with such vehemence that I could bring all my focus to the feelings coursing through me without missing what she was saying.

And I was feeling a great deal. The heat of anger gathered in my stomach like a bank of burning coals, and shivers of terror passed through my chest and intestines and ran goose bumps up and down my spine. I was aware of the speed of my feelings, how they raced through my body, the way they piled one atop another, like floes of river ice during spring breakup. No matter how much I observed the feelings, thoughts of "I, me, and mine" kept coming back and attaching to them. I felt fear and despair at the possibility of losing the relationship, terror at the potential for violence in the situation, anger at my friend for taking her anger out on me. Yet I also worked to free myself of these thoughts and others—like the image of my friend as an idiot for getting it all wrong, of myself as an idiot for being the friend of someone so off-kilter, and the what-ifs over whether she would abandon me or I her. I brought kindness to the feelings again and again, like a mother holding a hurt child close.

It took my friend almost half an hour and numerous reiterations of the story to rid herself of the accumulated rage and anger. Only then did her energy flag. By that time I found I had made friends with my own feelings. I didn't feel peaceful—the atmosphere was too charged with terror and sadness for that—but I did have a sense that I was welcoming back inside my body feelings I had sent into exile many years before. When my friend finally fell silent, I turned to her. I said only, "I am terribly sorry that you're in so much pain over this." I was taking her in, accepting her, just as I had welcomed my feelings. Amazingly, my friend started to weep. In a moment, the two of us were hugging. Somehow, in making room in myself for my feelings, I had also made room for my friend. In the space that opened between us, I was able to discuss the misunderstanding with her in a sympathetic, compassionate way, without accusation or blame.

I've seen documentaries about shamans, medicine men and medicine women from indigenous tribes, who take their strength from entering the darkness without reservation. I felt as if I had done the same thing. I came away with a confidence that I had the capacity to be with and to survive anything that came my way emotionally.

I had come to the core of Understanding. I realized that maturity arises more from being open to experience than from pushing it away. I had made a deep connection with the source of inner power that arises from owning up to all my feelings, no matter how difficult or frightening they may appear to be.

A PRACTICAL APPROACH TO THE PRACTICE

One of the most useful exercises for developing Understanding starts with listing on an 8-1/2 x 11-inch sheet of paper all the feelings around money you have and can ever remember having. Likely candidates are envy, greed, miserliness, anxiety, sadness, fear, jealousy, anger, despair, guilt, humiliation, and panic, but don't limit yourself to this list. If you've had other, more, or different feelings, write them all down. After you've listed them, see if you know where you feel the physical sensations of each emotion. Note the body locations next to the feelings.

Next, record the most memorable life story associated with each feeling. Pay attention to the structure of the stories, looking for patterns and repetitions, and to the qualities of the feelings, particularly how you experience them in your body.

Now write out the money stories most likely to arise from each feeling over the next few months. Prophesize. Again, note clearly how the structure of each story matches the quality of the feeling.

Form a commitment to let thoughts go and feelings be. The next time one of these feeling arises around money, promise yourself that you will let go of the stories associated with it. Plan instead to observe the feeling's sensations, bringing to them the attitude of the observer, the mother, or the warrior.

If your list includes nothing about the rat race, pay attention now to the ways you feel caught up in the endless pursuit of money. Record the feelings and the stories. Pay attention to your fears of never having enough and all the anxieties spawned by the rapid pace of modern living. While forming a determination to let thoughts go and feelings be, form an equal determination to discover what yearnings and feelings lurk beneath these anxieties and fears.

Review the goal exercises of chapter 6. Examine the feelings underlying your goals. Look at your yearnings and longings. Study your "shoulds." In each of these areas, it can be transformative to let thoughts go and feelings be when the stories and the emotions attached to them come up in daily life.

THE LESSONS OF THE WISE ONES

There is nothing like the experience of being with someone, older, wiser, and completely at peace with money. When Dante sees the gates of hell opening before him, he has the good sense to enter in the company of an ancient and trusted friend. The wise and accomplished poet Virgil serves as Dante's guide and mentor throughout the underworld. As a good mentor will do, Virgil let Dante know that no matter what he experienced during the time they were together, Virgil would be there for him. He was willing to look past Dante's thoughts and defenses to see the person he was underneath and to consider him with both unconditional positive regard and a confidence that he could get through whatever difficulties life chucked at him.

The practice of Understanding comes to us from a mentor like osmosis. It's not exactly that we start to think the way the mentor does, although that can help. It's more often that we begin to feel like the mentor. I remember when Sandra, an overspending client, first told me about her new friend, Rosalind, an older woman, retired and clearly at peace with money. There seemed to be a new glow, an ease and a lightness about Sandra herself. I'd been working with her for six months to no avail on her spending habits; her credit card debt just got larger and larger. But there were some things about this new friend that sounded promising. Rosalind lived a simpler life than Sandra. She dressed in a less expensive way, preferred pleasures like a walk in the woods to costly symphony tickets, displayed little attraction to pricey objects or big-ticket vacations. Within three months Sandra was paying off the new debt on her credit cards every month, and within six months she was significantly paying down the old debt.

When I asked her how it happened, she said, "Rosalind doesn't spend much and she doesn't get anxious about money. It was extraordinary to be in town with her, on Newbury Street, and see how much more pleasure she got in the weather, the walk, and our conversation than in looking at all the things she might buy. I like the peaceful feelings she has, and I think it's rubbing off on me around my spending. I didn't really know this before, but now I see how anxious I was and how I used buying things to quiet that anxiety. Rosalind's taught me something about quieting myself inside myself instead."

Over the years I too have sought out people I felt could teach me something about being at peace with turmoil. Some of these people have been counselors or psychologists, some pastors and spiritual teachers, some businesspeople, some random acquaintances. All of them have been mentors for me. For years I asked my friends, "Who do you know who's a really good person?" If someone sounded interesting to me, I would see whether there was a way I could meet him or her. Sometimes I was rebuffed, sometimes my attempts were awkward. Still, many of my most wonderful teachers have come from these endeavors.

Like the practice of letting thoughts go and feelings be, mentors can help us gain in Understanding. All of us have encountered our own vulnerabilities in the world of money. When we tell these stories to people we respect, and they in turn tell their stories to us, we help one another heal money's wounds. In confessing our own wounds we both recognize their existence and trust that another person can listen to them without judgment—acting, as it were, on a faith in forgiveness. In listening without judgment to others tell about their wounds, we practice an activity much like letting thoughts go and letting feelings be. We experience too a feeling comparable to forgiveness.

Again and again, people tell me how they feel used around money—by corporations advertising to sell their products, by lawyers filing suit, by governments imposing unfair regulations or taxes, by products and services that aren't up to snuff, by family members or acquaintances looking for a free ride. Building relationships with mentors around money helps us overcome these feelings by developing a rare sense of trust. Rather than looking at the world as a collection of people out to defraud us, we can treasure certain individuals we know are trustworthy. And if we can trust them, then perhaps it is possible that we can trust others and ourselves.

An exceptionally sharp businesswoman, Roxanne had built a booming benefits-consulting firm that catered to the high-tech industry in Massachusetts. Then she discovered that her major competitor was trying to woo business away by spreading malicious rumors that she got and kept accounts by bestowing sexual favors on key executives. In point of fact, Roxanne had always been scrupulously careful not to mix her romantic and business lives, and she was deeply hurt, offended, and enraged by her competitor's salacious falsehood. She confronted her competitor in private at an industry conference, but he denied he was saying anything untrue about her. Roxanne could tell from his very manner that he was lying through his teeth. So she went to see her lawyer.

"Look," he said to her. "It's clear and obvious slander. If you have a few hundred thousand dollars and five years of your life, I'm sure I can pin this guy's wings to the wall. But if you don't want to go to all that trouble, learn to live with it."

Roxanne didn't want the kind of trouble a lawsuit entailed, yet she did need help. She got it from her rabbi, who spent an hour with her each week, listening to her vent her feelings about the wrong, hurt, and humiliation being done to her. He passed no judgment, said only that her feelings were hers, that she had a right to them, all of them.

"After a few months, I felt purged," Roxanne told me in recounting this experience. "My rabbi guided me by holding out his hand and going with me where I needed to go. Slowly but surely I came to a clarity about the rage I felt. I found that I was actually more effective in business, less attached to my own stories, less caught by my feelings.

"The skunk who was slandering me fed into all my worst fears about how the marketplace really is. My rabbi's kind heart reminded me otherwise. He brought to mind all the good people I've done business with over the years. In fact, he put me in touch with precisely the quality I've always tried to come from—a quality of Understanding that connects me with myself and with my clients as well."

As we deepen in Understanding, we become increasingly able to connect with ourselves and others. Our relationship with money improves. As we forgive ourselves for our feelings, we are able to forgive others for theirs, passing on the self-acceptance we have learned to others who are opening to the same lesson.

In addition to individual mentoring relationships like Roxanne and her rabbi or Sandra and Rosalind, support groups focused on money can help. There are any number available, from Debtors Anonymous and Gamblers Anonymous to investment clubs. Currently I am training CFPs, therapists, spiritual advisors, and businesspeople from all over North America how to lead workshops in the Seven Stages of Money Maturity. Social support systems contribute to Understanding by giving us a safe place to share difficult fears, apprehensions, avarice, and guilt around money. A good community provides a zone where we are heard not in judgment but in compassion.

I once asked the participants in a CFP seminar to identify people who modeled Understanding for them. The list represented a wide mix: Mother Teresa of Calcutta, talk show host Oprah Winfrey, former president Jimmy Carter, actress Shirley MacLaine, the Dalai Lama, Chicago's Cardinal Bernardin, author (*The 7 Habits of Highly Effective People*) and business guru Steven Covey, and Catholic theologian and writer Michael Novak.

Do the same thing for yourself. List all the people you can think of who have modeled something valuable about Understanding. They can be people you know personally or public individuals who by reputation have expressed great power of the heart. After you've made the list, write a paragraph about each person. Record what it is about the individual that strikes you and what that person's life tells you about your own Understanding.

If your life lacks models of Understanding, find a few people to get to know. It doesn't matter whether they are counselors, spiritual advisors, or salt-of-the-earth people. Learning how to have a relationship with people who exhibit goodness around money is worth its weight in gold.

LIVING VIRTUE

If you want to go right to the heart of Understanding, without having to master the practice of feelings and thoughts and without the aid of mentors, just live a life of virtue. I don't mean the way we all think of ourselves as primarily virtuous people. Rather, be scrupulous, without exceptions. Live virtuously every moment of every day.

Living each day in an intentionally virtuous manner—a way of life that incorporates honesty, sincerity, integrity, trustworthiness, kindness, and all those other qualities we think of as good and desirable—builds Understanding as nothing else can. In addition to the good done by virtuous actions themselves and to the Understanding bestowed upon others, virtue creates a sorely needed kindness within and toward ourselves.

In Knowledge we learned that money has to be rooted in systems of virtue and integrity or else economies and cultures disintegrate. We know intellectually that this is true. In Understanding we take this Knowledge into our beings by becoming the virtue itself. If you doubt the benefit of virtue, then observe its effect: the ease that fills us and others when we act kindly, the suffering that springs from harsh and unkind deeds.

One day as I was walking along the street during the Christmas season, I passed a Salvation Army bellringer. A thought passed through my mind: "Give her twenty dollars." I hesitated, and another thought rose: "Twenty dollars? That's a lot of money to give to the Salvation Army!" Not a second later I slammed my foot against a raised crack in the sidewalk and stubbed my toe. As I was hopping about in one-footed pain, I got it. The universe had presented me with an opportunity for kindness. I turned away, however, and the painful consequences of my refusal manifested themselves immediately.

Unfortunately, virtue or the lack of virtue usually manifests its effects more subtly. I say "unfortunately" because it is not always easy to notice the subtle ways we build or weaken our own characters. Living with a heightened awareness of our ability to act virtuously requires us to observe closely the content and intention of our actions and to understand how every second of waking life affects our hearts and souls. We come to realize that self-interest is more complicated than economic theory would have us believe. The notion of self-interest in a market economy commonly raises images of crass material self-aggrandizement—J. R. Ewing working one more scam on an assembly of suckers or the stockbroker chanting a mantra of "earn 'em, churn 'em, and burn 'em." Understanding allows us to see deeper, to perceive how actions that deepen us and augment our wisdom work to our benefit. It is our very highest self-interest to experience the forgiveness of our sins, heal our wounds, end our suffering, even enter paradise. Indeed, living virtue in every moment is like living in the realm of the blessed. This practice belongs not only to the world's great religions but also to its most accomplished civilizations. And we can do it in every moment of the lives we are already leading.

Living virtuously pays off. It ends the rat race, deepens the sense of ease around money, and delivers a new freedom from care.

I discovered this benefit in a moment of sudden insight that I first mentioned in chapter 4. It came during the time when I was making my living as a tax preparer. I wasn't comfortable with that work. I found it difficult to charge people for doing tax work, and, as a child of the 1960s, I suspected—and feared—that my only motivation in making money was a minor-league version of J. R. Ewing's unfettered greed.

One morning a client called with a complicated and difficult tax question. I didn't know the answer off the top of my head, so as soon as the call was over, I scoured my tax library, devouring books in a long and difficult search for the answer. Afterward, I found myself wondering what I had been doing. "Was that greed?" I asked myself. "Desire for self-aggrandizement?" No, it wasn't, I realized. What I had felt during the long research to find the answer was generosity, a kindness toward a client who was troubled by a genuinely difficult complication in his economic situation.

This discovery surprised me. What did generosity have to do with business? This was hard-nosed work I was doing, an intellectual task focused on a financial issue. How could it be that in the process my heart felt open?

I started asking other small businesspeople about their motivations around work. Usually the first answer they came up with was something like "Oh, I gotta make a living" or "The kids need shoes."

But when I persisted, when I kept asking further questions that probed deeper into their motivation for working with clients and customers, they all finally spoke of generous actions, meeting the needs of those they served, and sharing kindness—like Thomas, the transplanted Georgian who imported furniture from Asia. This flew in the face of what economic theory seemed to say motivated people in the marketplace.

I looked again at my own day-to-day actions in business, focusing on how I felt as I went about the work of preparing tax returns. For years I had experienced guilt at what I assumed were my greedy motives. Certainly I needed to make a living and I had financial goals. Yet I did not feel greed. That realization lifted the guilt like a veil from my eyes, making me better able to act vigorously and effectively at work. In a moment I found myself able to stop fighting all the forces of civilization and to complete a tax return without feeling the tension of resentment and blame. Instead, I discovered that I could accept complicated feelings in myself and others and, with compassion, appreciate the moral ambiguities of human nature in the world of money.

Acting virtuously does not necessarily mean giving all our money to charity and living in voluntary poverty. It does mean living actively engaged with those around us and the moral dilemmas they present. It makes no sense to give away our capacity to realize a dream of freedom before we know what that dream is. Instead, living virtue asks us to pay close attention to every action of every day, no matter what we do, and to bring a consciousness of the consequences of our actions to bear on the choices we make.

TRY THIS—LIVING VIRTUE

To make virtue a part of everyday life, form a specific intention around virtuous action. There are a couple of ways to do this. One is to commit yourself for a particular period of time to doing nothing but virtuous actions. When you think of a virtuous action, do it; when you think of an action that violates virtue, refrain. Try this first for a day, then make it for a week or a month. Another is to promise to yourself that every single day—and that's every day with no exceptions—you will go out of your way to perform an unexpected act of kindness.

As you practice virtue, be sure to pay close attention to what is happening around and within you. Watch out for feelings and thoughts attaching to moments of suffering. Attend to the action's consequences, both internal and external, as well as its nature.

A FINAL WORD

Understanding involves the metamorphosis of suffering into something profound and spiritual. In mastering Understanding, we become more successful and at ease around money, but only after we come to see money as a powerful teacher and, like food, a necessary nourishment. Money teaches us by forcing us to encounter its Pain—the pain of economic difference, the pain of being without. Through it we learn wisdom, virtue, kindness, patience, clarity and joy, laying the foundation for personal transformation around money.

chapter 8

VIGOR:
THE STRENGTH TO CARRY
THROUGH

*It is vain to say human beings ought to be satisfied with
tranquility: they must have action, and they will
make it if they cannot find it.*

Charlotte Brontë

*I learned this at least by my experiment: that if one advances
confidently in the direction of his dreams, and endeavors to live
the life which he has imagined, he will meet with a success
unexpected in common hours.*

Henry David Thoreau

*People should not take self-control lightly, because if they do,
things can disturb them, and they have no sense of tranquil
stability. People should not be obsessive in attending to
affairs, because if they are, they will get bogged down by
things and lack freedom and lively vigor.*

Huanchu Daoren

*Would those who say it can't be done please get out of the way
of those who are doing it.*

Bumper sticker

Having faced the music, Mahealani felt her life begin to assume a shape something like what she wanted. As Pualani grew into a toddler and then a little girl, Mahealani moved ahead in her grocery-store job, buoyed by the persistence she had inherited from her father and the heartfelt interest in others her mother had passed on to her. First she became a checker. Then, when a position as assistant manager of the produce department opened up, she moved into it.

"But, you know, I was a lot smarter than that job," she told me. "They called me an assistant manager, but what I was doing was opening crates of everything from lettuce to papayas and putting them out. I wasn't so much managing as lugging. It was a little more money than I had made as a checker, but it was just another job, a way of punching the clock.

"But I was proud of moving ahead, and I have to admit I was learning something. When I got bored or tired, I found myself watching what people bought and wondering why they picked up what they did."

Tourists particularly fascinated her. They were drawn to items uniquely Hawaiian, such as papayas, mangoes, pineapples, macadamia nuts, and Kona coffee. And they wanted to be sure they were getting the real thing, the honest-to-goodness island edition of an item. Any number of times, a tourist approached her with a pineapple and asked, "Can you tell me—is this from around here?"

"Sometimes it was, and sometimes it wasn't," Mahealani said. "What struck me was how bothered the tourists were if something they expected to be true-blue Hawaiian actually wasn't."

Meanwhile, the financial situation at home was easing. Between her increased wages and Ricky's furniture-refinishing business, the two of them had paid off most of their debt and begun saving a little money. Mahealani discovered she was two months' pregnant, something she and Ricky had been hoping for. Life was going well until the day she found that the rumors flying around the store were all too true.

Mahealani worked for one of the last remaining independent groceries on Oahu. A major chain had bought the store and planned to consolidate operations with its own stores and trim staff. Mahealani received notice that in thirty days she was out of a job.

"I felt like one of those cartoon characters who steps out of his car and falls into the Grand Canyon," she said. "The new company was playing favorites with their own people, and they dropped me because I was part of the old company. I felt absolutely powerless. God, I thought, what the hell more can happen to me?"

Mahealani fell into a depression, a mood that Ricky shared with her. Just when their lives seemed to be improving, just when they had a new child on the way, something came along and kicked the legs out from under them. If anyone ever had good reason to feel bad, they did.

"Good thing I was pregnant. I probably would have started drinking otherwise," she said. "After the job ended, mostly I just moped around. I had a hard time getting out of bed in the morning. I felt like 'What difference does it make?' I had to dress and feed Pualani, but beyond that I thought nothing made a damn bit of difference."

Slowly her mood changed. "It was because I thought about what you said about entering the darkness, about learning from it, not letting it bowl me over. In the middle of this despair I started noticing little things, silly things, that started me thinking. Like how my mother used to make guava juice. Now I was craving it. And I remembered too how we used to mix fresh lilikoi with tapioca. I liked it so much, and I started thinking about that too."

An idea was forming in Mahealani's mind.

"I had to make money, but I didn't have a job. I began fantasizing about some kind of a little storefront or a roadside stand that sold only Hawaiian products, particularly ones made or grown by native Polynesians," she said. "The idea turned me on. As a people we had all these skills with local products, and the tourists were interested in them. What if we could offer those things to them and certify their authenticity? I had this feeling it might work as a business. I knew what the tourists were asking for, and I knew what my people could do. It was only natural to put the two together."

Mahealani pursued the idea further before Doreen was born and in the first few months following her birth. She made lists of possible products, such as guava juice, taro, lilikoi, soursop, breadfruit, persimmons, mangoes, star apples, avocados, and coconut ice cream, and she lined up people who could supply them and who were willing to take a chance on her entrepreneurial capacity. And she located a good spot for the stand alongside the main highway only a couple of minutes' walk from the house.

Ricky built the stand for her, with help from Pualani, who was fascinated at the sight of her father using power tools to shape raw boards into something with form and purpose.

"All of us got into the act," Mahealani said. "Ricky actually started taking off early from work to help me out a couple of days a week, and I took the kids down with me while I was setting everything up. When I actually opened for business, Ricky sometimes kept an eye on the kids for me, and sometimes he came to help. Sometimes all four of us were in the stand at the same time. It was great. I had my whole family all around me."

Still, Mahealani knew practically nothing about the nuts and bolts of business, from bookkeeping to tax law. Finding an energy in her she had not suspected, she took evening classes in basic accounting and finance at the local community college. On school nights Ricky cooked dinner for the girls and kept an eye on them so Mahealani could go to class, then she brought home what she had learned and taught him.

"I had a new feeling in me," Mahealani said. "School was fascinating. I couldn't believe I was getting excited about debits and credits. I woke up every morning thrilled with what I was doing. It amazed me how creative my life was becoming. There were so many new, different things to learn and understand. Every moment counted for something. Every moment was teaching me something new and wonderful."

Alexandria King, Derrick's estranged wife, struck out directly toward what she needed to support herself in her newfound independence. She enrolled in the master's of business administration program at the University of Santa Clara. Derrick expected her to fall flat on her face—and realize, as she was hitting the pavement, how much she needed him. "She was a classic liberal arts kind of person, a Spanish major in college when we met. I thought she was following some pipe dream that would blow away the first time she had to take a quantitative analysis class," Derrick said. "But she surprised me. She dug in her heels and got an A.

"And you know what—it upset me. Here she was doing well at the same kind of thing I did well at. I felt like she was throwing my own business success back in my face, telling me she didn't need me. 'My God,' I thought, 'I've been working my butt off all this time—and for what? What the hell's the point? If I've got a reason for being on this Earth, can anybody out there tell me what it is?'"

Lost in a despair as dark as any 3 A.M., Derrick went into counseling. Over a period of months, Derrick delved into his childhood and came to a far deeper appreciation of the suffering cycle of Innocence and Pain rooted in his background. He discovered that he had taken on the money messages and suffering of his father and that he had learned little from the connectedness and open-hearted quality of his mother. Her suffering frightened him.

Despite the therapy, Derrick's despair deepened. Nothing in his life seemed to make sense anymore, and his energy flagged. He cut back from his standard sixty- to eighty-hour weeks to a more usual forty hours. He did just enough to get by. He worried about his job, and he felt a concern that the other managers in the company would decide he was no longer a team player and might move to have him fired. Still, he didn't have the energy to return to his old ways of working at the expense of all else. Somehow he had closed the book on a former mode of existence, and he didn't know yet what was going to arise in its place. In the meantime, he felt only void, emptiness, a despair that consumed his entire being.

His mood had slumped as low as it could get when he phoned Alexandria and, using all the right phrases to ring her chimes, convinced her to give him a small chance, just the weekend after next. Reluctantly she agreed.

The next evening Derrick was sitting downstairs, in his big chair in the den where he usually watched TV.

"The set was off and the room was dark," he told me. "It was just me and all this blackness, like a blanket folded around me. I noticed my eyes were wet. I didn't want to admit it to myself, but I was crying. Then I admitted it to myself, and the tears really came. I must have sat there crying for a couple of hours. I felt like some part of me had finally come alive."

Derrick was grieving over the shape of his life. "I realized I was really pissed. It wasn't just that I wanted Alexandria back. I did. A part of me wanted her back more than anything else in the world. But more important, I wanted my own life back. If I had to, if getting my life back meant letting her go, I was willing to do it. I'd had it with sacrificing myself on the altar of somebody else's dream, whether it was my boss's twelve-hour days or Alexandria's home life or my boys' college educations. What I wanted was my own life, and that meant being engaged with my kids, going to soccer games with them, not being lost in dreams about their future. It meant finding some way to really connect with Alexandria, not just having her around as some kind of an accessory. And it meant working eight hours a day, not ten or twelve, with some time left over so I could think about what to do next with myself professionally. All this stuff scared me, but I felt I didn't have a choice. My old way wasn't a life. If I really wanted to live, I had to get on with it.

"Now I know what it means to speak of Vigor, inside my heart and my body as well as my head. I never knew before Vigor had a meaning for the whole of me. Now that I've felt it, I don't know how you could possibly have Vigor without the full engagement of the heart."

Susanna Swartz had a special way of describing the pleasure she took from fixing up her newly purchased Victorian house: "It's the most fun I've ever had with my clothes on."

She threw herself at the task with extraordinary energy. Trusting her own artistic instincts for the first time in her life, she drew up plans for what she wanted, then found and hired contractors to do the work. She developed a complex three-color scheme for the exterior paint, had the roof torn off and new slate laid down, uprooted and replanted the dying landscaping, making the front yard resplendent with lilacs, azaleas, and rhododendrons. She was equally thorough on the inside. Every wall was replastered and repainted, every curtain taken down and replaced. She tore out the kitchen and the bathrooms, installing modern appliances and fixtures that replicated the *fin-de-siècle* styles of the 1890s. And she had a special vision for the dance parlor.

She was showing me the space, now as huge, cavernous, and empty as a country church on Saturday. She described in detail the way she planned to redo the walls, suspend chandeliers from the ceiling, replace the buckling oak flooring with new, even build a small dais under the soon-to-be-refurbished rose window in the opposite wall.

Then she said, "You know, it occurred to me that when I get this big room done, I could use it for fund-raising parties. It will be very classy, the kind of space where you can bring the well heeled and the generous and talk them out of money to support the good causes I believe in."

She paused a moment. "Which brings up something I've been noticing," she began.

"What's that?" I said.

"When you and I did the financial goal work, I first rejected the idea of the house for two reasons. One was the guilt I felt over having money I hadn't earned. My fortune fell into my lap because of the family I was born into. I'm just lucky there was so much that a man as larcenous as my ex-husband wasn't smart enough to get all of it. The other reason against the house was I thought having a place like this was selfish. It was for me and me alone, I figured. It didn't feel right devoting those sorts of funds and all this energy to a project that seemed self-serving."

"And obviously you've been having a good time," I said.

"I've just loved it," she said, "the planning, the doing, getting wet paint on my hands. It's made me feel good inside, given me a kind of energy I've never felt before. The crazy thing is I've been thinking more about death, my death, as I do this. I've been aware that I only have so much time. I have to make the best of the life I have. And I realize if I can make this house into something special, I can use it to create some kind of a legacy around the causes that matter to me. I can redo this house in a way that both serves my own interests as an individual and does something to make the world a better place now and even after I'm dead and gone.

"It really turns me on to think and feel this way. Is there a name for it?" she asked. I was only too happy to reply.

"I call it Vigor."

⌐⌐

When I was growing up in the late 1950s and 1960s, perhaps the finest baseball player of the era—and the man I admired most—was Roberto Clemente, right fielder for the Pittsburgh Pirates. He was an excellent hitter and base runner, and in the field his sure hands and great speed gave him the ability to run down fly balls that would have been hits against an ordinary player. Clemente's most astounding asset was his throwing arm. He could make a long hard peg from the right-field wall to the infield with such speed that he threw out many a runner trying to take an extra base or score.

Clemente made it look easy; he played right field with the grace of a natural athlete who had been born wearing glove and cleats. But, out of the public's view, he worked assiduously at honing his skills. On his days off, when no one else was at the ballpark, Clemente still showed up to practice. A friend, who was not a professional baseball player, would hit ball after ball off the right-field wall and tell Clemente which base to throw to. Clemente became so adept at knowing exactly where he was that he could fire the throw almost before he turned around, giving him a jump on runners that often made the difference between winning and losing.

Roberto Clemente was an extraordinary talent, but talent was the smaller part of his greatness. He perfected his gifts through Vigor— the discipline, concentration, and focus that carried him toward his goals. Clemente had grown up poor in Puerto Rico, and he knew what it felt like to go hungry, yet his Vigor was more than an intellectual desire to escape poverty. It was a power that coursed through his entire being and made him who he was. When Roberto Clemente threw a baseball, he was giving his being voice. Vigor stated his identity in action. Clemente once said, "Anytime you have the opportunity to accomplish something and you don't, you're wasting your time on this Earth."

Vigor in the money world represents the energy to accomplish financial goals. It pulses through the mind, heart, and body, carrying one's whole being along. Vigor completes the work of adulthood on the path to Money Maturity.

Money Maturity is driven by sacrifice. In Knowledge, the sacrifice comes from saving and the hard work of learning itself. In Understanding, the sacrifice consists of patience with discomfort. In Vigor, we sacrifice our complacency and unearned ease to the purposes Knowledge has opened for us. Vigor arises from the dream of freedom, the pinch of necessity, and the desire to serve. It is not simple busyness, neither antic nor frantic. Instead, it springs from a profound inner aim. Without Vigor we are not productive and thus cannot give of ourselves to our communities and our dear ones. In Vigor we find who we are; we discover our identity and our selflessness. Here too we learn to speak who we are, without doubt and without obstruction, to give voice to the essence of our natures.

Vigor falls within the realm of the putatively "manly" virtues. While arising from our deepest roots, Vigor is as much the willow as the oak. It is a power, an attentiveness, that knows how to bend—the way Derrick King yielded to the shape of his life not from weakness but from strength, readdressing his Vigor to the needs of his heart that had gone wanting. Somehow, a mysterious new financial order flows from this redirecting of the heart, as it did for him, as it did eventually for Mahealani Sapolu.

Finding Vigor isn't easy, as I know all too well from working with clients over the years. Typically clients who lacked Vigor would sabotage their financial plans, whether by failing to complete financial tasks they had committed themselves to or by exaggerating to themselves and to me what they were capable of accomplishing.

When I first knew her, Connie was just such a client. A writer who edited a small literary magazine and dressed the part in jeans and sweatshirt, she had come in with her husband to see me during a couple of financial crises—the recession of 1982, when they were concerned about her husband's struggling business; again around the time of the 1987 market crash, when they were anxious over some investments. On both visits, I had asked them to fill out the ten-page questionnaire I give to all new clients at our first meeting. Connie and her husband made it through only the first couple of pages, and they canceled our follow-up meetings. Still, despite the paucity of information, a few things about their life became clear. Connie made practically no money from her literary magazine or the occasional free-lance writing assignment she took. She and her husband lived on the meager income from a small inheritance he received. The couple lived in a rent-controlled building, their lifestyle was simple, and the husband's business was always teetering on the financial edge.

Remarkably, the lack of money bothered Connie little. "Successful people cheat on the system," she told me. "That's how they got there. I wish I had their money, but I wouldn't want to do what they had to do to get it."

"Even if you had it, what would you do with it?" I asked her.

She shrugged.

"Perhaps that's the real issue for you," I said.

"What's that?" she asked.

"Your own lack of purpose."

When I next saw Connie, five or six years later after our second meeting, something had obviously happened. The jeans and sweat-shirt were gone. She was wearing a well-tailored business suit.

"Things have changed," she said. "I got a divorce in 1988, uncon-tested. I let him have it all, I just walked away. The assets were his to begin with, and I didn't want them. I wanted a life."

She reflected on our conversation years earlier. "You were right about my lack of purpose," she said, "only at the time I didn't want to hear about it."

At the time Connie was, in fact, deeply conflicted about money. Her lack of productivity plagued her even as she accepted a seemingly easy way of life, a reaction she now better understood.

"Joe's inheritance was enough, so I didn't have to work," she explained. "And I grew up thinking I'd never have to work. I had wonderful parents, kind, perhaps overly kind. Really they spoiled me, so I didn't have to do anything I didn't want to. Coming out of child-hood I had no image of what work might look like.

"When I married Joe, I put my energy into being jealous and crit-ical of everyone else. I guess my Vigor back then was the feeling of being right, but no action came out of it. I wrote very few short sto-ries really, just an hour a day most days, sometimes not even that, and I never got my magazine out anywhere near deadline. I felt guilty about not contributing more financially, but it took me hours to look through the help-wanted section and days to put together writing samples and redo my résumé. I spent most of my time reading *Newsweek* and the *Globe*, watching television, and talking endlessly to my friends on the phone. When I read *Newsweek* or the *Globe*, I was filled with critical jealousy at the reporters for their writing and at every author of every book that was ever reviewed. The little real work I did was in my husband's business. I liked what he did as a pio-neer in chemically pure products. Still, internally I criticized everyone there, including him."

"Sounds pretty bleak," I suggested. "What changed?"

"This stuff you call Vigor just exploded out of me during my sep-aration from Joe. I had gone into a very dark place. Then two things happened. One was I realized I didn't want Joe's money anymore. It didn't feel right to me to rely on him for my living, particularly when I wasn't married to him. The second thing was I discovered what I loved to do. It wasn't writing itself. What I loved was teaching people writing. Understanding these two things gave me this incredible burst of energy. I couldn't believe what I could accomplish in a day. I've got part-time high-paying employment at one of the best business schools and one of the best colleges in the Boston area, and I do free-lancing for some of the best companies."

She paused, then continued. "That's why I've come to see you. I've been saving like mad, and I've accumulated so much that taking care of it myself is making me nervous."

"I'll need you to fill out the financial-planning questionnaire this time," I joked.

"Already done it." Connie laughed as she pulled it out of her satchel. "I told you things have changed."

I could well relate to Connie's story. Particularly in the years after college, when I thought of myself as a struggling artist in need of an understanding world, I considered Vigor to be something someone else wanted from me as part of a job, not a vital expression of my own being, yet I never entirely lacked it. Even when I felt I was slaving away like a rower chained to an oar in a Roman galley, I kept my eyes on the prize. I reminded myself that I was headed toward what was freedom to me—the exploration of my soul. Work serves a purpose, I told myself. It will help me get where I need to go. This inner aim saved me from the dryness that Vigor without Understanding can produce.

As I pursued my financial and spiritual goals, I discovered that the two were, in fact, one and the same quest. I had encountered a further mystery of this endlessly surprising world. We labor under the illusion that our Vigor aims toward accomplishing some particular task or goal, like making a perfect throw from right to home or amassing sufficient net worth to live independently and follow our hearts. In fact, we are learning about and realizing Vigor as an inner development in our movement toward wholeness, Money Maturity included. We are discovering who we are.

ABSENT VIGOR, IS IT LIFE?

A lack of Vigor affects everyone at some time, in some way. The very poor, who depend for survival on various forms of charity and welfare, face a major challenge in finding purpose and energy. So do the very rich, who are tempted to rest on their trust funds and coast through life. Adolescents face the Vigor dilemma as they move toward adulthood and seek to discover a goal for their lives and the energy to put behind it. And for all the rest of us facing the weary tedium of daily tasks, Vigor is a constant issue. It can spell the difference between having a life and not having one.

Regardless of their background or stage in life, many people who struggle with Vigor feel overwhelmed by the world's patent injustice and unable and unwilling to act because of the corruption they recognize all around them. I have seen the same reaction again and again in my clients and seminar participants. Often that feeling is right and appropriate: The world can be woefully evil, crass, and cruel to its victims. But if that thought is used to immobilize and prevent us from seizing hold of Vigor and taking action, then we are simply throwing away our lives.

I encounter this dilemma among many of the participants in my seminars. One particular young woman comes to mind, a painter with a small inheritance. When we started to talk about her relationship to money, Zelda immediately complained about the bad deal the poor get.

"It's a thought I can't get out of my mind," she said. "Whenever the subject of money comes up, whether I'm buying something or somebody else is spending money, I find it impossible to get rid of the thought of poor people and how they don't have money. The inequity gets me. Why do some people have money and some people don't? That thought bugs me."

I too am concerned about the poor's short end of the stick, and my concern is one of the reasons why I'm writing this book. But why, when we were discussing how to get Zelda's economic house in order, was this topic coming up? I wondered whether she was feeling sorry for the poor as a surrogate for feeling sorry for herself or out of a sense of guilt at not having to work for a living. I responded intuitively to her that holding on to a structure of thought and feeling binds us to suffering and robs us of power. I explained further that people who identify with victims and hold resentment or blame toward others typically fail to tap their own Vigor and realize their life's purpose.

Zelda burst into tears. "I'd never thought of that. How did you know I have a major problem with Vigor?"

With my encouragement, she learned the practice of letting thoughts go and feelings be, and she followed it with considerable discipline. Over time Zelda was able to loosen the glue binding Innocence and Pain into suffering. As she did so, the energy in her doubled and redoubled. Her artistic output boomed, and she devoted many hours each week to volunteering in a community soup kitchen that fed the homeless. As she let go of blame and resentment, she could see the effect of her own vigorous action and feel inside herself the first seeds of the peace that would come with awakening.

If I had been blunt and direct with Zelda as soon as I heard her story, insisting she lacked Vigor, she would have become defensive. No one likes to be accused of lacking Vigor. Yet underneath much of our daily work lies a pretense to Vigor. The most common way we pretend to be vigorous is our devotion to frantic, endlessly busy lives. We are hiding from something, creating a flurry of activity to camouflage our lack of ease in the world of money. Crazy busyness, the fully booked, not-a-moment-to-lose air of always doing something or heading someplace fast lacks true Vigor's inner calm and deeper sense of purpose, the peaceful confidence of the self-definition and self-knowledge that spring from Understanding and form Vigor's core.

Alan, a student in a seminar of mine, came to understand this difference between mere busyness and Vigor and turned his life around in the process. He was very intelligent and polished, attractive, articulate, and knowledgeable, and for someone in his thirties who hadn't really made it in the world of commerce, his understanding of business was impressive. Obviously Knowledge wasn't the issue for Alan; Vigor was. In spite of his obvious capabilities, success seemed somehow beyond his grasp. He knew his shortfall sprang from a lack of energy and endeavor. To remedy that lack, Alan had apprenticed himself over the past few years to several businessmen he felt had Vigor.

Yet as he participated in the seminar, he came to realize that his mentors had busyness, not Vigor. They were more frantic than purposeful. This surprised Alan.

He was even more surprised when he did the overnight homework I had given the class on personal goals.

"Those exercises made me so angry, George," he said. "Here I am realizing my mentors had no purpose, and there I am with these exercises, discovering I have no goal, at least for myself. Every goal I have concerns someone else, not me. My kids, my wife, my parents, my friends—but there's nothing there for me!"

In spite of his smooth, brilliant surface and his many professional skills, Alan had never fully met the childhood darkness that blocked him. In his early years, Alan was inculcated with many negative, self-defeating messages about money that denied him the right to be successful and consigned him to playing second fiddle to other people's needs.

The key for Alan, as for so many others, was to find a purpose that would spark his vitality. As he and I discovered together, Alan wanted to feel part of a community and be seen as successful within it and in the larger world. The generosity characterizing his goal work was partly a sublimation of his own sense of purpose but also a clear statement of the importance he put on working with others. As he came to this realization, Alan's work efforts in the world shifted. Instead of looking for mentors, he sought out good people to partner with. Last time I saw him, he had found the success and partnering he was after as chief operating officer in a small but successful real estate development firm in Boston.

A lesson Vigor teaches us all is that we each must make a choice: either to be vigorous or to die on the vine. This was the choice Alan recognized. In the case of Mahealani Sapolu, losing her job when she was pregnant and not yet out of debt galvanized her Vigor. She was facing the threat of a kind of death. So was Derrick King. He understood that the life he most needed was dying around him, and only he had the power to take the action needed to achieve a resurrection.

Necessity varies from one person to another with the circumstances of life, yet a single reality makes us one: We all shall die. In the time before death stakes its claim, Vigor empowers us to work for ourselves, for our central purposes, and for others. In that work we discover Vigor's other wellspring in freedom, the determination to be fully who we are. On the way we discover many hurdles our souls must clear.

HURDLES AND PATHS

As we live out the story of our lives, each of us faces the challenge of overcoming adolescence, finding Vigor, and venturing into life. Vigor teaches us who we really are; without it, we can never fulfill our dreams or find ourselves.

The cliché is true—Knowledge *is* power—but by itself, Knowledge is insufficient to achieve Money Maturity. Attachment to Knowledge, which is fundamentally impermanent, leaves us insecure, too shaky to act with energy and resolve. Understanding frees us from attachment to Knowledge by softening the heart, creating the security and freedom from which Vigor can grow. Money Maturity requires all three: Knowledge, Understanding, and Vigor. Just one or two won't do.

Vigor activates Knowledge and Understanding. In Vigor what we know and what we feel are translated into accomplishments. Knowing about goals and budgets is one thing; actually saving money toward an objective is something else. Understanding difficult feelings within ourselves is one thing; taking action in a world of myriad conflicting pushes and pulls is quite another. Vigor is where the action is. Finally we have the energy to fill with light and accomplishment the world that to our adolescent eyes appeared hopelessly evil and shot through with corruption.

Men and women, I find, usually face somewhat different challenges around Vigor. Since we are enormously adaptable creatures, no simple gender stereotypes apply. I suspect too that Vigor issues shift from one historical and cultural period to another owing to the influence of socialization in different settings. Over the years that I have been working with money, the prototypical male who comes into my office is stronger in Knowledge and Vigor—Derrick King was a classic example—and weaker in Understanding, while the prototypical female is strongest in Understanding. Even now these stereotypes are changing, as more and more women pursue careers and the

Knowledge necessary to accomplish them. Usually I find that men need more Understanding in relation to their Vigor, whereas women need more Knowledge. Above all else I try to help people develop what they are lacking, whether it is Knowledge, Understanding, or Vigor.

Unless these three skill sets are fully developed, we cannot be complete human beings. To realize this completeness, it helps to know the common hurdles that cut us off from Vigor and the practices and awareness that can deepen our development in this stage.

WHAT GETS IN THE WAY

All the blocks to Vigor share a central commonality: They arise in suffering, in one or another form of clinging to Innocence or running from Pain. Baldly put, if you find yourself lacking in Vigor, you are living in projection. If you have yet to take the world as your rightful field of action, someone else has control over you—even as Susanna Swartz's father ran her life outside her conscious awareness. The most significant hurdles to Vigor arise in our individual psychologies as unique, ornate, and often surprisingly inventive ways of sabotaging ourselves.

BLAME AND RESENTMENT. Again and again I have found this fact to be true: Blame and resentment go hand in hand with a lack of Vigor, and a lack of Vigor goes hand in hand with blame and resentment. Splitting the world into "us" and "them"—perhaps in the form of "haves" and "have-nots"—creates the psychological setting for sitting on the sidelines and complaining rather than doing something. If your child wanders out into the street and you see a speeding car bearing down, you have a choice. You can sit on the porch and moan about how there ought to be a law against drivers who drive too fast or a legal requirement that Detroit build cars with special kid-deflecting bumpers. Or you can act, running into the street to pull your child out of harm's way. This is the difference between blame and resentment on the one hand and Vigor on the other.

FEAR. It is easy to be afraid of what we think is true—deep inside, many of us cling to Innocent images of failure. Immobilized by fear, we cannot imagine the ability to act effectively or to speak in our own voices.

Terrified from childhood regarding all aspects of money, Jay just did his job as a middle manager and kept a low profile. All the money he saved he put into bank certificates of deposit. When his accountant suggested various legitimate tax deductions, Jay demurred, saying he'd rather not get audited. In some ways Jay appeared remarkably normal and stable, but in reality he was quite uncomfortable, especially at work. There he was conscious of being judged both by his superiors and by his peers. Terrified of standing out, he never excelled. He came to see me because he recognized that his terror dominated investing. He heard almost daily of the extraordinary gains in the stock market, and he felt foolish at not taking advantage of them. Jay thought I might be able to help him. After working through his fears, we shifted his portfolio, and for ten years now he's averaged twice the rates of return he had been getting. He has $100,000 in his brokerage account he wouldn't otherwise have.

DEPENDENCY. Vigor is adult; it concerns standing on our own two feet as fully realized men and women. Anything that puts us in a dependent, childlike status and removes our personal responsibility blocks Vigor. Dependency takes a number of forms, one of them chemical. By creating addiction, drugs and alcohol rob the body and mind of the energy Vigor needs. Dependency also can arise in relationships. Dependency on government, spouse, or inheritance for income can rob us of Vigor, both because the situation eliminates necessity and because endeavor and reward do not match. People who identify themselves as victims lack Vigor, even when the circumstances that created the victimization no longer apply. One-down relationships, particularly those involving physical, sexual, or emotional abuse, drain Vigor by putting the victim in a position of powerlessness. These forms of dependency alienate us from the challenges of the moment, cut us off from our life's mission, and render us effectively dead.

SELF-DOUBT. The feeling of being down is often the result of blocked personal power, a belief that no matter what, we can do nothing to change how things are. Sometimes this attitude springs from low self-esteem, a feeling that "Oh, I can't do that anyway, so why try?" Perhaps we sell ourselves cheap or tell ourselves we don't deserve anything. One of my friends used to say "Money doesn't stick to me." And it's easy to come up with reasons for remaining in this disbelieving, disempowered state. "Why should I sacrifice to get ahead; I've sacrificed enough already?" or "Why should I work? I'd just be working for *them*" appears in various forms. Another variation is "But I don't need to go to adult ed. People should accept me for who I am."

VEERING FROM OUR TRUTH. Flawed integrity detracts from the deepest layers of Knowledge and hampers the development of Vigor. You may remember the story I told in chapter 5 about the hotel worker who was required to lie about room availability. Over the years his Vigor decreased.

Angela also faced a problem with Vigor, one she was not fully aware of. A recent college graduate with a liberal arts degree, she went to work for a client of mine as administrative assistant. Young, bright, and energetic, Angela did a great job, yet somehow she was late for work, sometimes quite late, day after day. She always had an excuse: traffic jams, a bus that didn't come, an alarm that didn't work, repairs on the subway, trouble sleeping, et cetera, et cetera.

Frustrated over the issue, her boss said, "Look, what can I do to help you make sure you come in on time?"

"Fire me!" blurted Angela, surprised at what was coming out of her mouth.

That unconscious outburst told her that this job was not where her truth lay. She really wanted to be in public relations. Within a few months of realizing this, she found a starting position in a PR firm, learning how to write press releases and pitch letters, phoning reporters, and loving it.

People stuck in dead-end jobs are often veering from their truth. I found my own version of this when my firm was short on cash flow and we took on a client who paid a high fee yet was disrespectful to everyone in the office. At first the presence of the money charged us with energy, but later we realized we all felt used. In the end we chose to let the client go and develop new business with clients we would prefer to deal with.

FAMILY KARMA. In the course of his therapy, Derrick King discovered that he was living as his mother and father did rather than seeking out what was true for him. The same reality held true for Susanna Swartz, though in reverse. She was living not as her father wanted her to but in reaction to his desires. In both cases, the family's values dictated the structure of the individual's life at a powerful, unconscious level and separated it from the psychic sources of Vigor.

RUNNING OFF TO TAHITI. Or any other wild, grandiose fantasy. Chapter 6 distinguished goals—which are dreams within achievable grasp—from fantasies—which have a sort of never-never land flavor whose impossibility mires us in Innocence. "I want to retire at age sixty-five with an annual income of $35,000 a year" is a goal. "The day after I hit the lottery, I'm packing my bags and disappearing in Polynesia" is a fantasy. A goal demands work; it has a way of mobilizing Vigor. Because fantasy is highly unlikely or unachievable, it undercuts our efforts and destroys Vigor. Why work hard for something you can never have anyway?

"MORE MONEY WILL SOLVE MY FINANCIAL PROBLEMS." This is one of a number of beliefs that take power and self-knowledge away from us as individuals and deposit it in some omnipotent outside force, in this case someone who will give us money.

In fact, money doesn't solve problems; people do. Most money issues require the application of Vigor, not the influx of more dollars.

PROCRASTINATION AND LETHARGY. Procrastination's curse is familiar: making up one excuse after another to avoid doing what must be done. Putting things off is not another way of doing them, whether it's taxes, budgets, balancing the checkbooks, investing savings, doing the job, filling out an insurance application, or paying the bills.

One of my clients was trying to renegotiate a mortgage at the same time her tax return was due. "I just felt so small in relation to the bank and the IRS. It feels horrible," she said. "So I put things off. I think I feel small in every way in relation to money. I'd rather not look at it, even if it means not getting things done."

Lethargy can be a particular problem in youth. If, in the early stages of life's journey, we spend too much time enjoying ourselves, we may waste the inner resources and the money needed to reach for meaning once we understand how crucial that quest is.

MERE BUSYNESS. A life of unending, frantic small stuff sucks off the energy that should be directed at our major goals, thus depriving us of Vigor. Whenever you find your days occupied by everything except what is most important to you, busyness is robbing your Vigor.

PATHS TO VIGOR

Vigor can be developed and learned, in much the same way that an athlete trains to perfect skill and boost strength and endurance. It starts with paying attention to what is blocking you and with forming a fierce commitment to not letting it interfere. For example, as I was writing this book, I realized that telephone calls significantly distracted me from the work of composing and drew off the energy I wanted to put into the manuscript. I made a plan: During the hours reserved for writing, I didn't pick up the phone. That simple discipline focused my Vigor on the task at hand.

No matter what trauma has kept us lacking in Vigor, we have a responsibility to learn from that experience, move forward from it, and become a stronger person because of the adversity. Without this commitment, we will not reach awakening.

We have seen the blocks and hurdles that leave people without Vigor. Here are some ways to discover the Vigor waiting in each of us.

EYES ON THE PRIZE. This is the primary quality we see in people with Vigor. Whether your model is Andrew Carnegie, Helen Keller, or Martin Luther King, Jr., all vigorous people share the capacity to focus on what they are after. This is why so much of the Knowledge chapter is devoted to clarifying goals. If we can tap into the place where our deepest goals reside, their accomplishment becomes a necessity that energizes Vigor.

Each of us needs this constant, clear sense of where we are heading and why. We must make reaching our objectives—the ones based on the goal work in chapter 6—a necessity in day-to-day life on the same order as paying the mortgage or feeding the kids. Through the course of the day, remind yourself where you are going. It is particularly important in moments of crisis or self-doubt to find the space where purpose resides—even when the stock market falls like a stone or your income tax bill is bigger than expected. Focusing on the goal to be achieved leads to a prioritized application of energy to change. You will discover that you know when and how to act as events manifest themselves.

I saw a stunning example of this in a client who faced an interesting dilemma. By age fifty he had saved over $400,000, but he felt beaten up and fatigued by his work as a specialized subcontractor in the construction business. He wanted to stop working, but he still faced the expense of college for his three sons. He and his wife, who worked with him in his business, fell in love with a house situated on an unusually large piece of land. Even though they had to extend themselves financially, they bought it. This man had an idea. He could divide the property and develop a portion of it, then sell the houses at a substantial profit. Even with college expenses looming, he saw that at the end of the project he would have enough money to reduce his own workload to half time or less within the next three to six years. Suddenly he was transformed from a fatigued middle-aged guy to an experienced man with extraordinary energy, clear about what he needed to do. Every day he went to work, both in his business and in his development venture, with will and passion, because he knew exactly where he wanted to go and what it would take to get him there.

DOING THE WORK YOU LOVE. There is an old—and absolutely accurate—statement that if you do what you love, you'll never have to work a day in your life. The point isn't that you'll suddenly get rich. It is that wedding love to task eliminates the grind we think of as work.

Every now and then I meet people who absolutely love how they make a living. Mahealani Sapolu was like that. Running her roadside stand became the core activity of her life, something that defined and energized her. When love and Vigor unite in this special way, we are ready for Vision and Aloha.

Many people ask me, "What if you can't do what you love? What then?" After the thousands of tax returns I did for a living over the years, I can well identify with the question. If you are in a job you don't love, don't let what you're doing for a living stand in the way of developing Vigor. See how your work can move you toward your purpose—even if it's as financially simple as paying the bills each month. Perhaps there are other ways you can use your job to serve your purpose—like doing well at it and saving your bonuses, or developing a budget and putting away 12 percent or 20 percent per year toward your goal of freedom. Perhaps the skills you develop on your job will stand you in good stead elsewhere. Continue to work on the development of Vigor by exploring your relationship to the rest of the suggestions in this chapter.

THE PRACTICE OF LETTING THOUGHTS GO AND FEELINGS BE. At first this practice may be particularly useful in freeing yourself of fantasies and magical thinking. Ridding ourselves of fantastical notions like immediate flight to Tahiti upon receipt of lottery winnings allows us to devote all our energy to real goals. Fantasies are the masquerades of Innocence. Unfortunately, right below the fantasy lies the Pain of feelings crying out to be felt before we can take true Vigor in. By creating an ease with and a friendliness toward all our feelings, the practice instills freshness and nimbleness into our lives. No longer bogged down by suffering, we can open to each moment in every hour of the day and grace them all with Vigor.

LESSENING DEPRESSION. Depression can be a complicated mental and physical disease. At its worst, depression requires medical intervention; if you think you suffer from clinical depression, you need to see a doctor.

Much of what we call depression isn't clinical, though. Rather, it is the emotional result of clinging to Innocent, idealized beliefs about how things are or how they should be. Remember the warrior practice in chapter 7. Working directly on the feelings arising from this clinging can release the thought, open the heart, and initiate the flow of Vigor.

A psychotherapist student of mine who followed this very strategy awakened to a powerful Vigor, saying "All my life I thought I was depressed, but I'm not. I've just been suffering." He had never understood the structure of his own suffering before or his own power in relation to it.

AUTHENTIC RELATIONSHIPS. True, trusting friends offer support, solace, inspiration, even the occasional heartfelt kick in the backside when that's what we really need. Such a relationship can come from a buddy or pal, a lover, a spouse, a spiritual teacher, a personal coach, even a counselor or therapist. The issue is less the nature of the role than the authenticity with which it is filled and the heart connection it allows.

Anne, a woman I have known since childhood, had tremendous talent as a woodworker, yet she preferred the security of a regular paycheck to going out on her own. Her boss was irascible and difficult at times, and it often seemed to Anne's husband and me that her best talents were languishing in her job situation. Then her boss died of a heart attack at fifty-one, and my friend faced a tremendous opportunity: a business, a set of clients, and tools and equipment her boss's estate was eager to sell on the cheap.

Anne, her husband, her best friend, and I huddled over a candlelight dinner at their home in Vermont to discuss her options. Anne recognized that Vigor was her problem. She confessed to her fears of making the move to self-employment. Everything scared her: the responsibility, the testing of her creativity, the freedom of being her own boss, even the money. She just wanted the security of working for somebody and getting a paycheck. Still, Anne's occasional sly smiles showed that she viewed this as the biggest opportunity of her life. Beneath her fear, she had a desire to be known for her creativity and her strong relationships with customers. When she spoke of the freedom of being her own boss and making the money her boss had previously made on her, a palpable rush of energy passed through her. Still, she hesitated.

"Look," she said, advancing her argument against herself, "I can't even buy things appropriate for the business. I need a new drill, and there's a recently introduced model on the market that does things I've never been able to do before. So I went shopping, expecting to pay $200, and I find it for just $50. First I felt happy I'd found it for so little money. Then this gnawing feeling welled up inside that I was getting away with something or maybe something was wrong. I looked closer at the drill and I saw 'Made in China' on it. Immediately I was afraid that I'd be taking advantage of these poor Chinese workers. Why, that drill may have been manufactured in a prison-labor factory. Much as I needed the drill, I didn't buy it."

Anne had a point, of course, about the injustice of prison labor, yet all of us at the dinner table had for years heard various stories that revealed how Anne blocked her Vigor. Like the chorus in Beethoven's "Ninth Symphony," we came at Anne from all sides, telling her she had to stay focused on her new dream and do everything she could to make it successful. Anne had the capacity to add to the world's beauty, pleasure, and goodness, and she mustn't let any of her thoughts stop her. As for the drill, she had no evidence that it had been made by prison labor. Failing to buy it actually reduced income in China and could cost people their jobs.

Anne got the picture. Her smile broadened. "You're going to be my team," she said, "my board of directors. Whenever I'm getting in my own way, I want to be able to call you all right then and get back on track. All right?"

All of us agreed. And, true to her word, Anne picks up the phone and gives one or another or all of us a call whenever she feels a challenge to her Vigor. The technique has worked, and her business has prospered.

FINDING YOUR VOICE. Voice is essential to Vigor; it lies at its very center. It is identity bursting from the soul to the surfaces we live on. When we act with Vigor in the world of money, our motivation is deeper than mere acquisition. Often our drive is self-expression. We are seeking to make our voices heard in the world.

Jay, the middle manager I mentioned earlier who lived in fear about work and investments, eventually overcame his fright on the job by learning to speak what he was feeling and thinking. The work group he belonged to seemed to him to be divisive and lacking in teamwork, and no one was admitting out loud what was happening. When Jay first brought the subject up, speaking out seemed to unleash more terror for him, but he soon realized that he was confusing terror with the unprecedented surge of energy he felt flowing into himself from speaking up. As Jay became more comfortable with this experience, his energy translated into Vigor. His productivity and his happiness level increased noticeably at work. It became easier for him to see what he was doing there and what he wanted to accomplish.

ELIMINATING DEPENDENCY, ADDICTIONS, AND OTHER BAD HABITS. Abstinence works. Probably everyone has seen recovering alcoholics become vibrant, responsible people. I've also witnessed people who were as miserly as Scrooge end their meanness and become, as Scrooge himself became, models of generosity. In a single moment they understood the unending tension they lived with, stopped hoarding, started giving, and suddenly filled with Vigor. I've seen people stop cheating and find an energy, spontaneity, and freshness they'd never imagined possible. In much the same way, people who have felt themselves victimized by parents, governments, spouses, corporations, or ethnic groups discover that this is their life, not someone else's. They go from feeling robbed of possibility and choice to taking the power into their own hands to make their lives happy and successful. Freshness, spontaneity, and Vigor explode from these people, as if they had been reborn into a new life. It is an event so powerful in its emotional impact that to experience it in oneself or to watch it in another brings tears to the eyes.

In cases of addiction to drugs or alcohol, a counselor or a Twelve-Step program can be a wise choice. Similarly, people caught in unhealthy dependent relationships benefit from counseling—either to change the current relationship or to make sure that the next relationship doesn't simply repeat the same old dependent pattern.

AN AWARENESS OF DEATH. Knowing that death isn't just something that happens to other people adds an extra pinch of necessity to our lives. Aware of our own transience and fragility, we realize again how critical it is to bring Vigor to each and every moment. In my own life, seeing time passing by and recognizing that, if I don't get on with it, I might not accomplish my life purposes constantly stimulates my Vigor.

Sometimes the awareness of death is particularly immediate. If the utility company threatens to turn off the heat because the bill is unpaid, somehow we find the Vigor to find the money to pay the bill.

FACING NECESSITY. When Loretta came to me as money management client, she was already in worse shape than she imagined. Some years earlier she had gone through a painful and difficult divorce from a wealthy man. She came out of the trial with the house and $1 million, which she began spending down. By the time she came to me she had only $200,000—far too little money for a woman of less than fifty years of age to live on for the remainder of her life. I tried every way I could to improve her situation, but the damage had been done. There was only one way left for her if she wanted to live without working: sell the family home.

"My kids will kill me," she said. "They grew up here, they think of it as their inheritance. Isn't there some other way?"

I just shook my head.

Loretta gathered her four children together and told them what she had to do. As she predicted, they were angry. Together they vowed to block the sale of the house and to withhold any financial help from her no matter how bad a bind she got into.

Loretta was humiliated, frightened, devastated. She felt even lower than she had during her divorce. Yet the experience of running up against necessity's hard wall tapped into her Vigor. She proceeded with the sale of the house, carefully invested the money, found a job, and created a new simple lifestyle for herself that has sustained her ever since.

It is a truth from the world of recovery that an alcoholic has to hit bottom before he or she finds the energy to get off booze. Financial necessity can do the same for us in discovering our Vigor.

GETTING PAID WHAT YOU'RE WORTH. Again and again I've heard the story of people who finally get paid what they think they're worth and their energy skyrockets. A woman and a man in a recent seminar, both from poor backgrounds, spoke to this. The man told about the thrill of his first job. Never before had he had any money to spend on himself. Now, even after meeting all his necessary expenses, he actually had money left over to spend on himself. The woman spoke of the energizing pleasure she felt the first time she was paid overtime. Receiving money for extra work made her feel noticed, valued, and important. Yet another self-employed woman spoke of the Vigor that arose when she finally began to charge what the market would bear.

Vigor also can increase when people switch careers and apply skills they have developed internally to better-paying jobs. The thrill of the financial reward charges many career-changers with vitality and Vigor toward their new endeavor.

INSPIRING STORIES. For some time I've made a practice of collecting videos, books, and magazine and newspaper stories about individuals whose contributions to the world came from dedication to what they believed in, persistence against all odds, and a willingness to be different. When I encounter doubt or a sense of defeat, I pull out my file of these inspiring stories about athletes, inventors, artists, entrepreneurs, teachers, caregivers, and freedom fighters. It's amazing how watching a video of Helen Keller coming to terms with her blindness and deafness fills me with energy and purpose. I get the same charge from reading about Confucius persevering in his work despite exile and rejection by powerful rulers. You can create the same sort of reservoir of inspiration for yourself by assembling a collection of stories that speak to you.

SHARPENING THE TOOL OF THE BODY. Vigor resides in the flesh as well as the mind and the spirit. In taking care of ourselves physically and developing strength and fitness, we build Vigor as well. A number of approaches help.

One is diet. While nutritional fads come and go, most authorities agree that a diet emphasizing fruits, vegetables, grain, lean meats and poultry, and low-fat dairy products—a diet rich in protein, complex carbohydrates, vitamins, and minerals and low in fat, sugar, and alcohol—contributes to health and energy.

Exercise is also a powerful tool. A huge body of contemporary medical research shows that a sedentary lifestyle is a health hazard, boosting the chance of sudden death by heart attack or stroke and increasing the risk of certain cancers. One of the best moves you can make toward Vigor is to turn off the TV, put down the remote, and head outside for a walk.

Style of exercise is a personal choice. I personally like tai chi, an ancient Chinese form of slow rhythmic movement, because it works specifically with currents of energy that enable Vigor. A great many people swear by aerobic long-distance workouts, such as running, jogging, fitness walking, swimming, and bicycling. Such exercise strengthens the cardiovascular system and builds muscle. It also has profound psychological effects. Long-distance workouts release brain chemicals called endorphins, which instill a sense of well-being and counter depression. I am also told by people devoted to this kind of exercise that the discipline of regular workouts as well as the psychological and physical benefits boosts the internal sense of energy and creates an awareness of physical and psychological power. If you can swim two miles a day four days a week, saving $200,000 over the next ten years doesn't seem like such a big deal after all.

ONE STEP AT A TIME. If you feel nervous about or overwhelmed by financial tasks and responsibilities, remind yourself that you don't have to do it all today or even tomorrow. Don't even think about "all" of it. Choose one small piece, like cleaning your desk, and accomplish just that. Often doing that little bit will give you the energy to do the next piece, which is to sort and organize your mail, which often gives you the energy to do the next piece, which is to pay your bills. Perhaps at the end of your bill-paying session, you notice that you have $1,000 more in your checking account than you need. That pleasant discovery gives you the energy to go on to the next task, which is to send the $1,000 to your discount broker and review your investments. It's so much easier to move toward your goals one step at a time than to feel overwhelmed at the beginning by every single thing you need to accomplish.

DIVE RIGHT IN. Sometimes we can get stuck in Understanding's kindness, sitting on the side of the pool, dabbling our toes in the water, practicing kindness to such an extent that Vigor has too little room to arise. If that's the case, hold your breath and hit the water. Mahealani did that when she refused the idea of bankruptcy. She made an on-the-spot commitment to a goal and held to it.

I've done the same often. Time and again during the writing of this book I hit roadblocks that tempted me to lethargy. I reminded myself of the old saying that even creative work is 90 percent perspiration and 10 percent inspiration, then I dove in again.

VIGOR FOR KIDS

Few people understand the critical important challenge parents face in teaching Vigor to their children. Of the three adult stages— Knowledge, Understanding, and Vigor—Vigor is the most difficult one to learn in later years. Vigor that isn't learned in childhood may never be learned at all.

Roger, a former client of mine, is a good example. Born into a family of moderate wealth, Roger had a small inheritance that supported him in a simple lifestyle.

"I always thought of money as a substitute for Vigor," he confessed to me once.

His mother possessed little sense of money, but she had a rich and generous imagination. His father was vigorous in the worst way. He lacked a heart, took out his frustrations in life on his family, lectured Roger over the necessity of working hard with such obnoxious insistence that Roger decided he never would.

As an adult, Roger could think up one good job and one virtuous deed after another yet never pull any of them off. Roger was highly intelligent and intellectually insightful, and he worked well with people. In other words, he possessed all the personal resources needed to initiate and succeed in his projects. But he lacked Vigor. He would think up a great idea, pursue it for a few weeks or months, then dismiss it with an "Oh, that didn't work out" or grow uncomfortable with the slow pace of the idea's success while simultaneously becoming enamored of yet another concept. The new plan won his attention for no more than a few weeks, until it too was sent packing. It was sad to see this attractive, talented man thrash about, unable to get his life on track and accomplish the good works he envisioned.

The study by Susan Mayer, first mentioned in chapter 6, points out just how significant parental modeling is in passing Vigor on to the next generation. Mayer, who herself had been a single mother and knew what it felt like to struggle against too many demands with too little money, wanted to understand the significance of a household's finances in shaping the later economic success of the children. Remarkably, she found that money counted for much less than parental character traits like hard work, dependability, and persistence. Children growing up with parents whose own lives embodied the concentration, focus, and discipline of Vigor were most likely to succeed, regardless of the family's income.

It has been my experience that a lack of Vigor falls with a particular vengeance on those who depend on others for their income. People who get something for nothing—whether from a wealthy spouse, an inheritance, or a government handout—can have a problem if their psyches receive the message that they need not earn their way in the world, that there is no connection between what they do and what they receive. This message robs them of the incentive to grow, to move toward a dream of freedom, to improve themselves. They risk dying on the vine, fruit that once promised sweetness only to wither away before it can ripen.

Of course, this problem affects all children in one way or another, because every child depends on others, often for years. Every now and then I meet parents who understand the importance of teaching their children about Vigor and helping them move from the dependence of childhood to the independence of adulthood.

Through a combination of hard work and idealism, Bob and Felicia had put together a travel agency that focused on ecotourism and employed seven people. Committed and thoughtful parents, they wanted to pass their attitudes on to their infant daughter, Carol. Money almost got in the way.

It happened when Bob's grandfather died. No one knew that this reclusive old man was worth $6 million, all of which went to Bob's father. Wanting to guarantee his only granddaughter's future, Bob's father had established an irrevocable trust that would give Carol $1 million when she turned nineteen. Both Bob and Felicia were in a rage over the "gift."

"She gets the money at nineteen outright," Bob said.

"Have you ever heard of such a thing?" Felicia continued. "What teenager have you ever known who was ready for $1 million to be plopped in their lap?"

Bob commented on how ironic it was that his father should do this to his granddaughter. "It was Dad who taught me Vigor. He had this wonderful attitude about pitching in and sharing work together. Whenever difficulties would come up, he'd always say 'Pray for rain and grab a hoe.'"

I shared Bob and Felicia's concern. A million dollars could rob Carol of the Vigor that had given them vitality and thrill by denying her the necessity to make something of her life.

Yet as we puzzled the problem out over the following couple of years, we kept coming back to the notion that money doesn't make the difference. People do. Bob and Felicia identified the character traits and values like commitment, sacrifice, patience, hard work, perseverance, determination, sense of purpose, endeavor, and strength of character they feared might be lost with a sudden inheritance of $1 million. They evaluated Carol's education in terms of how these traits would be developed, and both parents became particularly aware of the importance of their own gentle modeling of these characteristics themselves. This added a wonderful focus and Vigor to their own inner work as well as to their conduct with clients and employees.

Bob and Felicia are a wonderful model for raising children, whether rich or poor. Absent such good parenting, two factors in particular seem to drive Vigor—the pinch of necessity and the dream of freedom. Generally people from the middle class experience both, and thus do well with Vigor. They don't feel rich, yet they have generally seen examples of people who achieved freedom through hard work. In the case of the poor, some do well. Roberto Clemente came from an impoverished background, as did Andrew Carnegie, the nineteenth-century steel baron who endowed thousands of libraries across America. Additionally, statistics show that most of the poor don't stay poor; they move up, through their lifetimes and across generations.

In moving up and out, the poor face multiple barriers. Poor education is a common hindrance, for example. Sometimes too community attitude can serve to hold people down.

Virginia, one of my recent seminar students, shared very movingly what she had had to struggle with.

"In a way, I'm a victim of my success," she explained with a big grin that spoke of the thrill she felt in her work and the feeling that she was getting away with something.

"Why's that?" I asked.

"I grew up poor, I've been poor all my life. But in the last few years I've begun to make money, real money," she said, this woman who wore neither expensive clothes nor jewelry. "I've never been happier, nor have I ever worked harder." Her grin was wonderful and warm, yet her eyes seemed to be watching out behind her.

"So what's the problem?" I asked.

"In some way I feel cursed by my success. I mean, as happy as I am, I feel a little uncomfortable having money. A part of me learned in my community that money is evil and people who make money are bad. People are teasing me in front of others, saying 'She's the one who sold out.' It's as if, in their minds, nobody deserves to make money. My family calls me 'Miss Money-Bags.' If I weren't so happy, it would be a real drain on me."

I felt a true compassion for Virginia and her community, and I realized again how difficult the challenges to Vigor can be.

The rich encounter a different necessity than the poor do. Although they too face a limitation on time and life, they know where their next meal is coming from, and they don't have to sit around for hours in the county hospital's emergency room to receive medical care. Whereas the poor can be driven by a burning desire to escape the gutter or the ghetto, the wealthy need an overarching dream of freedom to motivate them.

The wealthy have a responsibility to train their children be attentive to their communities, to inspire them with Vision and Aloha, to encourage them in developing their talents, and to share with them inspiring stories of vigorous people. Without such a goal, so many resources are wasted, such human talent and financial power go for nought.

Whether you are wealthy, poor, or in between, you can do a great deal to bring Vigor and Money Maturity into your children's lives. Time and again I've heard from clients and friends how valuable their early experiences of making money were, whether it was through paper routes, lemonade stands, babysitting, or lawn mowing. Seeing at an early age how personal endeavor produces significant rewards and experiencing freedom both from money itself and from taking part in the larger world of money exchanges invigorates a child.

Understanding the significance of fair exchange, integrity, and equal relationships in the making of money also cuts through much of the powerlessness of adolescence that hampers the development of Vigor. Showing children, through your own life, how desirable it is to improve yourself, set goals, and accomplish objectives also helps them build the connections that link hard work, financial rewards, and the development of relationship skills that they will understand fully in later life.

You need not be a Marine Corps drill instructor; indeed, harshness can promote rebellion. Rather, show children the pleasure of working hard and the personal rewards of Vigor. Inspire kids to be whoever they can be. Tell them stories about John Henry, Mark McGwire, Harriet Tubman, Albert Einstein, Helen Keller, or anyone else, real or mythological, whose heroism and energy appeal to you. Let them know about the people who came from nowhere and changed the course of the world. Make sure they know too about ordinary people close to home who have succeeded and made a difference in the process. And tell your children they can grow up to make a difference.

TRY THIS: YOUR LIFE IN MONEY—VIGOR

The next step in your financial autobiography is to record where you stand in relationship to Vigor. You can use the following questions to guide your thinking and self-discovery:

> Who are your heroes and heroines of Vigor? Which ones have you known, which have you read about, which come from history or mythology? (Some candidates: Martin Luther King, Jr., W. Clement Stone, Teddy Roosevelt, Florence Nightingale, Malcolm X, Madame Curie, John Henry, Andrew Carnegie, Pope John XXIII, Mark McGwire, Vince Lombardi, Alexander the Great, John Calvin, the 1980 United States Olympic hockey team, the best teacher you ever had.) Write a few sentences describing the particular kind of Vigor each one manifests and what you find admirable about that individual and his or her Vigor.
>
> Whom have you known who was defeated and destroyed around

money? Who was lethargic? Make a list. What blocks to Vigor did they experience? What could they have done differently? What would you do in the same situations, and what steps could you take to tap into your Vigor?

What external circumstances leave you feeling weak and lethargic about money? What can you do to change your circumstances or yourself?

What circumstances make you feel strong and energized about money?

How do you rob yourself of Vigor? What can you do to change such undercutting?

In general, when you need strength, how do you find Vigor?

MEETING THE MOMENT, AND MOVING ON

Vigor works a miracle within us. We think this stage has to do with a goal, something we are working toward. Of course, the objective we are pursuing is important. Yet at the fundamental level of the self, the discipline, focus, and concentration of Vigor prompt an interior transformation. We are not simply striving toward something; we are making ourselves over.

Vigor engages us in every moment. We become like the novice monks of Burma who are sent to meditate in the forest, where the tigers prowl. Meditation under such circumstances builds an extraordinary awareness of each moment and everything happening within it. As we develop internally, we meet every moment simply, alertly. The world of money is where our tigers are. We know the hungry beasts pace nearby, and we discover where our strength lies—often in places we never suspected. Vigor makes the mind nimble and playful.

The central insight of Vigor is that life is meaningful. Because each moment is charged with purpose, Vigor creates meaning and strengthens the self. If our sense of self is cohesive and strong, we can take risks and enjoy them. We are engaged with the world comfortably and naturally.

It is one of the remarkable paradoxes of Vigor that in the midst of its strong sense of self develops the experience of selflessness. The Buddha himself spoke of the selflessness of moments as the third of the three characteristics of human existence. Remember we spoke of impermanence in Knowledge and of suffering in Understanding as the other two characteristics. Just as with impermanence and suffering, the Buddha felt that if we could see with absolute clarity into the self-lessness of one moment of experience we would awaken, as if from a dream.

Selflessness includes compassion, although it is more all-encompassing and particular than that. It doesn't mean a dysfunctional doting upon others at the expense of one's own needs and plans. Rather, it means a lack of attachment to individual moments of experience. Even as we grow stronger in the world, it becomes easier to let go, to allow every moment to come to us and pass through, without clinging, without suffering. The Vigor of Money Maturity generally arises first in meeting our own needs and those of our families. But the actual experience of Vigor coursing through our body, moment by moment, is free of preoccupations with self. It moves naturally beyond the concerns of adulthood and into Vision and finally to the surrender of all goals in the graciousness of Aloha.

I encountered this kind of selflessness in a friend who is a successful businessman. When I first met him, I didn't like him. He was tough, hard-edged, and ruthless in commerce. I didn't know that he was stuck—but he did.

"On the surface I was pretty successful," he told me recently, "but I didn't really like my work. I felt drained inside. I saw every business deal as a fight to the death—*mano a mano*, me over the other guy, I win, you lose. That kind of struggle drained me, it was like wrestling 600-pound gorillas all day.

"Then my six-year-old son almost died of meningitis. One night I woke up in the middle of a horrible nightmare about him dying. I was sobbing uncontrollably. It wasn't just that he had died in the nightmare. It was that he had died and I didn't know him—my own son! Over the next few months I shifted my energy from my business to spend time with my son until he recovered. In a way he was healing me, showing me what was really meaningful in life. When I went back to work full time, I realized that I didn't really know anybody I worked or dealt with. I began to approach deals with Understanding. I learned to care about the other person winning as much as I did, so both parties came out of every deal better off. I practiced this over and over, letting go my preoccupation with self. When I began thinking like that, both my Vigor and my business really took off."

Recently I attended a dinner for people interested in business ethics, and everyone at the gathering was fascinated by my model of Money Maturity. I was working through the stages, and when I reached Vigor, this one man's eyes lit up and he nodded in approval. He had, I knew, come out of the counterculture of the 1960s and was still connected with various New Age movements, yet he had also created a remarkably successful business. When I got the chance to talk with him later, I expected that he would tell me that many New Agers act in Innocent reaction to money forces and lack Vigor and that he himself had been forced to develop his Vigor in order to build his business. But he surprised me.

"For years I was the abbot of a Buddhist monastery," he said, "and again and again I saw what you said. The monks who achieved awakening had the most extraordinary Vigor. They didn't just play at being monks. They brought all the energy of their beings to every moment of meditation. It was an impressive thing to see and to be around."

The Vigor that carried my businessman friend into a newly selfless life after the near-death of his son and that bore those monks into enlightenment is the same energy that brings us Vision and Aloha, the topics of chapters 9 and 10.

TRY THIS: A MEDITATION ON VIGOR

The classic meditation on Vigor is Shantideva's meditation on death. He confronts death not as an evil but as the necessary foil to the central purposes of his life. Like Shantideva, when we do this meditation we come to reside in a place of virtue as well as Vigor. In my own life, I find it easy to keep my eyes on the prize by constantly reminding myself of the fragility of my life and the uncertainty of the time of my departure. In terms of the prize, every moment is now or never. Every major transition in our development—from childhood to adulthood to awakening—involves the death of old ways. Likewise, all the ways in which we hold ourselves back from Vigor are little deaths. Our fear of facing them holds us back from Vigor.

Death is the focus of my meditations on Vigor and vitality. I look directly at every conceivable way my death might come, whether imminent or distant, violent or peaceful, with friends or all by myself. Sometimes these meditations are quite moving. I understand them as metaphors for all the little deaths of wasted and transitional moments in my life. Learn a fearlessness in the face of all of death's manifestations, and nothing will hinder vitality and Vigor from rushing through you like the great river of life itself.

part three

AWAKENING

chapter 9

VISION:
SEEING FAR, INSIDE AND OUTSIDE

When a man is warmed by the several modes I have described,
what does he want next? Surely not more warmth of the same
kind, as more and richer food, larger and more splendid houses,
fine and more abundant clothing, more numerous, incessant, and
hotter fires, and the like. When he has obtained those things
which are necessary to life, there is another alternative than to
obtain the superfluities, and this is, to adventure on life now, his
vacation from humbler toil having commenced.

Henry David Thoreau

What does it mean to grow rich? Is it . . . to make a fortune . . . ?
Or is it, rather, to have a good family life and to be imbued with a far-
reaching and intimate knowledge of one's homeland . . . ?

Barry Lopez

The wise who are trained and disciplined
Shine out like beacon-lights
They earn money just as a bee
Gathers honey without harming the flowers
And they let it grow as an ant-hill slowly gains in heights.
With wealth wisely gained
They use it for the benefit of all.

Digha Nikaya
Translator, Gil Fronsdal

Cradle-born optimist and determined individual that she was, Mahealani wasn't surprised that her roadside stand offering only authentic island-made and -grown products soon proved a success.

"You know, even if I was nervous at first, I did expect to make a living out of the idea. I knew if I just had enough time, it was too good an idea to fail," she said. "What astounded me was the way it took off."

Within only a few months of the stand's opening, word got around, bringing a steady stream of shoppers, both locals and tourists. Business was so good that it was all Mahealani could do to keep up with demand. Her days were long rounds of waiting on customers and scheduling deliveries from the people who supplied her inventory. Evenings, after Pualani and Doreen went to bed, she did the books.

As sales picked up, Mahealani could afford to pay herself more, yet she had the forward-looking sense not to spend all her profits. Instead, she set a substantial percentage aside.

"I was seeing the beginnings of an idea," she told me. "If a stand could make it, then a full-size shop would too. It was the same idea, just on a bigger scale. And I figured I could involve my whole family and some of the local people. We could make this something good for all of us."

In her characteristically methodical and persistent way, Mahealani took the steps one by one to bring her idea to fruition. As her business savings accumulated, she added to the stand bit by bit until it was as large as a small store. Ricky bought used fixtures and used his furniture-refinishing skills to clean, paint, and restore the equipment. He also fashioned a street sign. "Mahealani's Authentic" they called their new establishment.

The store was indeed hers, and it became the center of her family's activities. Ricky handled the upkeep, maintenance, repair, and refitting work in his off hours and on weekends. Pualani and Doreen spent their time before and after school and day care at the store, sometimes playing as kids do, sometimes helping their mother and father. And when

Mahealani recognized that she very much needed an employee, she hired her sister, the one who had watched Pualani when she was still an infant.

"I didn't pay her much at first," she said, "because I still had to pump most of the money back in as capital. So I brought her in for minimum wage and a share of the profits. The first year that was practically nothing. The second year, it was a lot sweeter."

Mahealani discovered herself to be an effective promoter. She developed and printed exotic recipes for island fruits and vegetables so tourists would know how to use them to best effect. After all, not that many people outside Hawaii know what to do with lilikoi, ulu, and soursop. Mahealani attached small placards to shelves and displays that gave the proper Hawaiian name for each item. She expanded the product line to include household items crafted from native koa, kukui, and milo woods as well as baskets woven from coconut fronds and lauhala leaves. And, as her store's reputation spread, she advertised in Waikiki, urging tourists to steer their rental cars her way. Her store, with its authentic Hawaiian goods and strong family feeling, was a hit with travelers tired of concrete, plastic, and commercialism.

Maintaining an inventory of authentically Hawaiian products was no problem. A steady stream of would-be suppliers approached Mahealani daily. Inspired by her success, they wanted to take part in her business.

"One night I had this wonderful dream," she said. "I was in this place where there were all these circles, bigger and bigger circles coming out from the center, which was where I was. In the circle closest to me were Ricky, Pualani, and Doreen. Next came my sisters and my brothers, and beyond them were all the people who supply my store. Beyond them, in even wider circles, I could see all these other people, some of them locals I know, but also these folks from far away, like the tourists who come by.

"I woke up with this feeling that I was doing the right thing. I could see what needed to be done, and I was doing it."

Derrick and Alexandria King worked through their difficulties and reconciled. For both of them the separation had concerned finding their voices and claiming ownership of their lives against a situation that left them feeling robbed and trapped. Alexandria finished her MBA and began a career in international banking, focusing on emerging markets in

Central America. Derrick stayed with his job for a few months longer, until Alexandria got on her feet in the new job, then he established a marketing communications consulting business that allowed him more time with his boys.

Matthew King, Derrick and Alexandria's elder son, signed up for Spanish classes because his mother was becoming increasingly proficient in the language during her frequent trips south. "Homework help," he said, nodding toward Alexandria. The two of them practiced conversation together, and Matthew proved adept at the language, studying hard and moving quickly into advanced classes, which taught Hispanic culture as well as language.

"You ever heard of the civil war in Guatemala?" Matthew asked Derrick over dinner on a night when Alexandria was away on a trip to Belize and Honduras.

"Vaguely," Derrick said. "Tell me about it."

"For years there was a lot of fighting in Guatemala, mostly the army against the native Indians. They're descendants of the Mayans, you know. A lot of them don't even speak Spanish, they have their own languages. Over a hundred thousand people have died, and many Guatemalans have escaped by fleeing across the border into Mexico and Belize."

"Belize is where your mother is now," Derrick said.

"I thought so," Matthew said. "You know my teacher, Mr. Guzman, is originally from Guatemala. He said the really sad thing about all the refugees is how poor they are. They don't have much to begin with, and after they get away they have even less. The amazing thing is these people are really good artists."

"At what?" Derrick asked.

"Clothes for one thing. They make these really bright, totally cool clothes," Matthew said. He jumped up from the table, pulled his school backpack out of the front closet, and rummaged through it. He came back with an article cut out of a magazine. "See what I mean." Matthew pointed at the photos.

Derrick saw immediately what Matthew meant. The men sported shirts woven in blues, blacks, and reds, and the women wore white smocks decorated with exquisite embroidery.

"You'd think that people in this country would be interested in these sorts of things," Derrick said.

"They are," Matthew said. "That's what my teacher said. He says the

Indians' creations are sold at great profit in this country. The interest in clothes like these is increasing because people are really intrigued by indigenous arts and crafts. But I think maybe the Indians are being exploited. The people who do the work are getting just pennies for their effort."

"They ought to hire a marketing consultant," Derrick said, off the top of his head.

"You mean like you?" Matthew said.

"Like me," he said. "That's what I do professionally. Besides, I spent a couple of years in North Africa with the Peace Corps. I've got some experience in that kind of Third World setting."

"So say you work with these Indians. What good could you do?" Matthew asked.

"The Indians don't need help with their weaving; they're already very good at that. They need help in learning how to think like businesspeople. For instance, let's say the weavers got together and formed their own company to sell their clothing. They could market it in the United States, pay a fee to the people who handle the sales here, then divide the profits among themselves. They'd have a great deal more control over the process, and they would make a good deal more money," Derrick said.

Matthew thought for a moment. "I'll tell Mr. Guzman about it," he said.

When Alexandria returned home, Matthew picked up the conversation. He told his parents that his teacher knew a group of Guatemalan refugee weavers who lived in a village just across the border in Belize.

"As I was watching Matthew tell his mom about this, I had this wonderful feeling about him," Derrick told me. "Here was this kid, an adolescent who likes hip-hop music I can't stand, and he's got this fuzzy but laudable idea about helping Guatemalans he's never met. And I realized how little it would take to get these people up on their own two feet, and how we could do it as a family. Matthew was the one with the young person's outrage at injustice and the passion for doing something about it. Alexandria was going to Central America regularly, and I had the skills from the high-tech business to handle import and export, distribution, and advertising. I thought to myself, 'This is something we could do as a family. We could even make some money. As businesses go, this'll be a slam dunk.' Something about the idea felt inherently right to me.

"I said to Matthew and Alexandria, 'Why don't we encourage these people to form a co-op, and we'll start importing their clothes?' Matthew said, 'Yeah!' Alexandria said, 'Are you sure?' I said, 'I'm sure. We can do it together. It beats going to Disneyland.'"

Of course, the enterprise wasn't quite as easy as Derrick originally thought it would be, because the federal rules on importing textiles proved more arcane than he expected. Still, he put his mind to the task and mastered the regulations, figuring out exactly how to bring the clothing in from Belize in the most expeditious and least costly manner. He arranged with a small domestic clothing manufacturer to share warehousing space and order-taking through an 800 number. And, marketing communications consultant that he was, he developed a promotional campaign based on returning a fair price to the weavers for their work. He wrote and placed several magazine feature stories on the plight of the Guatemalan refugees and the artistry of their textile work, created a small direct-mail catalog, and designed magazine ads to promote the new co-op.

All the while, Alexandria had been working in Belize, taking time off during her business trips to visit the weavers Mr. Guzman knew and develop a plan with them. In the course of three visits to the village, she lined up a couple of dozen workers who wanted to take part, and she found a lawyer in Belize City willing to draw up the legal papers for a small percentage of the weavers' earnings.

The business started off slowly, yet almost from the beginning it paid its way. Derrick considered the weavers' co-op to be merely one of his accounts, yet he admitted that he drew particular satisfaction from working on it.

"This was the first time in my life that I was able to put my business skills to work to satisfy such basic human needs, like food, shelter, medical care, even a sense of dignity," he said. "Here I was, this business guy in the United States, actually making a buck and seeing to it that some people I'd never met were getting a fair shake."

Susanna Swartz went to sea to find her cause. A friend suggested a day's outing off Cape Cod to watch the humpback whales that summer in the area, and Susanna went along, just because she felt like a day somewhere different. At the time she wasn't really interested in whales.

"Before I went out, I thought of them as these big animated blubber balls. I mean, it was nice to save them and all, but who could get excited over such oversize creatures?" she said.

"I found out I was the one who could get excited. I never knew they were so graceful, so lovely to behold. They roll on the surface sometimes and toss their incredibly long flippers out, and the sight is beautiful. And the sound of a humpback breathing—it's deep and long and wet, bigger than a freight train, yet caressing, like night taking you in."

Susanna was hooked. And in her desire to know more about the endangered animals that lived so close off the coast of Massachusetts, she made contact with a group of young wildlife biologists studying the whales. They observed humpbacks all summer and took extensive photographs that allowed them to identify individuals and determine relationships among them, such as which calf belonged to which mother. They named each of the whales as they identified them and kept copious field notes on the movements and activities of every identified animal.

"As I talked with them, I realized we weren't talking about 'the whales' anymore," Susanna said. "We were talking about Binky and Captain Ahab and Mata Hari and Barnacle Bill and Sickle Tail. The humpbacks were individuals, with distinct personalities and ways of being in the sea. These young people had come to know the whales as if they were all members of the same family, whales and humans. I realized this was important work. This research was closing the terrible gap between our world and the world of nature.

"These biologists didn't know I had money. They thought I was just another middle-aged woman excited about whales. They thought I was being hypothetical when I asked them, 'If you had more money, what would you do with it?' One of them, this bright young marine biologist named Sean said, 'We'd spend seven days a week at sea, not just three. Three's all we can afford for chartering the boat we use for research. If we had more money, we'd have more time. Then we'd have that much more data and an even clearer picture of the whales.'

"I just nodded. But in my head I was already planning all the people I could inspire and the benefit I could give."

Susanna inaugurated her refurbished Victorian with the whale benefit. She turned it into a most elegant event, complete with champagne, canapés, and whale ice sculptures. A slide show depicting the individual whales in the study group played continuously in the dance parlor, and mounted poster-size photos of the animals hung on the walls. The house was packed with guests from Susanna's wide network of friends and donors.

"I even sent out invitations to the benefit to all my family," Susanna said, "not that I actually expected any of them to come. After all, I am something of a black sheep, and they all make an effort to stay out of my pasture. The amazing thing was my brother Roger showed up. He's the one who's closest to me in age, the one I really used to fight with. I hadn't seen him in five, six, maybe seven years. And there he was, just showing up."

Roger was in the audience when Sean gave an impassioned talk about the need for research on humpbacks and Susanna herself spoke of the experience of being transformed at sea in the presence of these great playful animals.

"Herman Melville called the whale 'the most devout of all creatures,' and I discovered what he meant," she said. "Looking at the whales, I felt the divide between me and them dissolve. Suddenly I knew, not just in my head but in my heart, that this is one planet and that all living beings are connected one to another. It felt wonderful not just to experience this vision of our world, but to do something to further it. I turned $15,000 over to Sean, which included the money I raised plus some of my own. As I did it, I knew I was making myself whole and I was helping the world heal, both at the same time."

THE VARIETIES OF VISION

All of us want our lives to be meaningful in profound ways that reach out into the world around us. We all carry images of things we might do, of who we might be, and we carry models of people who have inspired us. How can we accomplish these things in our own lives? What are the obstacles, what are the paths? As a way of approaching these questions, let us look first at the types of visionaries and then consider some examples of people who have come from humble beginnings to inspire us with their great Visions.

Visionaries come in all shapes, sizes, and styles. There are spiritual and religious visionaries, such as the Dalai Lama, Mother Teresa of

Calcutta, evangelist Robert Schuler, and Joseph Campbell, the scholar who returned mythology to modern consciousness. Other visionaries focus on community needs, as shown in the life work of Martin Luther King, Jr., and César Chavez and the peacemaking of former president Jimmy Carter. Political visionaries, like Abraham Lincoln and Nelson Mandela, bring their Vision to fruition in public forums. Some exhibit Vision in the development of products; examples are McDonald's founder Ray Kroc, CNN head Ted Turner, Mickey Mouse creator Walt Disney, and Microsoft founder Bill Gates. Artistic visionaries include Charles Schultz, creator of *Peanuts*; George Lucas, the force behind the *Star Wars* trilogy; painter Vincent Van Gogh; and architect and futurist Buckminster Fuller. Some visionaries work locally, others globally. Some are famous, and many others are utterly unknown, except to those whose lives they touch.

By no means are visionaries perfect people whose every step shines with indubitable sainthood. Bill Gates and Ted Turner certainly have their critics, and even Mother Teresa was condemned for, among other things, taking money from the Duvalier dictatorship of Haiti. Like everyone else, visionaries are real people, not without moral ambiguities.

Here are three examples of individuals whose unmistakably visionary actions have particularly impressed me, for various and different reasons. One was a professional athlete whose work seemed to have nothing to do with Vision. The second was a poor woman who spent her life in labor and service. The last was the richest man on Earth.

"GREATER LOVE THAN THIS . . ." Roberto Clemente proved himself the best player in baseball during the 1971 World Series that pitted his Pittsburgh Pirates against the Baltimore Orioles. In a hard-fought series that ran to a full seven games, Clemente provided leadership to the winning Pirates and came up with one brilliant play after another in the outfield, at the plate, and on the base paths. When it came time to name the series' most valuable player, there really could be no other choice. Hands down, it was Clemente.

Fourteen months later, an earthquake ravaged Nicaragua. Reports from inside the country indicated that relief supplies were being stolen by profiteers. Banking on his reputation as a leading figure in the Hispanic world and declaring that no one would steal from him, Clemente had an aging DC-7 filled with supplies in San Juan, Puerto Rico, and took off with it on a mission to Nicaragua. Unfortunately, the plane had been so overloaded that the engines caught fire and the aircraft plunged into the sea, never to be found. Everyone on board, including Clemente, perished.

Clemente understood himself as a citizen of the world, and he used his status to give back generously of his time and money to young people and to his fellow Hispanics. He died, at the young age of only thirty-eight, because he took his commitments seriously, attempting to turn his reputation into a zone of protection for Nicaragua's needy.

Clemente's death occasioned an extraordinary outpouring of grief, within the United States and across Latin America. The summer after he died, he was elected to the baseball Hall of Fame, the first Hispanic player to be so honored.

THE GIFT OF THE HUMBLE. Oseola McCarty lived a life that was the precise opposite of Roberto Clemente's. Outside her family and small community in Mississippi, she was unknown until the age of eighty-seven. And she made her living not in the bright lights of a major league baseball park but in ordinary housework, cleaning homes, washing and ironing clothes, and caring for family members. She never earned very much—laundry work is no way to get rich—but she spent even less, and the remainder she put, dollar by hard-earned dollar, into a savings account at the local bank. Over the more than seventy years of her working life, the money accumulated and earned interest. Ready to retire, McCarty found she had a six-figure nest egg.

She could have spent it on herself; after so much hard work, she certainly deserved the indulgence. Instead, she gave $150,000 as a gift to the University of Southern Mississippi (USM) to provide scholarships for financially needy students. She turned over practically the whole of her life savings to ensure students a chance at the college education that always lay beyond her reach.

The gift stunned the university. Former USM president Aubrey Lucas told the press, "I don't know that I have ever been as touched by a gift to the university as this one. Miss McCarty has shown great unselfishness and sensitivity in making possible for others the education she never had . . . The scholarship will assist students in achieving a college education, but it also puts students in touch with a person who has characteristics we would all do well to embody . . ."

McCarty's visionary generosity had a ripple effect. As her unusual story drew national and international media attention, business leaders and individuals added to her scholarship fund. By the end of its first year, the money had more than doubled, to $325,000.

Of herself, McCarty said this: "I can't do everything . . . but I can do something to help somebody. And what I can do, I will do."

MAN OF STEEL AND GENEROSITY. Andrew Carnegie started out as poor as Oseola McCarty. Born the son of a weaver in Scotland in 1835, he came to the United States as a teenager with his family and went to work in a cotton mill in Pennsylvania. He made his way up the ladder rapidly, working with Western Union and the Pennsylvania Railroad, until he went into business for himself. In time he set up Pittsburgh's Carnegie Steel Company, which launched the industry that became the economic heart of western Pennsylvania. By the time Carnegie sold the company in 1900 for $400 million—the equivalent of $7.6 billion today—he was the richest human being on Earth. He spent the remaining nineteen years of his life giving his great wealth away. When he died, less than 10 percent of his original fortune remained—and that too went to charities and foundations.

Carnegie was a complicated man, the sort of an individual who reminds us that the world is neither black nor white. He didn't build his steel business by being Mr. Nice Guy; he was a hard-headed, ambitious, and demanding manager who followed his own adage: "Put all your eggs in one basket, and then watch that basket." Carnegie appreciated the contribution of the working person to his wealth, and he made many seemingly pro-labor statements. Yet during the pivotal six-month strike by the Amalgamated Association of Iron and Steel Workers against his Homestead plant in 1892, Carnegie took off to go fishing in Scotland. While he was gone, Homestead plant manager Henry Clay Frick brought in 300 Pinkerton strikebreakers, who assaulted union members with billy clubs, brass knuckles, and handguns. Ten people died. Carnegie never forgave Frick for bringing in the Pinkertons, yet he himself had conveniently turned his back on the workers' plight and he profited from the union's failure.

The Homestead strike serves as a dramatic backdrop against the main philanthropic work of Carnegie's life—building a system of public libraries. In the late nineteenth century, public libraries were few and far between. If you wanted to read a book, you had to buy a copy or rent one from a pay library. The tools of literacy were largely unavailable to people of limited means. Carnegie envisioned a network of free libraries in every city, town, and village, places where anyone and everyone could read the world's great books at no cost. Virtually uneducated himself, Carnegie wanted to provide all Americans with the means to a self-education as profound as they could handle. He spent a major portion of his wealth on building more than 2,500 libraries in English-speaking nations and stocking them with books. The system of community libraries in the United States, which we now take for granted, resulted from the visionary generosity of Andrew Carnegie.

Carnegie also established a number of philanthropic organizations that continue his good work to this day. As an example, the Carnegie Endowment for International Peace is one of the world's most articulate and powerful proponents for nonviolent solutions to conflicts between nations.

Carnegie believed that an individual who died rich died disgraced. In his 1889 book, *The Gospel of Wealth*, he summarized his philosophy of community responsibility:

> This, then, is held to be the duty of the man of wealth: first, to set an example of modest unostentatious living, shunning display; to provide moderately for the legitimate wants of those dependent upon him; and, after doing so, to consider all surplus revenues which come to him simply as trust funds which he is strictly bound as a matter of duty to administer in the manner which, in his judgment, is best calculated to produce the most beneficial results for the community.

WAKING UP TO OURSELVES AND
OUR COMMUNITIES

We are used to thinking of Vision as being the realm of larger-than-life characters like Carnegie and Clemente, but the actions of Oseola McCarty remind us that perhaps even people of humble means—even you, even I—can become visionary. In fact, all of us have experienced visionary imaginings, in which we roll back disease, end wars, save endangered species, and eliminate racism. Yet where we simply imagine, a person with Vision accomplishes his or her objectives. There is no obstruction.

What is Vision, and how can we accomplish it? Of the two stages of awakening, Vision is the more active and community-oriented aspect, Aloha its quieter and more personal side. Vision entails coming to each moment of life with the focused awareness of someone who is vital and alive. What propels us through life is no longer the deadening, blinding suffering caused by the dance of Pain and Innocence, but the full consciousness of every moment supported by the skills of adulthood and a calling toward what needs to be done. In Vision, we act to benefit the community and the environment—whether that arena is as small as my mother's backyard or as grand as the whales, the oceans, the entire planet. Vision and Aloha reframe our destination in life. We shift from pursuing a dollars-and-cents kind of retirement to accomplishing wholeness in our beings, communities, and surroundings, fully engaged in money's ebbs and flows. In awakening, our moments with money become moments of clarity and compassion.

Vision and Aloha shift the pointer on the compass of our lives once again from the outside—the place where we acquire—to the inside—the place where we give. In Vision we feel the blessing of being connected with community. In Aloha we feel the soul's blessing. Vision gives us a depth of seeing; Aloha, a depth of love. Vision is at peace and accomplished; Aloha is simply at peace.

It would certainly be nice if we could leap from our earliest imaginings into visionary action. Yet it is one of the paradoxes of spiritual development that before we are free to give our beauty to the world, we must experience the self-strengthening of adulthood. Only when we have developed the personal power of an identity that is truly our own are we able to direct that power toward our communities with a natural, flowing generosity.

Money has given us this gift. Because money turns on human exchange, it draws us into dealing with our fellow humans. Each exchange provides an opportunity for integrity, virtue, generosity, and strength. It builds the skills of adulthood and increases the consciousness of community that flowers into Vision. Vision, along with Aloha, is our reward for the hard work we have done. As we reach a point where we have produced more than we personally require, we discover within us a capacity to reach out, often much farther than we ever imagined, to meet the needs of our families, our communities, perhaps even the planet itself.

What sets Vision apart from the personal goal work of chapter 6 is inspiration, the deep soulful urge to focus all of our energy on a goal that reaches beyond our beings into a context larger than ourselves. Wanting to have a family is a personal goal, but working with all our skills to build families that are uniquely cohesive, supportive, and loving is visionary action. We all know Vision when we see it. It is driven by inspiration, and it fills us with inspiration as well.

Each of us carries within a capacity for Vision. In fact, most of us are unfulfilled visionaries frustrated by such childhood messages as "If only they'd listened to me" or "If only they'd done it my way." Our actions in the world and in our businesses become visionary when all the skill sets of Knowledge, Understanding, and Vigor are activated within us. When we see something that needs to be done in the world, we simply do it—because we know how.

Here are three examples of people who have brought Vision into their daily lives.

Anne, my woodworker friend, changed in ways she herself had not imagined possible when she summoned the energy to go into business for herself after the sudden death of her boss. It was as if in claiming a part of the world she was actually claiming a part of herself. She felt a new responsibility for the world around her.

Anne worked in a small village with numerous shops like her own surrounding the large green in the town center. One day Alicia, her five-year-old, was spending the afternoon with Anne in her woodworking shop. Wanting to focus on her work, Anne told Alicia to go out into the green to play. Alicia obeyed, then returned in a few minutes.

"Why are you back so soon?" Anne asked.

"It's boring out there," Alicia said, rolling her eyes, as only a five-year-old can express complete ennui. "There's nothing to do."

Anne realized Alicia had a point. The green was a tree-dotted, rolling open space, pretty to look at but hardly engaging of the energies of small children. As Anne fitted a cabinet together, she began both remembering and imagining. As a child she had loved playing outdoors, clambering and climbing, swinging and sliding. What if the green offered an inviting, challenging environment for children—a playground to be sure, but one that fit in with the trees and hillocks of the setting? Alicia would hardly be the only child to use it. A number of mothers worked in the shops on the green, and all of them would appreciate a play space for kids, as would the customers. As Anne awakened from her reveries, she found herself at a drafting table sketching her ideas. She knew she had the woodworking skills to build the apparatus for such a space. And she had friends who could pitch in—a landscape designer expert at fitting structures to natural environments, a lumberyard owner who regularly contributed materials to community causes, a child psychologist who had written a dissertation on play and wanted to bring her ideas from the academy to the real world, plus a dozen or so parents who would invest their own sweat and money into building something wonderful for their children.

The obstacle in the process was the planning commission, which at first was opposed to the idea. Yet Anne was undaunted, choosing a path of patient persuasion. She and several friends committed to the playground visited each commission member repeatedly, listened carefully to their objections and concerns, made a number of changes to accommodate their points of view, and, vote by vote, changed the commission's position from no to yes. By the time Alicia turned seven, she had a space in the green that kept her occupied for hour after playful hour.

Anne achieved her Vision because of her work at the tasks of adulthood. She knew her own skills and those of her friends. That was Knowledge. In terms of Understanding, attention to her own feelings allowed her to deal both with her allies and the town councilmen. And the Vigor she had discovered in launching her own business gave her the energy and self-confidence to persevere and accomplish her goal.

Kathy and Belle, two friends who founded The Ariel Group, a theater-based consulting group in Cambridge, found that Vision inspired them to greater acts of Vigor and greater mastery of the Knowledge side of money than they had ever thought possible.

A professional actress for many years, Kathy had spent the last decade cofounding, managing, and acting in a small professional theater in the Boston area. Although the theater was thriving and her work challenging, she was frustrated by the emotional ups and downs of the acting life and the long hours of work with little financial reward. To supplement her income, she began offering acting classes to the theater's subscribers and audience. When many of those who attended turned out to be business executives and professionals, a light bulb went off in Kathy's head.

"As I watched the students work and improve, I saw what a powerful impact actors' skills can have on people from all walks of life, both personally and professionally. People literally transformed themselves. They engaged the world in ways they'd never thought possible," Kathy said.

Belle, a cabaret singer by background, had a similar revelation when she began teaching voice to nonsingers, promising that anyone who can talk can learn to sing.

"It was so exciting to watch people who had been told all their lives that they couldn't sing realize they actually could," Belle said. "It made them question all the other things they thought they couldn't do."

When one of Kathy's students, thrilled by the change acting and singing were making in his life, insisted that she and Belle come and teach a workshop in the Fortune 500 company he worked for, it became obvious that they had a business possibility. At first they weren't sure they wanted to go that route, however. They were artists, after all, suspicious of the business world. Then they were inspired by the thought that, just as in their workshops yet on a larger scale, they could make a real difference in people's lives. This became their guiding principle: to teach only what would make people better both inside and outside.

"It's been critical to all of us," said Kathy, referring to the troupe of twenty-five actors and actresses she and Belle have now put together, "to understand the work we do in personal communications as including the development of honesty, generosity and individual integrity."

Things began to snowball, and before long The Ariel Group's list of clients read like a story on America's leading companies in *The Wall Street Journal*. Although Kathy and Belle thought they knew nothing about running a business, in fact they had both developed sophisticated money-oriented skill sets—Kathy from running a nonprofit organization, and Belle from managing her own self-employment. Still, they needed additional expertise. They hired a Harvard MBA to guide them through the strategy and financial challenges, a lawyer for legal issues, a computer specialist to set up office systems and to teach them how to use the full potential of their personal computers. The financial rewards have helped, but it has been the Vision of making a difference in people's lives that has enabled Kathy and Belle to work the long hours and make the necessary sacrifices to advance their careers.

Ashoka: Innovators for the Public, an organization founded by one-time McKinsey & Co. consultant William Drayton, searches the poorer parts of the world for what he calls social entrepreneurs—people who have everything they need to achieve their Vision except capital. Ashoka provides that, giving each Ashoka fellow a monthly stipend that allows him or her to devote energy to the idea and seed capital for the project.

Ashoka looks for people who have a clear sense of the social problem they face, are championing a cause that may spread regionally, have the skills and maturity to figure out what they need to do, and demonstrate strong ethical backbone. As Drayton told a *Forbes* magazine writer, "We are looking for the Andrew Carnegies and the Steve Jobses of the social arena. They have to have knockout ideas that can become a new pattern for the society as a whole. They have to be thoroughly trustworthy. The world already has enough corrupt leaders. Ashoka does not want to add to the supply."

Operating on a modest annual budget of about $7 million—raised from local chapters and donated by corporations and foundations—Ashoka fellows have chalked up impressive accomplishments: returning confiscated savings to Brazilian investors, preventing South American cattle ranchers from using banned carcinogens in feed, and building 3,000 low-income housing units in São Paolo's slums for about half the private-market price.

⌶⌷⌸

Without all three skill sets of adulthood, visionary action rarely takes place. Had Ashoka and its fellows, The Ariel Group, and Anne lacked Knowledge, Understanding, or Vigor, they would not have accomplished what they did. Without a unique economic idea, the ability to work with others, and energy and endeavor behind their work, nothing could have been achieved. Once again we see that money alone does not solve financial problems. People do—people with the skills of adulthood.

Think for a moment what happens if any of the three skill sets is missing. Remember the woman in chapter 5 who was furious at the prices in natural-food stores. Her anger evidenced the energy to do something about her concern, but without Knowledge of the industry or the economic system, she was powerless to take action.

An artist I knew in Boston had a wonderful vision of how subways should look, creating adventure, energy, and ease. At the time Boston was revamping its subway system, he put together an assembly of sketches and paintings that held me in awe and wonder for most of a day. This artist, though, couldn't work with people. His bad reputation preceded him, and he never got the opportunity to grace the subway's walls with his work. His failure in Understanding has stolen a ray of light that might have brightened many lives.

We have all known people with Vision who lacked Vigor, the quintessential Monday-morning quarterback who talks a good game but can't find the energy to play it. Vision without Vigor is no better than an opium smoker's dreams.

Vision is not a separate stage that can be mastered independently. To some extent Vision flows naturally out of the development of Knowledge, Understanding, and Vigor. To some extent it is kept alive by reminding ourselves of it as we go through life, by keeping alive the capacity to dream. Derrick King serves as an example of what happens to Vision that isn't kept alive. His years in the Peace Corps signaled an interest in a world larger than his own personal goals, yet he repressed that interest in order to carry on with what he considered his "responsibilities," binding himself into a straitjacket. It took a marital crisis and an inspired son to bring Derrick to a place where he could risk Vision again.

Vision reaches well back into our lives, into early awareness. It appears in our fantasies, in those early impulses to be generous or heroic, to become a firefighter, a teacher, a parent, a professional athlete, a physician. These impulses, strong and significant as they are, lack the power to move us to true Vision, however. Only when we have assembled an adult maturity founded on significant development in money skills do we have the tools to act in a visionary manner. As our money path becomes clearer and we reach more of our Knowledge-based goals, the visionary part of us finds it easier to discover its voice and to accomplish its objectives.

TRY THIS: ACTIVATING VISION

Activating Vision entails discovering who the visionary inside you is. Review the goal exercises in chapter 6. See if you can distinguish between ordinary, personal goals and visionary ones, those that somehow involve your communities—anywhere from your backyard, to your family, to the globe itself. Consider also the following questions:

Who are your heroes and heroines of Vision? Which ones have you known, which have you read about, which come from history? Name them, then write a few sentences describing the particular kind of Vision each one manifests and what you find admirable about that individual and his or her Vision.

What is your visionary sense of yourself? How do you see yourself now as a visionary? As you look into the future, what Visions would you like to make real?

What blocks stand in the way of your Vision? What can you do—in terms of Knowledge, Understanding, and Vigor—to remove them from your path?

If you had all the money you needed, how would you give to the world in a visionary way? How can you ensure that your giving will not rob its beneficiaries of their ability to develop Knowledge, Understanding, and Vigor?

How do you need to act to accomplish your Vision? What have you inherited, learned, acquired, and understood that can help you in the pursuit of your Vision?

CULTIVATING VISION

As noble as our Visions are, they often feel much larger than our lives. Amid the tedium of daily tasks and the burden of economic necessity, what part can Vision play?

When I was a young man seeking my place in the world, I drew on two sources of visionary inspiration. One was the art and literature I had studied; the other was my spiritual work. I tried to put the two together in various book projects, but the Vision was unsustainable. My financial situation was too unsettled and penurious to give me time, and the skills of maturity still needed a great deal of development. It took a long time and many failures to learn how to join these two areas of inspiration in the writing of this book.

For years, without really knowing what I was doing—in my mind, spirit and art were split irreconcilably from job and work—I did what many people do: I learned how to bring Vision into my day-to-day labor, first in doing tax returns, later in financial planning and money management. This was no easy row to hoe; tax work, like many occupations, humbles a visionary. The work was humdrum and, with the April 15 deadline rigid and ever-looming, always filled with the stress of time pressure. It also linked me to the Internal Revenue Service, the most hated bureaucracy in the United States, and enmeshed me in endless streams of numbers and regulations notable for their loopy and unnecessary complications. Yet something of Vision did emerge for me. When I turned down accounting positions with the national firms of Arthur Andersen and Coopers & Lybrand, I realized I was saying no to the usual way of doing tax work. I wanted to make something different of it. It wasn't just numbers to me. I needed to make tax work human by knowing my clients as fellow human beings. Remarkably, I soon discovered that knowing my clients well turned up countless deductions and credits that a more superficial approach would never have revealed. For more than a third of my new clients I was able to file amended returns for the prior three years, when they themselves or another preparer had done their taxes, and get money back. Important, too, only by getting to know my clients and sharing in their lives could I stomach, much less enjoy, the work of doing taxes. Dedicating myself to connecting with my clients and solving their problems gave me the energy and enthusiasm to learn all the complicated ins and outs of deductions and credits. It made me a more accomplished professional and a better human. Moreover, it was visionary in a way that applies to every job and occupation.

This concern for the people I worked with carried over into my financial planning and money management career. My clients' goals for themselves, including their visionary objectives, formed the core of my relationship with each of them. At the same time I created two seminars—"How You Might Retire in Twelve Years by Saving Twelve Percent Per Year" and "The Seven Stages of Money Maturity"—to help people discover what was most meaningful to them and accomplish it in the quickest possible way.

Even as my passion to help people with their money issues grew, I kept alive my older Vision. In fact, I was learning new skills in writing and figuring out how to navigate the world of publishing. I began to realize that now, after over fifteen years of effort, I possessed what I needed to write the book I had once only dreamed of. Not only did I want to integrate money into the whole of our lives and end the separation that so plagued me as a young man, but I also wished to share this Vision with the widest possible audience. Maturity made the impossible possible. Now I had the Knowledge, Understanding, and Vigor as well as the money to make the four-year commitment needed to gather materials for *The Seven Stages of Money Maturity* and draft the manuscript. While I certainly do slip back into the knot of suffering from time to time, the experience of writing itself has been typical of Vision—working without blocks or obstructions, just a steady, gentle, yet relentless moving forward moment after moment.

THE NATURE OF VISIONARY ACTION

How do we act with Vision in the midst of our ordinary lives? To qualify as visionary, an action need not be aimed at the salvation of the planet. My mother was a visionary, a Christian teacher who lived out her truth in the context of her backyard, her home, family, and church. Hers was a small world, yet she didn't let its size limit her. When Mr. Johnstone stepped off his garbage truck, her Vision flowed into that circumscribed universe. Mahealani Sapolu's Vision centered on her family, first in a purely personal way, then in a manner that connected into a larger community.

Recently a friend of Hawaiian ancestry took me to visit a *heiau,* the ruin of an ancient holy site, near my home on Maui. The structure had been built by the ordinary people, who gladly gave of their time to build the walls. "Every stone was a prayer," my friend said.

His statement reminded me of the great Gothic cathedrals of Europe, each of which was built by craftsmen who willingly devoted months and years of their lives to build these monuments of faith. For them too, every stone, every pane of stained glass, was a prayer, a visionary action connecting them to their community and to their shared sense of the Divine. Laying a stone or fitting a pane was ordinary, but the inspiration behind it made the act visionary.

Like those ancient Hawaiians and medieval craftsmen, each of us can act with Vision in the ordinary, daily, humdrum details of our lives. Now that you have revisited the goal work of chapter 6 and given thought to the nature of your own Vision, consider where your Vision might manifest itself—even in the smallest and most seemingly insignificant of places. Give thought in particular to how you might implement your Vision with your family or in your community, as Anne did with the playground on the green. Consider the money skills necessary. And consider too the people who might help you.

Your job is an important arena for Vision, in terms of products you make or sell and relationships with customers, vendors, and fellow workers. Consider how you might implement Vision in each of these areas.

Elaine, a friend who is a seamstress, exemplifies extraordinary Vision in an ordinary undertaking. A talented worker with a longing to do more than she did, Elaine was rummaging through a box of old clothing at Goodwill one day when her fingers touched several old wool sweaters at once. The sweaters were moth-eaten, worn in the elbows, stretched at the necks, but Elaine's skilled fingers noticed something. Most of the wool in each sweater was perfectly fine.

Instantly she got the idea of making something fine and colorful from discarded sweaters. Elaine foraged at flea markets, swap meets, and secondhand shops, and she asked her customers to bring in old wool clothes, giving them a 10% discount as an incentive. Soon she had more old wool than she knew what to do with. Soon too she had employees, as the colorful hats, mittens, and coats she made from recycled wool became an instant hit among Christmas shoppers.

Money and work connect us all in a vast matrix of exchange and interaction. If we bring a Vision born of adulthood into our work, we help those around us. With Vision and Aloha, we can do anything and everything as a gift—run a home (as Susanna Swartz shows us), drive a bus, walk the high iron on a construction site, wash the laundry (like Oseola McCarthy), compete in a triathalon, frame a house, design the world's next great computer operating system, manage a mutual fund, balance a set of new tires, perform open-heart surgery, or mop up the operating room afterward. Each and every action of daily life performed with a consciousness of the human context and done with the intention of helping others draws our Vision into the world and makes it a better place.

It's not what we do. It's *how* we do it. Sometimes, as I learned in my tax business, we don't have the strength or the skills to implement our larger Visions. Still, each of us can build on what we know to make our smallest actions visionary, even if it's just the way we lift the bricks. When we fill our lives at home, in our communities, and at work with Vision, what a wonder this world becomes.

VISION'S INNER WISDOM

Vision is a type of wisdom. Whether we are rich or poor, Vision reaches its fullness only where we no longer experience obstructions around money. We see our financial suffering clearly when it arises, perceive its roots in Pain and Innocence, and through Understanding know how to end it. We know with equal clarity the role money plays in our lives and the way to employ it vigorously in the pursuit of our most profound purposes. Seeing deeply without, we find good works to be done wherever we look. Seeing deeply within, we partake of the quiet that forms our true home and lay the foundation of Aloha's pure blessing.

In the Eastern traditions, Vision resides in the sixth chakra, the so-called third eye, in the pineal gland in the middle of the forehead. This is the eye of intuition, an organ of powerful focus that sees deeply both within and deeply without. A Buddhist master perfects this profound seeing to experience each individual moment as it arises and passes away. These passing moments are perceived as vast teachings—not thoughts or ideas or scientific laws, but pure experiences of sensation and impermanence as vast in their teachings as *War and Peace,* the cantatas of Johann Sebastian Bach, or Billie Holiday's blues. Such moments are gifts waiting to be received, waiting to be given away. They rise and fall like waves on the sea, reflecting the fire, passion, and transience of our inner world. Each of our individual Visions arises in such moments of insight and intuition.

In the realm of money, Vision is as immediate and spontaneous as it is forward-looking. See if you can recognize the balance between comprehending your purpose and meeting each individual moment of experience as you act upon the world. When you do this, something wonderful happens. The inner and outer, the present and the future, meld into one; the split between self and world resolves. When our aim is clear and our goal pure, we move ahead without flinching, without obstruction between thought and action, without leaving behind the tracks of suffering.

chapter 10

ALOHA:
BLESSING, PURE AND SIMPLE

timepieces can be bought but not the morning.

W. S. Merwin

The thief left it behind: the moon at my window.

Ryokan

Suddenly I realize
That if I stepped out of my body I would break
Into blossom.

James Wright

Ricky Sapolu couldn't believe his eyes. He looked once, then again, just to be sure. He nudged Mahealani with his elbow.

"You know who that is?" he whispered.

"Who?" she said, startled by his hush.

"Him." Ricky cocked his head in the direction of a man impossible to ignore. He was a tall fellow, big across shoulders and around belly, with huge hands and a wide calm face under a thick shock of graying hair pulled back into a ponytail. There was more to him than simple size. When he took a step, he moved like king, a man familiar with majesty.

"That's Raymond K," Ricky said.

"Here?" Mahealani asked. She knew who he was by reputation: the most respected and powerful elder in the native community on his home island. "What's he doing on Oahu?"

"Beats me," Ricky said.

"You sure it's him?"

"Positive. I met him maybe ten years ago. He's the kind of a guy you remember."

Mahealani felt both flattered and fearful. It pleased her that a community leader from an outer island would stop by her store. At the same time his presence frightened her. What if he didn't like what she was doing? In his youth, Raymond had earned a militant reputation as a fierce spokesman for the ancient ways of native Hawaiians. More recently Raymond was known as a resolver of intractable disputes, the man called in to settle conflicts that otherwise might escalate into endless bitterness or violence. And he was a kahuna, a healer who knew everything there was to know about plants, animals, and artifacts Hawaiian. Suddenly insecure, Mahealani felt almost certain Raymond would condemn her store as commercial and amateurish.

Long anxious moments passed as Raymond continued his regal tour around "Mahealani's Authentic." He moved slowly, contemplatively, stopping now and again to pick up an item and roll it around in his large, sensitive hands. Suddenly he turned and moved toward her.

"I know you're Mahealani," he said.

She simply nodded.

"I could tell just by looking. You carry yourself with the pride of a woman who owns something of value," the elder said. He swept his hand out in a half circle, as if drawing the entire store within his grasp. "This is great, what you are doing." He fixed his dark eyes on Mahealani. "I wish we had something like this back home."

"It felt like he was looking right through me," Mahealani said, in describing the experience, "a man of great power seeing into my soul and loving what I was doing. My soul moved, yes, it moved. It could feel his blessing. What I felt from him, way down deep in me, was Aloha."

It was Alexandria's idea that Derrick come with her on a trip to Belize. "You've been working with the weavers for over a year now," she said. "You really ought to meet them."

"Okay," said Derrick, more than a little curious about the weavers whose clothing he had been marketing. "I need some time away. Let's take the boys too. They need to see something outside the U.S.A., get a little perspective."

Yet it was Derrick himself who benefited most from the change in national viewpoint.

"I felt it as soon as we left Belize City and headed toward the Guatemala border, the four of us in this rented four-wheel-drive," Derrick told me. "The roads aren't very good down there and it isn't much of a highway anyway, but I found the country fascinating. At first it was a coastal scrub forest, then we came into this lush green country with low rolling hills."

The main road took Derrick and his family along the Macal River, where in the late afternoon local people gathered on the bank under a canopy of tall overshadowing trees—the men to talk, the women to wash clothes, the children to frolic in the green, swirling current. As the Jeep passed by, the people paused and waved, their faces wide with smiles.

"Something about them impressed me. In part it was their physical beauty, their raven-black hair on brown skins. It was also those smiles, an openness I didn't expect in people who have been through terrible horror."

Alexandria headed the Jeep off the main road and up a small track that led through a patchwork of fields cleared from the surrounding rain forest. The heavy, humid air crackled with the calls of parrots and toucans, at once harsh and exotic. In one clearing a group of small houses with thatched roofs stood on stilts, up off the ground, silhouetted against the backdrop of tall trees. Alexandria pulled up next to one of the small houses and parked. Immediately a small Indian man came out to meet her. The two of them spoke in rapid, animated Spanish.

"Can you understand?" Derrick asked Matthew.

"Some," he said, listening to the interchange. "He's Alejandro, kind of the head weaver."

Derrick nodded. He knew the name. He stepped out of the Jeep.

"I was carrying this envelope with the last couple of months' earnings in cash," Derrick said, "and I wanted to give it to him. When I look back on my motivations, I realize I was being something of a cultural imperialist. I imagined myself as a beneficent gringo with two college degrees giving all this money to an uneducated Indian refugee, who of course should be eternally grateful to me for being such a brilliant businessman that I'm helping him earn what he thinks is a fortune. Boy, did I have that all wrong."

"How so?" I asked him.

"I gave him the money, and Alejandro didn't even open the envelope," Derrick explained. "He took my hands in his—he's a small man and he has tiny hands, but there is a power in them. I knew I couldn't have pulled away from him even if I'd wanted to. Then he looked into my eyes. I had this feeling he was riveting me in place, that I was in the presence of someone who had extraordinary personal power, not from having money but from the quality of his being. Over and over he said to me 'Gracias, gracias,' and Matthew, still playing the translator, said, 'He's thanking you.' And I thought, 'He's doing more than saying thanks. He's blessing me.'"

"Roger—he's my brother, you'll remember, the one who showed up at my benefit—well, he came back again. Just showed up at my house two nights ago," Susanna said. "And he wanted money,"

"I thought he had money," I said.

"He used to. That's what he wanted to tell me about. He inherited a great deal, just as I did, but then he managed to lose it, in one bad business deal after another," she explained.

As Susanna told the story, it was clear Roger was trying to make her feel sorry for him. By his telling, he had suffered one of the worst strings of bad business breaks in human history. Every venture he took part in went sour, and always he came out with much less money than he went in with. Now the last of his fortune was gone, and he was facing bankruptcy. Unless, of course, Susanna wanted to help him out.

"And I really thought about it," she said. "I could see the pain in Roger's eyes. When we were young and his life seemed to be dedicated to causing me trouble, he was full of this cocky confidence. Now he was broken. He had no fire left, no spunk. It was sad.

"And then I began to realize he was in the same kind of a place I had been in around my divorce. I knew I couldn't make it any easier for him. He had to face this as it was. Giving him money would just draw out the pain. It would rob our relationship of power. I started crying, and I said to him, 'I won't give you money. But I will be your friend.'

"'So what the hell's that worth?' he yelled at me. "'You're just like the rest of this screwed-up family. It's as if your one purpose on this Earth is to cause me grief.'"

At first her brother's tirade frightened Susanna. Hearing him rail took her back to childhood and adolescence, when every event in the family made her feel small and worthless. Yet she stood her ground, refused to give in to his demands for money, and continued to offer friendship.

"I told him how it was just like that when we were growing up," she said. "Then he gave me this amazing look. 'You mean it was tough for you too?' I actually had to start laughing. Roger had this idea that my father was easy on me, where he had been hard on him and my other brothers, always pitting them one against the other, making them struggle for his approval—which of course he never gave. 'God,' he said, 'it was such a constant pain in the end to grow up under that hard old man,' and he softened. His whole demeanor changed."

Susanna and Roger compared memories of childhood. Soon they discovered that they had suffered similarly under the weight of their father's demanding authoritarianism and their mother's pervasive weakness. Forced to compete against each other, they had overlooked something important.

"We could have been allies," Roger said.

"We were in it together," Susanna said.

"And all this time I've assumed you were hostile to me because that's just the way you are," Roger said. "What a hell of a lot of time we've wasted."

"About forty years," Susanna said. "So now we start over."

They hugged, their faces soft and wet with tears. And they kept on talking, sharing experiences and memories and discovering in these further remembrances even more common ground between them. They continued through much of the night, stopping only to catch a few hours' sleep before the sun came up and Susanna brewed coffee, sliced strawberries, and warmed croissants for breakfast.

As they were eating, Roger said to Susanna, "You know, when I asked you for money, I felt toward you just the way I used to feel toward Dad. I thought you have more money than I do, so you owe it to me. I'm sorry I made you into him."

"We've both done a lot of that," Susanna said. "It's time we claimed our own lives. I know you feel bad about yourself right now. That doesn't change the fact that you're a good person. You have everything you need to get out of this hole you're in. God knows, I've been royally screwed up around money and I understand how hard it is to get it all straightened out. One thing I can give you as you work all this out is my friendship and love."

When Roger left to drive back to Providence, he didn't actually say good-bye. He wanted to be sure that this time together was a beginning, not an ending.

He said, "Sis, you've given me more than I came for, more than money. I'm sorry for all the misunderstandings, for being so wrapped up in my own struggles that we couldn't be friends." Then he paused. "You know, you're not half bad after all. I'll be seeing you again soon."

"In that instant of awkward silence before he actually turned to walk out the door," Susanna told me, "I felt a connection between us, wonderful and deep. It was something like a discovery, and something like a feeling of grace."

Given or received, Aloha is unmistakable. It is humility, kindness, and blessing that passes from one person to another. Aloha lacks economic distinction. It can be given by a poor person to a rich one, like Alejandro to Derrick, or vice versa, like Susanna to Roger. Aloha arises from the interior place where we have emptied ourselves of attachments to objects and stories and can give ourselves spontaneously, genuinely, and lovingly to another. In Understanding, we had to work at such kindness. In Aloha, it flows without effort.

Once, at a conference for certified financial planners, a number of us were lounging around late in the evening, sharing ideas and notions. Somehow the topic of Aloha came up, and a string of inspiring stories unrolled.

I told about the wealthy retired professional who invited six people over for dinner, myself among them. He was by far the richest man in the gathering, yet, in his apron, he waited on us all hand and foot. He didn't merely cook an elegant meal, surprising all his guests with his extraordinary culinary skills. He filled every moment with an uncommon grace—pouring wine, playing music, serving all the meal's many courses, prompting conversation among people who had been strangers, and encouraging everyone to enjoy. He was deferential, wise, endlessly curious and involved in others. All evening long I felt that I had been blessed by a gracious servant.

After that evening, I pursued a friendship with this man because I wanted to know what made Aloha so easy for him. He did indeed teach me, through his constant example of generosity, selflessness, and interest in others. A rare illustrated book in his library fascinated me, and a couple of days later it showed up in the mail, an unexpected gift to me. Animals trusted him. When wild birds came to his backyard feeder, they let him approach closely, knowing he meant them only good.

Another one of us spoke of a single older woman in her apartment complex who used mealtimes to bring the other tenants together and bridge the gaps between them. Every evening she invited people over to eat with her. It was a motley crew—old people, latchkey children, recent immigrants, the lonely and desperate, people who expected nothing and got less. For some of the people who came to dinner the meal was their only human contact of the day, and they were regular attendees. Others came now and again, whenever they needed the family feeling they sensed there. The apartment building became a community of tolerance that spread Aloha among everyone who ate at the older woman's table.

My friend Lynne told the story of her father, who was shopping for fishing tackle one day when he spotted a young boy eyeing a shiny new Mepps bucktail spinner. The lure cost only a few dollars, but Lynne's father could tell from the way the boy handled it that he both wanted it desperately and didn't have the money. Without a second thought, he bought the spinner for the boy.

The youngster, stunned by his sudden good fortune, said, "Thanks, mister. I promise I'll pay you back as soon as I can."

"Don't worry about paying me back," Lynne's father said. "Someday, when you're grown up, do the same thing for a boy like you."

Another person told of how after growing up poor then making it big in the city, she went back to her rural home to see her grandparents. In childhood she had received conflicting messages: People with money were evil, but it was important to escape poverty. Now that she was richer than either her parents or her grandparents, she was unsure how she'd be received. In spite of her anxiety, she felt immediately the warmth of their welcome and their home.

Her grandfather said, "I'm proud of what you're doing. But keep this in mind. It's not how much money you have, or even whether you have money. The question is: Does the money have you?"

Hearing this, she relaxed into grateful tears. She understood the meaning of the wisdom her grandfather had passed on to her. When it comes to a choice between money and your life, he was saying, choose your life.

And finally there was the story of the poor uncle who made up for a father dead at a young age. He took the three fatherless daughters wherever they needed to go, whether to the dentist's or to school dances (where he waited outside in the car to take them home afterward!), and he shelled out for school supplies, prom dresses, and other necessities when money was low. The woman who had received these kindnesses saw her uncle as a good angel who came to her on wings of kindness in time of need.

When the stories ended, the room filled with quiet, peace, relaxation—a rare feeling among the wired, type-A anxious personalities who handle other people's money for a living. Something of the Aloha we were telling about had taken up residence within us. We were learning how to trust.

Aloha cools the mind and calms one's whole essence. It delivers the gift of an end to suffering, an acceptance of feelings coupled with a letting-go of the struggle attached to thoughts. Such a gift feels like a blessing. And it can be as simple as a smile, a gesture, a look given by someone who knows beyond words what we are going through and accepts both it and us, with unconditional positive regard.

As the very name indicates, Aloha is for me inextricably bound to the land of Hawaii, where it is part and parcel of the indigenous culture's way of being. While it often comes with the ease and grace of a warm smile or a helping hand, sometimes Aloha's deeper expression has to be won.

Lei was one of my first clients on Maui and a woman who had been taken advantage of by numerous financial advisors. Having been too trusting already, she was guarded with me, nervous and awkward. At first she was in denial that she'd been used and betrayed by others. Then, as the truth broke down her denial, she became angry and filed lawsuits. Even though her rage intimidated me and seemed to run counter to the warm Aloha friends told me she possessed, I stuck with her. Then I walked into her house one April day to a chorus of "Happy Birthday" and a big warm hug from Lei. After her bad experiences with financial advisors, she was hesitant to tell me how pleased she was with my work. To express her appreciation, she had rounded up all my friends to throw a surprise party for me. The islands are like that.

When I first began going to Hawaii, I had little money, so I usually slept on the floor of Buddhist temples, enjoying the hospitality of kind monks. Invariably, as soon as I met people who lived on the islands, they invited me into their homes and let me stay with them for free. This kind of easy kindness, so natural to Hawaii, drew me back to the islands again and again and led me to begin living there part of each year. When I returned to the intellectual energy of Cambridge, I felt as if I were carrying the Aloha of Hawaii with me and sharing it, smiling at the people I met on the street, offering a ray of sun through winter's cold dark. Aloha isn't something you hold on to; it's a blessing you love to give away.

Aloha often comes from people older than we are, particularly in childhood. To many children Christmas is the season of Aloha, a rich blend of warmth, gift-giving, and family blessing. For others Aloha comes in their early practical experiences with money outside the home, often in their first jobs, where they least expect to encounter acts of generosity. A friend of mine talks still of how a stranger came up to her first lemonade stand and bought up her whole inventory with a $5 bill, a generosity that filled her with delight. Thomas, the furniture importer who had a paper route in his grade school days, once said to me, "The customers who kept me going were those few special people who were warm and kind no matter what. I remember this one woman who had hot chocolate ready for me on a particularly cold, nasty afternoon. Even when I was low and felt undeserving, she and the others appreciated me in a kind and gentle way. I often think of my furniture business as a way of giving back—not just to them—but as a way of expressing thanks for all of the kindnesses I've received over the years."

Abby, a participant in a recent seminar, told about an unexpected blessing attached to one of her earliest memories of money. The school bus dropped her off a few blocks from her house, and she walked home along a route that passed a *Boston Globe* newspaper dispenser in front of a corner grocery. She put her finger in the hole where the money went, and every now and then she pulled out a quarter. She felt as if she had uncovered buried treasure.

As an adult she went back to the neighborhood for a visit, and she ran into the old man who had operated the corner grocery when she was a child and was still at it. They got to chatting, swapping stories about the old days over Cokes, when the shopkeeper said, "You know, I remember you clearly."

"Yeah?" Abby said skeptically. "What do you remember?"

"Well, the school bus dropped you off up the avenue, and you always came down the street on that side"—he pointed—"cut across the alley, then waited at the stoplight for the 'walk' sign."

"That's right," Abby said, her skepticism replaced by amazement that the old man, whom she knew only in passing, remembered her childhood in such detail.

"Of course, then you'd stop by that old *Boston Globe* box out front and put your finger into the money slot. I thought that was just the cutest thing. So lots of days, when it was about time for your bus to arrive and the store wasn't busy, I'd put a quarter in that machine for you to find."

UNATTACHED KINDNESS

Experiences like Abby's remind us that something deeper is at work in this human world than the Nobel prize–winning efficient-market theory or the laws of supply and demand.

A businessman I think of as a visionary argued with me the other day that Vision is a higher stage than Aloha. In the course of the conversation I caught sight of a discomfited part of him I'd always suspected but couldn't quite identify. This visionary businessman had trouble receiving kindness, I realized, and was filled with compassion for him. It is strikingly difficult for people active in the world of business to find Understanding, much less Aloha. So extreme is the development of Vigor and Knowledge in the corporate world that we lose sight of the power of kindness.

As I try to help people across the country with their relationship to money through workshops, talks, and seminars—work I think of as visionary—my struggle is to bring a deep sense of Aloha into a task that imposes all the demands of a complicated business yet brings many people who want to confer with me. As valuable as I hope the contents of the workshops are, it is in the individual exchanges within the workshops that the deepest work is done. This profundity has nothing to do with what we talk about or the Seven Stages, but with the space we open to each other—the trust, the generosity and acceptance, the openness and vulnerability with which we approach each other. It has something to do with magic, with mysticism, and with the ordinariness of the "secrets" Abby's shopkeeper seemed to know. It has to do with bringing and receiving a gift that reaches all the way into our souls, strangers though we may be. The demands of the world sometimes make it difficult to find our Aloha, but nothing is more powerful and profound than these moments of generosity and kindness.

In the realm of money we are too used to thinking that Knowledge is everything, that money is simply about the facts of insurance, investments, budgets, economics, estates, and balancing the books. But Knowledge is uncertain, fragile, and incomplete. It's no way to live a life.

Kindness, though, takes everything in. No matter how much you know or own, in the end all the rest falls away . Only kindness counts.

In the history of the West the most enduring figure of Aloha is Francis of Assisi, medieval mystic and founder of the Franciscan order. Francis offered unending kindness to everyone he met, even the despised and the outcast. Francis's vow of poverty allowed him to look at the deeper truths of life. We too take the same vow when we enter Aloha. There we are no longer "a wealthy person," "someone who demands respect," "a parent with authority," or even "a person with money." We stand stripped and pure, in the poverty of our own spirit, willing to give it all away. To enter Aloha we must give away our apparent riches and our identities. Some people might see Francis's vow of poverty as an act of Innocence, but it was in fact the result of profound Knowledge about money, specifically its ephemerality. A man of great Understanding and exceptional Vigor, Francis did the work of Adulthood in coming to Aloha.

I saw the same process develop in a friend of mine with the wonderfully archangelic and artistic name of Raphael. Like his namesakes, Raphael was both an angel and an artist. He brought a grace to life, although not originally in the manner he had intended. He wanted to be a painter, but financial reality led him to work as a consultant. Raphael trained administrators in community colleges, then managers in big corporations, how to be creative in their work.

Raphael appeared happy in his occupation, yet I wondered if he still had the desire to paint. I ribbed him a little. "If you ever do retire to paint, you'll probably be so bored that you'll sign on for another big corporate gig before the first month is out."

Raphael fell silent, wearing the face of a serious man who has received a rebuke. "Don't you think," he said, "that it's hard enough to learn how to live in peace with oneself?"

The change came for him one night on the road, when he was alone in a cold hotel room, dog-tired from another twelve-hour day of teaching executives how to be creative. "How ironic," he thought to himself. "I work so hard showing them to be creative that I feel utterly emptied." He and I had spoken of Aloha, and Raphael realized that was what he needed—an infusion of Aloha. Shaking with fatigue, he pulled himself off the bed and headed out into the night.

His wanderings took him into a bookstore, where he found a small volume of watercolors. He bought it and headed back to his hotel. As Raphael thumbed through this book of scenic paintings, he understood suddenly that painting was his Aloha. Capturing small, wondrous moments in nature's blessing and passing them on to others through painting—this was the Aloha of his life. When he looked at paintings, Aloha came to him, across continents, across centuries. And when he painted those selfsame moments, then he bestowed Aloha on his viewers. Before he fell asleep, Raphael knew the time had come for him to be a painter.

Within a year he had quit his job, halved his budget, and devoted himself to spreading Aloha. He painted watercolor after watercolor, and when someone liked one of his paintings, he gave it away.

"Earlier in my life, I would have had to be paid for my work, to be recognized and rewarded financially," he said. "Now it's important for me to give, in every way I can."

When Raphael comes to see me, he always brings as a gift a small object of great beauty, a watercolor, a piece of succulent fruit. He lives out the creativity he used to teach, not in the service of corporate or organizational goals but simply as a way of passing along the blessing.

Once, as he and I went to lunch in Harvard Square, he stopped to talk with anyone who wanted his attention, even panhandlers and solicitors for various political causes.

"They're here for a reason," he explained to me. "We tend to think that they're asking for something from us. But I like to assume that it's the other way around. They're here to give us something, so I stop for a moment to find out what. I figure they've come to teach me something, something I ought to be grateful for."

Yet, for all the sweetness in Raphael's story, he remains grounded in the practical world of money. He knows where his roots are, and he's as clear about his budget and his investment goals as he is about his painting.

"Money taught me this, George," he said. "Without taking the hard knocks of money, I never would have learned how to be strong in my convictions, how to accept and understand this world as it is. I would have always doubted myself in some way if someone had just handed me the freedom to paint as a young man. There is a rigor that comes from entering the fire of the world. I wouldn't have it any other way."

Sadly, the experience and the example of beautiful human beings like Raphael are all too rare. After all, how can one small kindness—or even one great generosity—make a difference against all the suffering of a world in which trillions of dollars change hands every day? Holding to such Innocence, we make ourselves small and powerless. We cling to our notions of ourselves rather than trusting enough to give ourselves away to others. We deny Aloha by clinging to its putative impossibility.

Yet, truth be told, every kindness matters. It is said that the orbital leap of an electron on the other side of the galaxy can affect the outcome of a game of pool here on Earth. If that is true, then how much more powerful is the single beat of human heart? How much must an act of kindness weigh upon the Earth? It is said too that the flap of a butterfly's wings in Tibet can be felt in the swirl of a thunderstorm over Lake Michigan. Aloha is like that. It starts small and reaches out in circles of blessing. It changes us deep within. And it moves the world.

ROCKS, HARD PLACES, AND THE PRACTICE OF ALOHA

Aloha isn't a substitute for economic endeavor but a part of it. Since every exchange of money is in fact a reciprocal giving of gifts, Aloha can be an inherent part of every financial dealing. A seminar participant told me about a man who, when he sold his company, gave his employees $100,000 apiece. This man always answered his own phone calls, talked up good causes, and, even though he had been through his share of ups and downs, made everyone he dealt with feel as if he or she were the most important person on the Earth. Think of how wonderful our world would be if each of us could take even a small piece of his blessing inside ourselves.

Sometimes Aloha comes from the most unexpected quarters. When I was in my thirties and needed roof repairs done to my house, I hired an older craftsman, a Dutch immigrant named Cor, to handle the work. Cor was in his sixties and on the verge of retiring, and he had a reputation of being very money-wise—frugal and savvy, and possessed of a gritty integrity and honesty in business. He also told me something I needed to know. Cor's father had been an international banker in Holland, and although he had died when Cor was young, he impressed his son with an ethic that made the handling of money an activity of supreme moral order. I was trying to establish a money management business, struggling with the regulatory requirements and the long hours. Yet I was troubled by popular cultural notions that all things financial are crooked and dirty.

"No, no," Cor told me. "It is quite the opposite; money work is the highest calling. What you are doing is good."

It was a blessing for an older man who stood for the integrity of money, who believed in it and in me, someone who had gone through his own struggles and put in his own long hours, to pass on the torch of the integrity he had received from his father. Cor's Aloha gave me the strength to move ahead.

When Tony, a longtime family acquaintance, retired in his fifties from a career as a structural engineer in the housing industry, he went to live in a small city in the South and run a homeless shelter. A classical music buff, Tony was taking in a Mozart symphony at a university in a nearby town when he struck up a conversation with the man sitting next to him. This fellow lived in the same city as Tony, and he had a reputation as a hard-bitten conservative businessman, not the sort usually interested in social causes. Tony was surprised that the homeless shelter intrigued the businessman, who later told Tony that his younger brother, a schizophrenic, had died while out of communication with his family and living on the streets. The businessman still felt the deep sadness of that unnecessary death.

"At the time I wasn't so sure about my career change," Tony said. "It was hard to be a Yankee in the South working at something so new and demanding. My newfound friend's enthusiasm for my work made me feel that I was doing something worthwhile. He gave me a kind of Aloha."

Tony and the businessman bumped into each other on the street from time to time. Tony felt the same blessing each time.

Then came the sudden, fierce flood that swept through the city's downtown, including the homeless shelter, destroying all the computers, files, and other equipment in the basement office. The businessman phoned Tony to ask about the extent of the damage. Two days later Tony found a generous check in the mail to cover replacement costs.

"It wasn't just the money," Tony said. "It was that a man from outside my usual world was supporting me. His Aloha meant more to me personally than the several thousand dollars he gave."

The challenge each of us faces is to discover Aloha in the midst of money and to act with it even as the exchange remains economic. When a client presents a difficult personal and financial problem to me, I look for a way to be giving and gracious, but I still charge for my consulting time.

Aloha can't be rushed, but it can be practiced—a task that sometimes isn't easy. I once told a respected mentor that I often didn't feel kind. He responded wisely. Kindness, he said, is most deeply appreciated and most powerfully learned when it springs from a place of vulnerability within. Those instances in which we act in spite and in the midst of our vulnerable spots present us with particularly potent—if scary—opportunities for Aloha.

Some years ago, when I was hosting a large fund-raising party for a cause I believed in, I found myself in conflict over a bill I had paid the caterer. Before the event, he had billed me for an advance against food for an agreed-upon number of people plus a number of other services. I paid the advance, then he gave me an additional bill at the end of the event, which I paid on the spot. Later, when I was reviewing the additional bill, I discovered a number of details that bothered me. The music charge was higher than what the caterer and I had agreed to, and he had billed me for ten people more than the number we had decided on. I felt terrible about paying the bill in a rush without thinking more about it, yet I knew the caterer to be an honest man. I debated whether to call him or just to let it go. Finally I knew I had to call, and I wrestled with how to talk to him candidly about the problem and at the same time bring kindness to the interaction. When I got in touch with the caterer, I told him how much I appreciated his work and the beautiful job he had done with the food and music. I went on to detail what I took to be our understanding, explained my oversight, and said I was willing to compromise. His response was most gracious, and he too compromised. He gave on some items, I gave on others, and in the places where conflict remained, we split the difference. The attitude between us was one of cooperation, a willingness to accept the other with complete kindness even around areas of disagreement. When I got off the phone, the Aloha that had passed between us left me feeling blessed.

THE REAL AND THE FALSE

A caution: Be patient. Do not leap to a false Aloha. Stay with yourself and your inner work. Extend a loving kindness to yourself. Aloha arises with ease and naturalness only when we have developed sufficient Knowledge, Understanding, and Vigor to support it. Francis of Assisi was one of those uncommon people who achieve Aloha early in life. For those of us in the common, unsaintly run of humanity, Aloha arises more slowly. It develops only as we do sufficient work on our inner selves, when giving becomes as natural as breathing and is no longer a guilt-driven response to an external "should."

I once had a client who inherited a small fortune and promptly gave it all away to friends and deserving charitable causes, an act that seemed like Aloha. He wanted to continue to contribute to his community through literacy and conservation work, but he discovered that these activities were so little valued financially that he couldn't make a living at them. He came to the horrible realization that he had given away the resources he might have used to finance his literacy and environmental ambitions and support his family. Remorse and regret filled him; he suffered terribly. It took him years of inner work around money to understand that the real reason he gave away his inheritance wasn't generous at all. He dumped his wealth because of the terror he felt at facing the shame, desire, guilt, and an ancient anger at his father the inheritance roused in him.

His was a classically false Aloha. If we give something away without feeling free to give, then we are giving away a crucial part of ourselves. We aren't in Aloha. In fact, we aren't even in Adulthood. Rather, we are clinging to some blind Innocence.

How do we know when our giving is enough, too little, or too much? When Aloha is true, we know intuitively, without asking. Dealing with the world of money has required us to know our own boundaries. In Aloha and Vision, the tools of Adulthood are developed to the point where we know where our limits lie around money and time. Then we can give just the right amount, easily and generously. And we find we can give in every moment and never run out.

THE PRACTICE OF ALOHA

People with Aloha enjoy the greatest ease and comfort regarding money and are least plagued by money's endless worries. Here are some formal ways to build this awareness.

As the fruit of the other six stages of Money Maturity, Aloha is developed by strengthening our understanding of all seven. Return to the lessons of each stage and look at how the development of Money Maturity in every step along the way affects the development of Aloha in your life. For instance, if you find yourself acting in a thoughtless way around money, don't let yourself get away with it. Look at it. Ask yourself what messages or thoughts prompted you to act that way. Learn what feelings you were unable to welcome within yourself to cause you to act in that way.

Knowledge is very helpful in the development of Aloha. Without Knowledge we have no idea how much we can give without causing harm to ourselves or our families. When we are able to set appropriate financial boundaries, we can then focus on all the different ways we can give. Without appropriate boundaries, guilt and uncertainty around giving plague every opportunity for generosity.

The practices of Understanding are particularly useful in bringing Aloha into our lives. For instance:

- Make a commitment to do an intentional act of kindness every day. Go out of your way. Be creative. Do something kind you wouldn't ordinarily do.
- Whenever you think of giving, give all that you imagine—immediately. Try this yourself. Don't hold back, either by waiting or by giving less than you thought of. (Obviously I don't want you to attempt this exercise if you're likely to give away the possibility of freedom for yourself.)
- Bring kindness to yourself in every moment. Do it internally, quietly. Notice how you approach the tiniest moments of suffering within. Create a forgiving space that offers the same kindness to everyone and everything in each moment.

Aloha is a kind of prayer without ceasing, an unending contemplation of generosity and gratitude moment by moment. The practice of ceaseless kindness in every moment of our lives, a central lesson of Understanding, readies us to meet every opportunity for Aloha as it arises.

Often failures to be kind or generous come from a laziness of spirit. Go back to the Vigor exercises. Work on them.

On the other hand, the most beautiful acts of Aloha and the ones most long remembered are often combined with visionary actions. Seek within your own Vision for opportunities to give the blessing of Aloha.

As to Aloha itself:

- Form a resolve to act with Aloha, learn Aloha, observe the Aloha of others, and seek out friends and mentors with Aloha. The mentors we met in chapter 7 are frequent bestowers of Aloha.
- Pay attention to each day's exchanges, looking for the Aloha they contain. If you can't find Aloha in a given exchange, ask yourself what you can do to create or facilitate it.
- Devote some time to considering how you would like to be generous if you felt yourself completely free of economic or emotional constraint. Would you even think of dedicating your life to generosity? How would generosity or kindness fit into this

new world of freedom? The gift could be money, time, or yourself. Think of simple daily ways you can give as well special one-time occasions for generosity.

- List all the areas where you aren't generous. Would you like to be? What needs to change inside yourself? Be honest. Remember, we're talking here about our maturity, which is much easier to change than the whole world.

TRY THIS—YOUR LIFE IN MONEY: ALOHA

The final step in your financial autobiography is to record where you stand in relationship to Aloha. You can use the following questions to guide your thinking and self-discovery:

Who are your models of Aloha? Which ones have you known, which have you read about, which come from history? Write a few sentences describing the particular kind of Aloha each one manifests and what you find admirable about that individual and his or her Aloha. How can you act like your model in the ordinary daily life of commerce and responsibility?

More often than not, we are moved most by small acts of extraordinary kindness witnessed or experienced. What actions of Aloha have you seen or felt? Write a description of each act of witness or experience.

What would ideal Aloha feel like—both giving and receiving? In what kinds of settings or moments is it most effective? Where does it have the most effect?

What kinds of reciprocal gifts of Aloha can you imagine between yourself and those who differ from you—richer or poorer, of a different color, older or younger, more powerful and more famous, or penniless and unknown? Make a note of each gift, both giving and receiving.

Encouraged by community leaders like Raymond, Mahealani Sapolu steadily expanded her business. She opened a second location on Oahu, and her sister took the business to Raymond's outer island. The second Oahu store thrived, but the other store didn't do as well, simply because Mahealani's sister lacked local community and family connections. Still, Mahealani became a successful businesswoman, with an income now vastly greater than she had ever imagined. She put more and more time and effort into working with and supporting a number of nonprofits dedicated to preserving Hawaiian culture and the unique flora and fauna of the islands. She has also worked hard with me to spread the message of Money Maturity.

Derrick King overhauled his life. First he put together a string of scholarships and loans to finance his sons' college. Matthew, the more academically gifted of the two, was admitted with a generous scholarship to Cornell, where he majored in Spanish and Latin American history, while David, the younger son, graduated from the University of California at Davis in computer engineering. With their sons' futures taken care of, Derrick and Alexandria moved to Belize to be closer to the people they had become so attached to. She expanded her work in investment banking in Central America, and he grew the export business. Both of them are able to travel to the United States regularly to maintain good contacts with their children.

As for Susanna Swartz, she taught me a necessary lesson.

CYCLES

Much to her pleasant surprise, Susanna continued to heal the wounds in her family, creating an important relationship with Roger, and her charitable fund-raising work grew in scope and ambition. Her Victorian house was as much a community center as it was her home.

Whenever I went to see Susanna to talk about business, I felt personal pride in the change she had effected in her life. She had gone from being an anxious, resentful person trapped in a cramped apartment by her own ghosts to a mature community leader. She had learned a great deal about handling money, and she displayed an increasing depth of character. Susanna had shown herself to be a good person, someone I was terribly fond of.

One afternoon, about two years after her reconciliation with Roger, she and I met on her patio to discuss her investment accounts. It had always bothered me that so much of her portfolio was taken up with the family company stock she had inherited from her father. She stood to inherit even more of this stock when her mother, still alive but aged and ailing, passed away. That inheritance would push her portfolio, already out of balance, into a positive tilt. For years I had suggested to her that owning so much of a single stock was the same as putting almost all her eggs in one basket. I proposed to her repeatedly that she sell a substantial portion of the stock, pay the capital gains taxes, and reinvest the net proceeds of the sale into a variety of other stocks and mutual funds, achieving a diversification that stood a better chance of protecting her assets in the event of an economic downturn that might cause particular harm to the family company's fortunes. However, the family stock had done well despite my warnings, so well, in fact, that Susanna's relative percentage in it had increased significantly.

In the course of our afternoon meeting, I repeated my concern about Susanna's large holding of a single equity. In the tone of voice one uses for changing the topic, she said, "Do you remember what you advised me way back when about working with a financial advisor?"

"I assume you're referring to the importance of both the personal side, of liking and trusting the person, and the professional side, of understanding their expertise and acumen," I said.

"Well, partly," she said. "I was thinking more of something you said once, something to the effect that if I didn't follow my financial advisor's advice, I should change advisors."

"Yes, I did say that," I said. "It's important." And I still thought it was. Refusing to follow an advisor's advice fosters mutual distrust that must be healed for the relationship to go forward. And if the relationship can't go forward, then it should end.

"For years now, George, you've been advising me to sell my family stock, and I just can't do it," Susanna said. "I realize I'm doing exactly what you told me about: I'm not taking your advice. So I've decided to end our relationship."

For a moment I sat stunned. I felt as if I had just turned a corner and been run down by a garbage truck.

Susanna stepped into my silence, explaining herself further. "I've learned a great deal from you, so much so that I feel confident I can handle my affairs with my accountant and my attorney. You've helped bring me to where I am, and I thank you for that. Now it's time for me to move on."

As the shock lifted, I realized I wasn't totally surprised. The family stock had always been a sticking point between us. Still, I felt deeply disappointed at losing a client I cherished. I parted from Susanna as graciously as possible, mouthing the expected courtesies, but moments after I left her house, I sank like a pebble in a pool. I was trading a sense of shared Vision and Aloha for the pain of a broken relationship. And I was losing money. As one of my largest clients, Susanna accounted for 5 to 10 percent of my annual income, which was about to evaporate.

As I drove from Winchester back to my office in Cambridge, I reached for all sorts of questions and explanations, each of them sprung full-blown from my own Innocence: "How can she do this to me after all I've done for her? What a mistake she's making, the fool. She's going to regret this. God, she's stupid. And I was so brilliant! Heavens, can't she see what an idiotic move this is?"

Like a drowning man slipping under the waves, I was reaching for something to cling to, something to keep the Pain at bay. Then I turned on myself. "I must be a lousy investment advisor. Wow, did I blow this one. Once word gets around, everybody's going to jump ship the way she did, and I won't have any clients left."

Anger, sadness, and fear kept cycling through me. As I came slowly to recognize those feelings, Understanding began to kick in. Rather than cling to questions and disparaging thoughts, I made myself available to the feelings themselves, dropping the barrier of Innocence. I opened the door to disappointment, that river of sadness and grief that pours over us when we part from someone we care for.

Slowly, as Understanding took hold, Knowledge also came into play. In my head I calculated how much income I stood to lose, and I began cooking up strategies, each calling on Vigor, to pull in new clients to make up the loss. I returned to Knowledge to explore what I could learn from my experience with Susanna. Perhaps I was wrong to push for my investment strategy when her feelings around selling the family stock ran so high. Perhaps I should have ended the relationship earlier myself, or maybe I should have proposed handling only her assets apart from the family stock. As I revisited my history with her, I realized I needed to be more flexible, let go of my own preconceptions, and give myself a greater ease around client relationships. As this Knowledge dawned on me, I discovered a deeper confidence in my skill at bringing Understanding to bear on my work with individual investors, and I found I was ready to act with greater Vigor in this arena in the future. Letting go of the part of me that had to be right and perfect with clients boosted both Understanding and Vigor and gave me a subtly different Vision of how my work benefits clients. The experience humbled me. I found myself inclined toward a gentle acceptance of imperfection, both my own and Susanna's. In that acceptance, Aloha blessed me.

There is more to this incident than its details. It teaches an important lesson: We never really finish the work of Money Maturity. Rather, we cycle back through the stages as circumstances challenge us in new ways, constantly reencountering and re-creating ourselves, always learning and feeling more than we have learned and felt before. The Seven Stages are never over. They are always just beginning again.

part four

SPECIFICS

chapter 11

KNOWLEDGE AT WORK: SHARPENING OUR MONEY TOOLS

*A workman who wants to do his work well
must first sharpen his tools.*

Confucius

卐卐

*The student said, "What does enlightenment mean?"
And the master replied, "What is the price today
of a pound of rice?"*

a Zen story from thirteenth-century China

RESOURCES: WORKING WITH WHAT WE HAVE

Getting ourselves from here to there—this is the essence of financial planning. Setting goals tells us where we want to go. The next step is determining what we have to work with that can help move us along toward the objectives we have chosen.

What's the difference between inner and outer resources? How can I improve my inner resources?

Generally, outer resources can be stated easily in dollar terms (e.g., my house is worth so much, I make a salary of so many dollars a year) and may be a part of your net worth. (See the next question.) Inner resources refer to those qualities of your being that contribute to or detract from your ability to achieve financial goals. The link between integrity, financial success, and Money Maturity makes inner resources as important as outer resources.

Review the competencies chart from chapter 6. Congratulate yourself on your strengths, but pay particular attention to the areas where you feel stuck and in need of change. Professional help may be useful. In skill areas, for example, such as ignorance about investing, you can sign up for a class at a university extension or an adult education school or take a seminar offered by a financial planning firm. Character-based issues can be addressed with the help of a pastor or counselor or by immersing yourself in the teachings of *The Seven Stages of Money Maturity* around adulthood and awakening (chapters 4 to 10).

If you find yourself resisting this task, keep in mind that resistance usually is rooted in the suffering that arises from the endless dance of Innocence and Pain. The issue here is one of the heart, not the head.

This part of the process may be resolved only as you work through the stage of Understanding in chapter 7.

Net worth sounds like a complicated calculation. What does it involve?

While the details of determining net worth may take some work, it's basically a simple act of adding up the pluses, subtracting the minuses, and seeing what's left over.

TO START, TOTAL YOUR ASSETS.   If you use a personal computer finance program, you can use it to tote up your assets with a relatively small effort. The next solution is a paper-and-pencil approach using the following assets and liabilities lists. Or you can begin working with a financial planner, and let that professional figure your net worth. However, even if you use a computer application or a professional, it's important to know the basics of this determination.

Begin by listing all assets, particularly anything you can turn into cash. Typically, assets include cash, bank accounts, stocks, bonds, mutual funds, annuities, and real estate as well as antiques, collectibles, and other items that are readily marketable. Use the following list as a guideline, adding categories as needed to fit your specific situation.

ASSETS

Cash
   Savings accounts
   Checking accounts
   Other _____
   Subtotal

Securities
   Mutual funds
   Stocks
   Bonds
   Certificates of deposit
   Other _____
   Subtotal

Retirement plans
   Company pension
   401(k)
   Individual Retirement
   Accounts (IRAs)
   Other _____

Life insurance cash value
Real estate, current market
  value
Value of self-employment or
  business you own
Other assets
Automobile(s)
Valuables
Furniture, equipment, personal
  possessions
Other _____
Subtotal

TOTAL ASSETS

ADD UP YOUR LIABILITIES. Liabilities include any and all money you owe on mortgages, credit cards, personal debts, student loans, auto loans, and the like. Use this list as a guideline, again adding categories as needed to fit your situation.

LIABILITIES

Current bills (list)

Loans
   Auto(s)
   Credit cards
   Lines of credit/personal loans
   Education loans
Other _____
Subtotal

Real estate loans
   Home mortgage(s)
   Other _____
Subtotal

Federal and State Taxes

TOTAL LIABILITIES

NOW YOU CAN FIGURE YOUR NET WORTH. It's this simple: Subtract total liabilities from total assets. What remains is net worth. As an example, if you have assets worth $250,000 and liabilities of $150,000, your net worth is $100,000.

In addition to calculating the specific dollar figure of your net worth, this exercise makes you more conscious of what is happening in your financial life. As you do this exercise, note which of your assets are earning a rate of return in the form of interest (e.g., savings accounts, bonds, and certificates of deposit), rents (e.g., rental property), dividends (e.g., stocks and mutual funds), and capital gains (from, e.g., real estate, stocks, and bonds; a capital gain refers to the increase in value of an asset held over time). Be careful to note which liabilities are costing you the most money. Home mortgages, which generally have tax-deductible interest, cost far less after taxes than do credit card balances. Pay attention, too, to any assets you are slowly consuming, such as savings accounts you are drawing down or stock accounts you have borrowed against. This aspect of the net worth calculation is an important facet of Knowledge because it begins to make the connection between your resources and your goals. Assets that are posting a return can help move you toward your goals, while the ones you are consuming move you in the opposite direction.

Now I know my net worth. What does it tell me?

Net worth is important for two reason. First, it tells you in objective dollar terms the tangible resources you have to work with to fulfill your goals. Second, it lets you know just how close you are to enjoying the freedom to follow the path you have chosen.

The whole point of building a larger net worth is to provide the wherewithal for living expenses while you do what you most want to do. Invested in stock, your net worth should return 9 to 12 percent a year, as long as the market follows historical averages. As a rule of thumb, in all but the worst of times, you can deduct 3 percent for inflation and another 3 percent for federal and state taxes and figure on an annual living allowance equaling 3 to 6 percent of your net worth.

For the sake of example, let's say you have $300,000 in stock market investments, whose annual returns should average between $27,000 and $36,000. Of this, about $9,000 will be lost to inflation and another $9,000 will be claimed by taxes. That leaves a yearly living allowance in the $9,000 to $18,000 range. All by itself, that's little to live on, but you may be able to add in some self-employment income, Social Security, job pension benefits, or inheritance, even some home equity principal over time.

To highlight the dramatic effect of an increase in net worth, let's raise the amount in our example to $1 million. Now returns average $90,000 to $120,000, with losses to inflation and taxes equaling $30,000 each. That leaves living-expense funds of $30,000 to $60,000 annually, approximately equal to a moderate income in the economy of the late 1990s.

Remember, though, that the 3 to 6 percent rule is only a guideline. Some asset categories we will be looking at in the following pages have yielded 18 to 22 percent in total returns over many decades. On the other hand, sometimes the market does poorly over extended time frames, and during such periods you would have to take less or risk spending down your net worth.

Budgets have always struck me as somewhat mysterious. What exactly do they consist of?

A budget simply records how much money is coming in and where it is going out. A budget makes no judgment; it's a tool that tells the truth. And once you learn how to use a budget well, it becomes an instrument that helps deliver your lifelong dreams. A budget is a key tool in increasing savings and boosting net worth.

The basics of budgeting are simple, a matter of stating income versus expenses on an annual basis—what you make in a year and what you spend in the same year.

First, list all sources of income, including gifts, rents, interest, wages and salary, income from self-employment, and pensions. And don't simply guess at the numbers. Go back through your deposit records to bank and brokerage accounts. Then do the same for your expenses, which are usually paid in one of three ways: cash, check, or credit card. Investigate and list your expenses over the prior twelve months by each payment method. Cash is the hardest to track, because many of us fail to save receipts or keep a record. If you must, estimate, but don't just guess. Put a small spiral notebook in your pocket, purse, or backpack, and get into the habit of writing down every cash expense over the next few months. Keep this list according to the expense categories you have created, and figure what percentage of your cash you spent on each category. Use this value to determine how to allocate your cash expenses over the past year.

The following categories can serve as a guide; add or delete to fit your circumstances.

BUDGET

Income	Charitable donations
Wages or salary	Clothing and clothing care
Income from self-employment	Auto expenses
Dividends	Auto loan
Interest	Gas & oil
Rent	Repairs
Pensions	Savings for new car
Gifts	Other (list:) _____
Other (list:) _____	Subtotal
Total Income	
	Other transportation
Expenses	Groceries
<u>Check Credit card Cash</u>	Meals out
Rent or mortgage	Services
Utilities	Medical and dental expenses
Telephone	Income taxes
Furniture, fixtures, and repairs	Other (list:) _____
Insurance	
Home	Total Expenses
Car	
Health	Net Savings (Income less
Life	Expenses)
Other _____	
Subtotal	Retirement savings %
Entertainment	Emergency fund %
Vacations	
Childcare	Investing fund %
Education	

Most people who do this exercise experience shock or surprise at the amount they have paid in particular categories. Reactions like "I never knew I dropped so much cash at restaurants" or "No wonder I have a lot of CDs; I spent $2,127 on them last year" are not uncommon.

Typically, too, this exercise underscores your ability or inability to save. The net savings number tells you where you stand. Obviously, the larger this number, in both absolute dollar terms and as a percentage of your income, the more you have to work with toward realizing your goals. If you have no savings at all, you're on a treadmill, running faster and faster toward a future that never gets any closer.

In the last chart, I've divided net savings into three categories. "Retirement savings" include tax-sheltered accounts, such as IRAs, Keoghs, and 401(k)s. The "investing fund" contains money you plan to invest for the long run (generally, five years or longer). Into the "emergency fund" goes money for surprises (such as unexpected house repairs) and for shorter-term needs, such as unemployment or health emergencies.

How can a budget help me reach my life goals?

Working through a budget increases your awareness of the categories you might be able to reduce as a way of increasing net saving—essentially, sacrificing in the short term for what you want in the longer term. When saving became particularly important for me in the 1970s and 1980s, my own budgeting work turned up three categories where I spent much more than I realized: clothes, books, and eating out. When I went through my shelves and closets, I was amazed to discover how many shirts I had yet to wear and books to read. I made a rule for myself never to buy on impulse and to wait for twenty-four hours after a shirt or a novel caught my interest—and be sure I really wanted it—before I bought it. This practice helped cut my expenses and build up my net savings.

When I am taking clients through this exercise, I suggest that they develop two lists of expenses. The first, a realistic budget, is based on current needs and spending patterns. It largely represents your financial situation as it now stands. The next list, a bare-bones budget, strips away the fluff and cuts out the fat. This budget pares expenses down to the minimum that would sustain your household if hard times struck or you decided to save the absolute maximum toward your future goals.

Some clients—those who have the resources to reach their financial goals easily and who, like Susanna Swartz at first, are denying themselves a lifestyle that would make them more creative and productive members of their community—I ask to develop a third and final list. This so-called easy street budget represents the expenses needed to bring more fulfillment into their lives.

EXPENSES	Realistic	Bare Bones	Easy Street
Rent or mortgage			
Utilities			
Telephone			
Furniture, fixtures, and repairs			
Insurance			
Home			
Car			
Health			
Life			
Other			
Subtotal			
Entertainment			
Vacations			
Childcare			
Education			
Charitable donations			
Clothing and clothing care			
Auto expenses			
Auto loan			
Gas & oil			
Repairs			
Savings for new car			
Other (list:)			
Subtotal			
Other transportation			
Groceries			
Meals out			
Services			
Medical and dental			
Income taxes			
Other (list:)			
TOTAL EXPENSES			

Most people think of financial planning as concerned primarily with investments. But, as you work through these budget exercises and understand their implications, you will see why I think of financial planning as driven by goals and based on a budget. No matter how much research and analysis you do on investments, the moment you put your money down you lose control over the external circumstances that will ultimately result in a net gain or a net loss. By contrast, the one element you can control is your spending habits and budget. If you reduce your spending, you instantly become richer and have more choices. If you increase your spending, you automatically become poorer and have fewer choices.

**I've worked very hard at getting my budget down,
yet I'm still making little headway at raising my net worth.
What do you suggest?**

Even without scrimping harder or earning more, there are various ways to increase savings. They require nothing heroic, only attention and discipline.

DON'T SPEND RAISES OR WINDFALLS. If you're making it now, you'll continue to make it if your salary increases or Uncle Joe dies and leaves you a Palm Beach condo in his will. Instead of living it up with any extra money that comes in, add it to your savings. Because of the effect of compounding, saving even a relatively small amount per month can have a major effect on your net worth over time.

PAY THE TAX MAN NO MORE THAN HIS DUE. When I was doing tax returns for a living, I used to surprise clients by holding up a $10 receipt and asking, "What do you see?" They usually answered something about a receipt for office supplies or some other business expense. I'd say, "I see $4.60 in cold cash."

"What do you mean?" clients asked.

"Look," I continued. "You're in the 25 percent federal income tax bracket, you pay a 15 percent self-employment tax, and the state of Massachusetts takes another 6 percent. That adds up to 46 cents of every dollar you earn going to government. For every $10 deduction I can document with a receipt, you save $4.60. That's why, when I see a deductible receipt for $10, I see $4.60 in cash in your pocket— and so should you."

Some clients understood right away. A few objected. "Still, keeping all those receipts is a right royal pain in the whatever," they said.

"If you saw a quarter on the sidewalk, would you stoop to pick it up?" I asked.

"Sure," they answered.

I held up the receipt again. "Every receipt for 55 cents or more is worth at least a quarter to you. Think about it that way, and you'll start keeping receipts."

You also should strategize with a tax-savvy accountant—who can be worth his or her weight in gold—on ways of deducting more of your expenses. Basically, anything you can deduct you are buying at a discount.

Take advantage of tax-deferred retirement plans such as Individual Retirement Accounts (IRAs), Self-Employed Individual Retirement Accounts (SEP-IRAs), and Keogh plans. Money put into these accounts is exempt from taxation until it is withdrawn after retirement. In most of these accounts you save the tax bite on the original contribution and on the account's returns until you begin using the money late in life. A Roth IRA, which offers many advantages over the regular IRA, is taxed on deposits, but no taxes are due when the funds are withdrawn and you are not required to withdraw funds at age seventy and one-half, as with other retirement vehicles.

Unfortunately, our tax codes are extremely complicated. Currently, the Internal Revenue Code totals more than 7 million words—which is about ten times as long as the King James Bible, both Old and New Testaments, and is far more difficult—and much less rewarding—to read. Even more cumbersome are the many volumes of government regulations that purport to "explain" the Internal Revenue Code plus the steady flow of judicial decisions on disputes between the IRS and taxpayers that explain current interpretations of tax regulations. Fortunately, you don't have to know it all by yourself. Instead, hire someone who does.

It is a sad truth that governments discourage the popular development of Knowledge—and encourage the hiring of lawyers—by making laws and regulations far more complicated than necessary. The constant accretion of laws and regulations unwittingly deters people from mastering Knowledge, and thus they work to retard the growth of Vision and Aloha. This is a long-standing issue. James Madison, one of the framers of the U.S. Constitution and an author of *The Federalist Papers*, wrote in 1788, "I believe there are more instances of the abridgement of the freedom of the people by gradual and silent encroachments of those in power than by violent and sudden usurpation." He had a point.

BUY ONLY THE RIGHT INSURANCE, AND NO MORE. With insurance it's easy to be penny-wise and pound-foolish. Protection is important since inadequate insurance may jeopardize all your savings. A good general rule is to insure adequately against disasters and to self-insure small losses—that is, pay them out of your own pocket.

Car insurance is a good example. Being at fault in a major collision with serious injuries is an absolute catastrophe that can cost hundreds of thousands, even millions of dollars. Obviously, you would have to be crazy to get behind the wheel without automobile liability insurance. But there's no reason to shell out the higher premiums to pay for small claims like broken windshields or dented fenders or for towing and car rental while your car is in the shop. Such are the sorts of events against which you can self-insure. Raising your insurance deductibles—the amount you pay before the insurance company takes over—cuts your premiums and will save you considerable money over time.

Americans typically overinsure their lives and underinsure their potential disabilities. If a breadwinner dies, income decreases, but so do expenses. (After all, the dead don't eat, turn on the lights, or go to the dentist.) But if a breadwinner is disabled, by an accident or a sudden medical emergency like a heart attack or stroke, income goes down while expenses, particularly care for the disabled person, are likely to go up.

Insurance is a thorny and difficult budgetary area to address. Many of us find it emotionally difficult to consider scenarios of disease, disaster, and other untoward events and figure out how they would affect our households. It adds insult to injury that we don't know whom to talk to about insurance except insurance salespeople. Since they have a built-in conflict of interest, their trustworthiness is open to question. You never know whether an insurance salesperson's recommendations are professional advice or a sales pitch. As a result, many of us avoid salespeople and overlook necessary insurance expenses in our budgets.

Together with researching insurance options through *Consumer Reports* and other consumer and personal finance periodicals (see the appendix for a list of recommended titles), hire a financial-planning professional who works on an hourly basis and doesn't sell insurance. (Information on locating such professionals is discussed later in this chapter, starting on page 355.) He or she can help guide you through the process of analyzing your situation, determining your insurance needs, and buying the most suitable policies.

Down with credit card debt. Many people have no idea how much money is draining away through their credit cards. When I first began teaching my twelve-years-at-12-percent class, one of my students, who was also a tax client, announced proudly that she had indeed socked away 12 percent of her income in an investment plan. I felt immensely pleased at her success—until I did her tax return. There I discovered that she hadn't really saved the money at all. She had instead charged thousands of dollars of basic expenses and was paying interest to boot.

Because it must be paid off with what could have been future savings, credit card debt can be very costly. Unless the item charged is a business expense, the interest can't be deducted. Even then, the sometimes extraordinarily high interest charges—rates in the 18 to 20 percent range are still not uncommon—make credit cards unpalatable sources of funds. If you pay a third of your income in taxes each year, you will have to earn 30 percent on your investments in order to have 20 percent left over at such high rates.

If you have debts already or if you have to borrow money for an unavoidable need like medical expenses or tuition, it is better to use a second mortgage on your home borrowed either as a lump sum or through an equity line of credit. Interest rates are usually much lower. Also, under current federal income tax rules, home mortgage interest is generally deductible, which lowers the effective interest rate further.

INVESTMENT: GROWING MONEY

What does rate of return mean?

An investment's rate of return includes income from interest and dividends as well as any increase or decrease in the asset's principal value. Suppose, for example, that you own a mutual fund that generates $1,000 a year in dividends. Suppose, too, that stock prices are currently rising, so that over the next year the market value of the mutual fund rises 10 percent. The yearly total return on the fund would include both the $1,000 in dividends and the 10 percent increase in the asset's value.

It is the total rate of return on an investment, as opposed to its so-called yield or income—such as rent in the case of real estate or dividends from stocks—that interests us most in choosing investments. Total rate of return allows us to gauge how well an investment is doing and what effect it is having on our net worth.

Does a high rate of return really make that much difference? And does a higher rate of return affect my savings substantially?

Absolutely—and this effect becomes even more pronounced over time owing to the power of compounding. Say you invest $100 at a 10 percent annual total return. At the end of the year you have $110. Instead of taking the money out, you leave it in the investment. At the end of the second year you have $121; the third, $133.10; the fourth, $146.41; the fifth, $160.71. In five years at 10 percent annual return the money has grown a total of not 50 percent but almost 61 percent. That's the power of compounding.

Over the long term compounding is extremely productive. If a one-time investment of $2,000 at an average annual return of 11 percent is made when a baby is born, that individual can retire at age 65 with a net worth of $1,766,134—a very nice nest egg to live on.

The effect is dramatic. The following graph relates compounding and time to show how great a difference a higher rate of return makes over time.

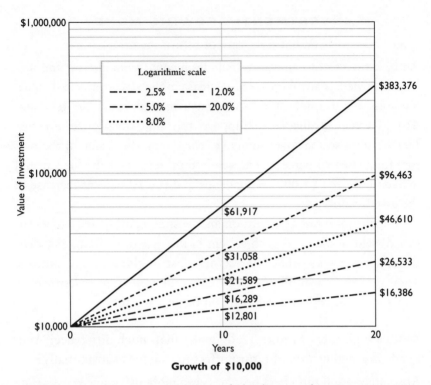

Growth of $10,000

If you put the money in a mix of checking and savings accounts, it will generate perhaps 2.5 percent per year. In ten years—if you withdraw nothing—you'll have $12,801, and in twenty years, $16,386. What happens if, instead of low-yielding bank accounts, you put the $10,000 in asset categories with much higher returns? Should your investments return an average of 20 percent annually, you will have $61,917 in ten years and an astonishing $383,376 in twenty. The difference between total return rates of 2.5 percent and 20 percent at ten and twenty years is $49,116 and $366,990.

I don't have a lump sum available for investing, just a little money I try to save every year in an IRA. Does this approach do me any good?

Yes, it does—particularly if you begin saving early in life. Compounding is so powerful at increasing resources that an early start can make a huge difference. If a twenty-two-year-old invests just $2,000 a year at 12 percent total annual return for six years, then leaves the money until retirement at age sixty-five, he or she will have

$1.2 million. But if the same individual puts off investing until age twenty-eight, it will take an annual investment of $2,000 for the next thirty-seven years to reach the same $1.2 million at age sixty-five. Six years of compounding makes that much difference.

Even if you don't have a lump sum to begin an investment program, regular savings can still build up impressively. Say you put $2,000 in a tax-free Individual Retirement Account (IRA) every year.

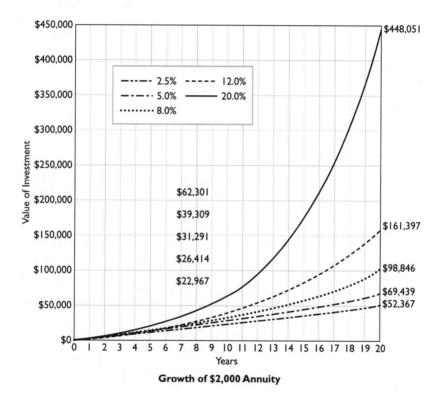

Growth of $2,000 Annuity

In ten years at 2.5 percent, you'll have $22,967, and in twenty years, $52,367. Again, raising the total rate of return to 20 percent makes a huge difference. In ten years you'll have $62,301—or $39,334 more—and in twenty years, $448,051—or $395,684 more.

The point made by these hypothetical calculations is obvious. If you have a long time frame over which to invest—for example, if you are looking ahead to retirement in twenty or thirty years—it is foolish to go for anything less than a high rate of return.

Given that high rates of return are valuable, how can I get them?

One guide is the historical record posted by different classes of investment assets. The next table lists the long-term returns of various asset types for much of the twentieth century. Look first at the column listing annual total return.

Asset Categories:
Long-Term Returns and Risks

	Asset Class	Annual Total Return	Standard Deviation (Risk)
Stocks	S&P 500	12.6%	16.6
	Small Stocks	14.8%	26.1
	U.S. Small-Cap Value Stocks	19.8%	32.4
	Japanese Stocks	15.5%	35.1
	Emerging-Market Stocks	16.3%	30.5
	Venture Capital	16.6%	33.7
Bonds	Treasury Bills	4.7%	3.2
	U.S. Long Treasury Bonds	5.3%	10.4
	U.S. Intermediate Bonds	5.7%	6.4
	Corporate Bonds	5.7%	10.0
Collectibles	Gold	5.1%	26.2
	Silver	4.7%	54.2
	Art	8.5%	15.0
Real Estate	Residential Housing (including rents)	7.1%	4.1
	Farmland (including crops)	10.0%	7.2
	Commercial Real Estate (including rents)	7.3%	5.6

Source: Morgan Stanley and Dimensional Fund Advisors. This table covers the period 1945 to 1996 for all categories except emerging-market stocks (1950–1996), commercial real estate (1960–1996), U.S. small-cap value stocks (1926–1996), and art and gold (1945–1991).

There is an obvious conclusion to be drawn from the data on total return: Gaining the highest available return means investing in stocks. Every asset category that returns over 10 percent annually is an equity, some kind of ownership in a company in the form of stock. The highest-returning stocks are those held in the smallest companies with high book-to-market ratios (so-called small-cap value stocks), a concept to be explained further in this chapter.

After stocks, the second best investment returns come from real estate. That's true, however, only if rental income or crop value is included. Simply buying houses or accumulating idle farmland yields only a mediocre return.

The biggest surprise in this table is the low return on bonds, both government and corporate. Unlike stocks, which represent ownership (or equity) in a company, bonds represent loans investors make to governments or corporations. Essentially, bonds are debts. On average over the past fifty years, bonds have paid only about 1 percent more than the rate of inflation, while the blue-chip stocks represented by the Standard & Poor's 500 Index (S&P 500) run about 7 percent better than inflation. That gives stocks a sevenfold advantage over bonds. Bonds, however, do provide investment protection against the risks of deflation—which lately has been threatening large portions of the world economy—disinflation, and depression, and they can have an important place in a well-diversified portfolio.

Why do stocks do better over time than real estate or bonds?

That's a good question. Is the historical superiority of stocks over bonds and real estate a random effect, the result of chance? Or does it reveal something inherent in the nature of these different investments?

The difference has to do with the connection between the investment and the storehouse of human creativity embodied in commercial enterprises. When we invest in commercial real estate, we house that creativity. When we invest in bonds, we lend it money. But when we put our savings into stocks, we buy that creativity. Stock is a form of ownership in the most productive, most creative part of the economy.

Through Knowledge we see that the stock market is a barometer of human creativity. After all, it has given us electricity, light bulbs, automobiles, refrigerators, telephones, personal computers, the Internet, penicillin, arthroscopic surgery, and Bach's Brandenburg concerti on CD, among millions of other benefits. In essence, stocks return more because they produce more.

Stocks have the best record of return. But aren't they risky?

You're right—all investments entail some degree of risk. Risk, you will remember, represents the uncertainty around a given asset's expected total rate of return. The table on page 332 uses a statistical measure of risk called standard deviation—the higher the standard deviation, the greater the degree of variation in the investment's return over time. Treasury bills, or T-bills, which are government bonds with the shortest repayment term, have the lowest risk of all the assets listed here, a mere 3.2. This safety from risk is what makes T-bills attractive as an investment. They are a good place to put money that simply cannot be risked or that will be needed within a few months or years—for example, money you are saving toward the down payment on a house. There's another thing to note about bonds. Even though longer-term bonds, such as corporate bonds and U.S. government bonds, return only slightly more than T-bills, they carry two to three times the risk. Market conditions affecting the direction of interest rates can have a strong effect on the value of longer-term bonds, yet they affect T-bills only a little. Unless you are confident that interest rates are going to be moving downward, which will push the value of longer-term bonds up, you should buy shorter-term bonds and avoid the risk.

Risk measurement also explains the appeal of real estate. Residential housing is only slightly more risky than T-bills—a standard deviation of 4.1—but the rate of return is substantially higher—7.1 percent compared to 4.7 percent. Thus, for taking only a little more risk, you can make more than half again as much in total return.

At the other end of the scale, risk explains the powerful gambler's appeal of gold and silver. Both precious metals have long-term rates of return in the same low range as bonds, but their risk level is astronomical by comparison—which means that sometimes they are big losers, sometimes big winners. If you bet right, you can walk away with a bundle. Bet wrong, though, and you'll lose your shirt.

The stock market is riskier than other kinds of investment. Is there any way of gauging how likely I am to lose and how much the loss could be?

Again, we can use historical information to find the answer. The next chart shows information on gains and losses in the bellwether Standard and Poor's 500 (S&P 500) stock market index over the period 1926 to 1996.

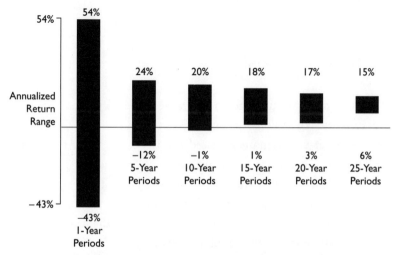

How the risk on common stock investments is reduced by lengthening your investment period. Common stock returns 1926–1996

In a single year, stocks have made as much as 54 percent and lost up to 43 percent. Yet as the time period of the investment lengthens, the amount of loss per year drops substantially. For anyone holding the investment for twenty-five years, maximum annual return has been 15 percent and the minimum 6 percent. At such a long time horizon there is no loss.

The next table explores your chance of losing or gaining within certain ranges over time. It also shows how holding on to stocks for longer and longer periods increases the likelihood of attractive returns.

What Are the Odds?

Making or Losing Money in Stocks by Holding Period

If you hold	Your chance of losing money	Your chance of making 0–10% per year	Your chance of making 10–20% per year	Your chance of making 20%+ per year
1 year	26%	18%	20%	37%
3 years	14%	28%	39%	19%
5 years	10%	31%	49%	10%
10 years	4%	42%	53%	1%
20 years	0%	37%	63%	0%

Source: *Newsweek*, November 10, 1997, p. 38.

The most likely occurrence on this table is the 63 percent chance—nearly two out of three—of making between 10 and 20 percent annual return if you remain invested for twenty years. At that time frame, in fact, the chance of losing money is a reassuring zero. But look what happens if you stay in the market for only one year. Then your chances of losing money are a little over one out of four. Clearly, holding on during short-term losses has paid off in the long run in the form of a positive if not spectacular return.

It can happen that investing in the stock market will produce a huge one-year loss. The following chart, which we saw first in chapter 6, shows the ups and downs in stocks from 1789 to 1997.

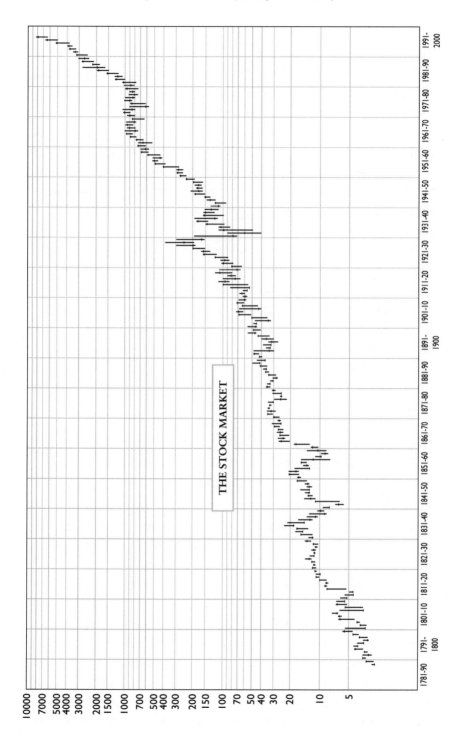

THE STOCK MARKET

As you can see from this graph, huge one-year losses are rare. They were most common and extreme in the period between 1929 and 1942, the era of the Great Depression. The historical conditions that led to these massive swings in value are not present in America today. Even if they were, a similar collapse in economic activity or the stock market is unlikely. Awareness of the policy blunders made in those years led to regulatory reform for the U.S. stock market and changes in securities law that eliminated many of the mechanisms contributing to such volatility. It is to be hoped that the current crisis in Asia and other emerging markets will lead to similar kinds of regulatory reform.

In the stock market you should expect one losing year in every four or five. However, even over a five-year period, there is a 10 percent chance of a loss. Of course, if this level of risk daunts you, you can load up on T-bills until your comfort level for your whole portfolio (stocks plus Treasuries) rises enough for you to trust your riskier investments. But before you do that, it pays to learn something about risk and to understand an approach to investing based on a model of stock market behavior that won the Nobel Prize for economics in 1990.

You said in chapter 6 that a Nobel prize–winning theory of stock market behavior can serve as an investment guide. Would you explain these ideas?

Merton Miller, Harry Markowitz, and William Sharpe, who are the only economists ever to win a Nobel Prize for work on stock market behavior, developed a fascinating model called the efficient market theory. Stated crudely and superficially, the theory doesn't sound efficient at all. It says that if you tack the stock listings of today's *Wall Street Journal* on your kitchen wall, throw darts at it, and then buy the stocks you hit, you will do just as well as if you had spent hundreds of hours analyzing annual reports and other financial statements to come up with a list of winning stocks. It sounds amazing that an essentially random process of selection can be just as successful as one guided by diligence and analysis. It is even more amazing that an idea so seemingly absurd would have won the Nobel Prize, the world's highest award for scientific achievement.

In truth, however, the theory underlying Miller, Markowitz, and Sharpe's work is remarkable and profound. Their model reflects an understanding of how markets work as information systems.

Let's assume that you're my client and I've been helping you put together your investment program. As you're eating breakfast, you read the business pages of your daily newspaper and see a report that Ford Motor Company appears likely to announce a loss of $1 billion in the financial quarter just ending. This poses a real concern to you because you're holding several thousand dollars' worth of Ford stock. Immediately you pick up the phone, give me a call, and say, "George, you've got to sell my Ford holdings today. The paper says they're going to take a big hit."

My response may surprise you. "It probably won't do you any good," I say. "It's too late. The news has been out for at least a few hours, and practically everybody has already heard about it. The price for Ford stock right this minute already reflects the likelihood of this loss. Truth is, if industry analysts last week thought Ford was going to lose $2 billion, the stock may actually go up because the company's loss looks to be less than expected."

The theory of the efficient market is an elegant statement of this reality. As news and other information enter the stock market, the market immediately adjusts prices to reflect the new data. You yourself cannot beat the market; in fact, nobody can. It's simply too fast and too accurate. Most studies suggest that you can't accurately anticipate significant moves in the market, and you won't be able to find an indicator of current value more accurate than price.

To the extent that the market is a sophisticated data- and information-crunching machine, the efficient market theory demands our respect. And if there are inefficiencies in the market—blind spots where information doesn't penetrate and where extremely astute people can make money by knowing something nobody else does—we are going to have to be extremely sophisticated to find and exploit them. In fact, given the computerized sophistication of today's money managers, the odds are overwhelming that no individual investor on a regular basis can get out in front of stock price movements.

The efficient market theory says that neither you nor I can beat the market—but we can join it. If our investment portfolio consists of just one stock, that stock can go bankrupt and our portfolio value will shrink to zero. Adding a second stock to the portfolio lowers the portfolio's volatility. Moreover, if we buy a whole portfolio of stocks and hold on to it for a long period of time, our trading costs (i.e., commission on each stock-buying or -selling transaction) are minimized, and we won't have to pay capital gains taxes on stocks sold. In fact, if we were to die with this portfolio intact, our heirs get a step up in basis, which means they never have to pay capital gains taxes on the portfolio. Maybe the efficient market theory isn't so dumb after all.

For those of you offended at the thought that the market is smarter than you are, take heart. The efficient market theory isn't the final word. It is more like the first word, the foundation to be considered carefully when you are constructing an investment portfolio. Newer theories built on the model of market efficiency suggest we can beat the market's overall performance by a substantial margin by investing in certain categories of stock.

But which stocks should I buy? And how is risk in stocks related to return?

Let's start with the relationship of risk and return. The rule of thumb on risk parallels the guiding principle of bodybuilding: no pain, no gain. The higher the potential return of an investment, the more volatility one would expect in its return. Recently, however, this connection has been questioned by economist Eugene Fama of the University of Chicago, perhaps one of the most brilliant and respected experts on stock market behavior.

Fama began his work because of a study done by William Sharpe, one of the Nobel prize winners for the efficient market theory. Sharpe took a hard mathematical look at the relationship between risk and rate of return and came up with a correlation of about 70 percent between them. That is, crudely speaking, seven times out of ten, the higher the rate of return, the higher the risk.

Eugene Fama thought that a 70 percent correlation was remarkably low. After all, common sense tells us that the connection should be very close to 100 percent. If the relationship is markedly less certain than that, then there must be something else going on in the market other than a simple connection between high return and high risk.

Teaming up with Ken French, now a professor of economics at Yale, Fama rigorously analyzed stock market behavior from 1964 through 1992. Instead of a straightforward connection between risk and return, Fama and French found that the value of stocks varies with three factors. They vastly increased the accuracy of Sharpe's original model, developing a system that accounted for 95 percent, rather than 70 percent, of the stock market's outcome.

The first of the three factors is exposure to the market. As an investor, you expect a higher return over time for entering the stock market, one significantly higher than the safe, low-risk return of a Treasury bill, for example. Say a stock makes 11 percent in a year when T-bills are paying 5 percent. The equity premium in this instance is 6 percent, and it compensates stock owners for bearing the extra risk of the stock compared to a T-bill. Stocks usually pay an equity premium, but not always. Some years they decline in value. So investors demand an equity premium over time to compensate for the substantially higher short-term risk they are assuming.

The second factor Fama and French uncovered is the size of the company. Small companies and large companies behave differently in the stock market. On average, small company stocks fluctuate more and produce higher returns than large company equities. Since small companies don't have the commanding market shares or deep pockets of large companies, they are more vulnerable to economic hard times, technological shock waves, and industry reversals. Investors in small company stocks require a higher rate of return to compensate them for assuming the higher risk of these equities.

The third factor, the book-to-market ratio, was a surprise. Book-to-market ratio is a relatively complex calculation that involves comparing the accounting value of a company (the asset value of the firm minus its liabilities, divided by the number of its shares of stock outstanding) to the company's value on the market (how much a buyer in the stock market would pay for a share). If the stock has a high book-to-market ratio—that is, if the market value of the company is low compared to its book value—the stock is called a value stock. (Value stocks are also often defined as having low price-to-earnings ratios, low price-to-sales ratios, or high dividend yields. Fama and French, however, found the book-to-market ratio to be the most telling about stock market behavior.) Value stocks usually are companies that have fallen on hard times and aren't expected to do well in the near future. If the situation is reversed and the company's earnings have been growing rapidly, the equity is called a growth stock. Many growth stocks are established companies that have discovered new, rapidly expanding markets for their products. Growth stocks also are found with new products in fast-emerging economic sectors, which these days are represented by information systems, Internet applications, and biotechnology, for example.

It was here, in the comparison of value stocks to growth stocks, that Fama and French made their most astounding finding. They discovered that, over the long term, value stocks delivered a substantially greater rate of return than growth stock, without substantially increasing volatility.

This discovery turned heads throughout the ranks of academia and professional money management. In terms of the three-factor model, the relationship between market exposure and return was hardly surprising, nor was it earth-shaking that small companies did better than large companies over time. The experience of most investors supports these concepts. The big shock came with the understanding that value stocks outperformed growth stocks by a huge margin—even though they often offered a lower degree of risk as measured by standard deviation. If Fama and French were right, you could boost your return and lower your risk by investing in value stocks rather than growth.

Fama and French's original study covered only twenty-nine years of the United States stock market, a small slice of the global economic pie, raising concern that perhaps their findings have limited applicability. Further analysis, though, has shown that Fama and French have uncovered something that holds true for other periods and places as well. Research into the U.S. stock market back into the 1920s finds the same three-factor correlation. Analysis of the foreign markets of Europe, Japan, and the emerging nations has come up with similar findings. If we can count on any stock market strategy to deliver high returns, the research of Fama and French is a likely candidate.

The theory says that a value-oriented investment strategy should return the most of any approach to the stock market. Does this hold up in practice?

This next chart shows how well a value-oriented approach has worked in the stock market's real world for the thirty-three years from January 1964 through December 1996.

Investment Dimensions: Size of Company and Financial Strength

Historical Returns
January 1964–December 1996

U.S. Large Cap Stocks   U.S. Small Cap Stocks

	Large Value Strategy	S&P 500 Index	Large Growth Strategy	Small Value Strategy	CRSP 6-10 Index	Small Growth Strategy
Annualized Compound Return (%)	14.85	11.27	10.29	18.09	13.38	12.32
Annual Standard Deviation	17.69	15.71	17.09	24.27	25.42	27.50

Growth Strategies: Jan. 1964-Present: Data courtesy Fama-French, includes hold ranges and estimated trading costs.
Value Strategies: Jan. 1964-Mar. 1993: Data courtesy Fama-French, includes hold ranges and estimated trading costs; large value excludes utilities.
                   Apr. 1993-Present: Dimensional's Live Value Portfolios net of all fees.
                   Source: Dimensional Fund Advisors, Inc.

For both large and small companies, a value-oriented strategy out-produced a growth strategy: 14.85 percent versus 10.29 percent with large companies, 18.09 percent versus 12.32 percent with small. If we look at real returns—that is, the rate of return with inflation sub-tracted—the value strategy delivers nearly twice as much as the growth approach. And the volatility of the value strategy is almost the same as the growth strategy's—a standard deviation of 17.69 com-pared to 17.09—for large companies, and actually smaller—24.27 compared to 27.50—for small ones. Although small stocks are clearly riskier than large, the annual rate of return of 18.09 percent with a small-company value strategy is strikingly higher than the 11.27 per-cent of the S&P 500 over the same time period.

Although the Fama-French theory is no more the last word on stock market behavior than was the efficient market theory, it deserves the serious attention of anyone who wants to invest toward the goal of realizing his or her own dream of freedom.

Do any other asset categories produce as well as domestic value stocks?

The next table highlights four other stock categories with long-term returns in excess of 18 percent per year.

Four More High-Returning Categories

stock category	return	years
international value	20.4%	1975–1996
international small company	21.5%	1975–1996
U.S., PSR < 1.0, high relative strength	18.14%	1954–1994
U.S., PSR < 1.5, high relative strength, 5 years earnings growth	18.22%	1954–1994

Source: Dimensional Fund Advisors and O'Shaughnessy/Compustat

The first two categories in the table were uncovered as a result of research undertaken to examine the validity of the Fama-French approach in markets outside the United States. The second pair came from research by James P. O'Shaughnessy using Standard & Poor's Compustat, the most complete database of American stock market information over the past forty years.

The abbreviation PSR in the second two categories refers to the price-to-sales ratio. A low PSR is, like a high book-to-market ratio, a sign of a value stock. The PSR is determined by dividing the market value of a company's stock by its annual sales. The other description in the second two categories, "high relative strength," means that the stock was among the best performers in the stock market over the prior year. High relative strength combined with five years of earnings growth generally indicates a growth stock. Thus O'Shaughnessy has contributed a way of combining growth and value criteria that have produced outstanding stock market returns.

While the international categories in the table were derived from Fama and French's research, some money managers and academic researchers are now exploring whether O'Shaughnessy's categories have as profound an implication for investing as do Fama and French's.

The returns you highlight are terrific, but I'm still nervous about risk. Are there measures I can take to lower the chance of losing money?

A portfolio of investments aiming at the highest possible return often carries a significant amount of risk, but different assets can be combined in such a way that the risk of the portfolio is lowered without sacrificing return. This is accomplished through asset categories that have a low correlation with each other. Correlation measures the extent to which two sets of data move in tandem. Two asset classes can have the same expected return, but, if they have a low correlation with each other, they will respond differently to the forces that move the market. The good news is that, over time, the same high return will be achieved for the combination of assets as each asset would have attained on its own, but with much less short-term volatility. Thus, while an asset may be considered risky all by itself, it actually can be used in conjunction with other assets to reduce the risk of a portfolio. The next chart will help you visualize how this works.

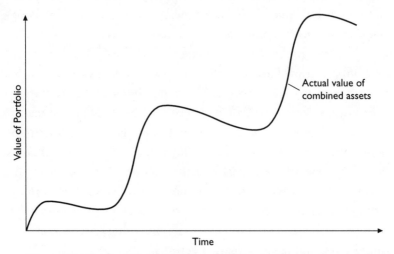

Correlation. Theoretical volatility of a portfolio of two asset classes with high historic annualized returns and perfect correlation

This graph represents the fortunes over time of two hypothetical asset categories that perform exactly the same way. When the one falls in market value, the other does too; when the first rises in market value, the other follows behind. These two asset categories are said to be perfectly positively correlated (+1.0), like sunrise and daylight. Were you to mix these asset categories together as a diversification strategy, you would gain nothing in risk protection.

This next chart shows the varying fortunes of two asset classes that behave in precisely the opposite way.

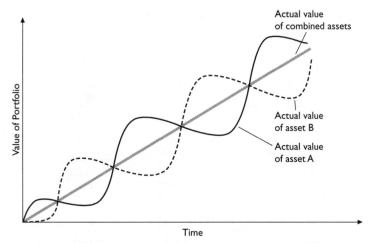

Correlation. Theoretical volatility of a portfolio of two asset classes with high historic annualized returns and negative correlation

The correlation in this case is perfectly negatively correlated (–1.0)—when one asset category loses value, the other gains. Diversification into these two categories offers exceptional risk reduction. Say both categories returned an average of 18 percent annually. If you divided your investment equally between the two classes, the whole portfolio would earn at a steady rate no matter which way the market moved. This portfolio would carry no risk at all.

That's the theory. Reality is a bit trickier since portfolios are never so perfectly negatively correlated. But the basic point holds—the more you split your investments among asset categories with less than perfect correlations, the more you can reduce your risk, even when the market is volatile.

This is precisely the reason why many investors put some of their portfolio into stocks, some into bonds, and some into certificates of deposit and money market funds. Typically, these categories move with low relative correlation. Mixing bonds and cash with stocks provides a measure of protection against a downturn and gives a portfolio earning power in case the market stagnates or slips.

Because of the returns, I'd like to invest principally in stocks. Will buying different kinds of stocks afford any protection against risk?

Diversifying into different kinds of equities is a wise, risk-reducing move. The following chart compares rates of return among three categories of stocks—U.S. small-company equities, the S&P 500 index, and the international stocks in the Europe, Australia, Far East Index (EAFE).

5-year periods beginning	US Small	S&P 500 INDEX	EAFE ($) INDEX
1/69	−10.1	2.0	7.4
1/70	−15.4	−2.3	1.6
1/71	−3.1	3.2	10.6
1/72	1.7	4.9	5.5
1/73	0.7	−0.2	2.6
1/74	23.3	4.3	12.2
1/75	41.7	14.8	19.3
1/76	37.4	13.9	17.1
1/77	25.8	8.1	16.0
1/78	26.1	14.0	11.7
1/79	28.7	17.3	10.1
1/80	18.2	14.8	10.4
1/81	15.1	14.7	15.6
1/82	17.3	19.9	28.8
1/83	9.5	16.5	34.9
1/84	6.7	15.4	35.8
1/85	10.3	20.4	36.5
1/86	0.6	13.1	18.4
1/87	6.9	15.4	9.0
1/88	13,6	15.9	1.7
1/89	13.3	14.5	2.3
1/90	11.8	8.7	1.8
1/91	24.5	16.6	9.7
1/92	19.5	15.2	8.5
# of times on top	11	3	10

Returns: 5-year overlapping returns, annualized
Jan. 1969 – Dec. 1996

The shading indicates the particular five-year periods when the performance of a particular asset category led the other two. As you can see, the range of returns in each category is very wide. The three categories have traded the lead many times. It is practically impossible to know which group is poised for the best performance at any given time and which is about to fall, but it is a simple matter to divide holdings among all three and benefit from the rise in each one, while reducing the risk of doing poorly by holding only the category that is doing worst.

There is clearly a benefit to diversifying among asset categories. For example, mixing U.S. and international stocks, which lack perfect correlation, can both lower risk and raise rate of return. The next chart graphs these two categories for the years 1969 to 1996.

The rate of return on foreign stocks (EAFE) was higher than

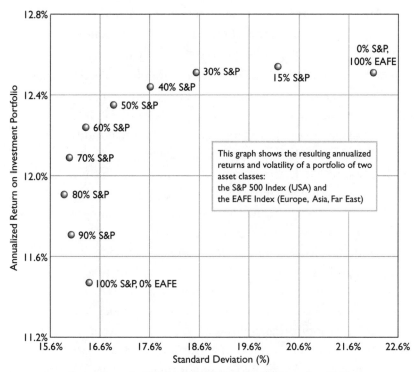

Return vs. volatility: January 1969 through December 1996

United States equities (S&P 500) during most of this period, but the risk and volatility in domestic issues was lower. Combining the two creates a substantial advantage. The risk level of an all-domestic portfolio was the same as one with 40 percent foreign and 60 percent domestic, but the rate of return went from 11.5 percent to 12.3 percent, a significant boost for no added risk. The lowest possible risk, as measured by standard deviation, came from a mix of 20 percent international and 80 percent domestic. The annualized rate of return at 11.9 percent was still more than half a percentage point higher than the all–U.S. portfolio.

While there is no absolute assurance that the correlations between asset categories for the past thirty or forty years will hold true for the next thirty or forty, we can be sure that asset categories poorly correlated with each other will provide significant risk-reducing benefits for investors.

Are there other ways I can increase the rate of return on my investments? How should I structure a mutual fund portfolio to accomplish this?

The best way is to reduce costs. Investing entails two major expenses: trading costs and taxes. Obviously, cutting both types of costs will help your money grow faster. Trading costs can be reduced or eliminated by using discount brokers and no-load mutual funds, a topic to be discussed later. Cutting taxes takes planning.

The best way to keep your tax bill as low as possible is to keep tax-efficient mutual funds—those that have little turnover in portfolio and pay little in the way of dividend and interest income—outside your retirement accounts and put more actively traded funds, with higher interest and dividend income, inside retirement accounts, such as IRAs, Keoghs, SEP-IRAs, and 401(k)s. The tax-efficient funds I use most often are called index funds. They deliver most precisely the advantages the efficient market theory and the three-factor model describe. Index funds try to capture the returns of a particular asset category—or index—by buying a representative portion of all the stocks in that index. Index funds deliver two other advantages besides tax efficiency. Their performance tends to be in the top 25 percent of all mutual funds over any ten-year period, and they charge by far the lowest fees of any class of mutual funds—which also helps increase returns to you.

MUTUAL FUNDS, BROKERS AND ADVISORS, AND THE FINANCIAL-SERVICES CONSUMER MOVEMENT

Is it best for me to invest on my own? Or should I seek professional help?

There's no right answer. Some people want to learn everything they can about investing and manage their own money. The activity gives them a sense of satisfaction and pleasure. Other people want to know something about investing, but they also want the expertise of a specialist to rely on. To yet other people, learning the nuts and bolts of money is pure pain. They want to turn it all over to somebody else.

It's important to know where you are in Money Maturity so you can make the choice that's best for you.

Getting professional help interests me. What are my choices?

For a long time, Americans looking for help with investing turned to full-service brokerage firms like Merrill Lynch, Prudential, Paine Webber, and Dean Witter. The brokers working for these companies generally have earned their livings from commissions on the stocks, bonds, limited partnerships, annuities, and mutual funds they sell. Although they are often very professional and knowledgeable about their products, many brokers, even at the best firms, lack the breadth of expertise to tailor investments to clients' complex needs. In investing, one size doesn't fit all. On top of that, brokers are caught in an inevitable conflict of interest. Although they give financial advice, they are paid only if they sell investment products. This arrangement can lead brokers to recommend financial products that are unsuited to particular clients but pay substantial commissions. In addition, many clients find themselves unwilling to share their own painful vulnerabilities around money with someone who is trying to make a sale. That unwillingness, and growing concern about conflicts of interest, spawned a consumer movement in the financial services industry.

The key to the consumer movement, which has revolutionized the investment industry, has been the growth of the financial-planning profession. Earning the professional designation of certified financial planner (CFP) requires an educational program in insurance, investments, tax planning, retirement planning, and estate planning with a series of five three-hour tests followed by a comprehensive examination that lasts a day and a half. By contrast, brokers can become qualified by taking one course and passing one exam. A prescribed amount of work experience is also part of earning the CFP, and significant continuing education is required to maintain certification.

Equally important, CFPs like myself are aware of the conflict of interest involved in selling investments. More and more of us have turned away from commissions and make our livings by charging a fee for our advice, much like an attorney or an accountant.

Interestingly, this shift parallels what happened in the medical profession about a century ago. Many people these days consider financial advisors to be slick snake-oil salesmen with no integrity, while they consider doctors to be professionals with integrity. It wasn't always this way. In the nineteenth century physicians charged no fees; instead, they made their money by selling medicines. It was, in fact, doctors' questionable business practices that gave us the phrase "snake-oil salesman" in all its meaning. The economics of the profession made doctors untrustworthy, since it was in their self-interest to sell unneeded nostrums to perfectly healthy people. When the medical profession reformed itself around the turn of the century, one of the key changes was the institution of fee-for-service practice in place of medicine merchandising. Separating sales work from professional advice transformed medicine.

Fee-only financial planners are following the same path. The fee-only planner essentially sells his or her expertise, usually on an hourly basis or for a fixed percentage of assets under management.

The National Association of Personal Financial Advisors (NAPFA) has taken a visionary role in the financial-planning movement by being the professional organization whose membership comprises fee-only (no-commission) financial planners. NAPFA and the financial planning profession in general have led the consumer movement by educating both clients and the community at large in ways of investing, often at a fraction of the fees charged by full-service brokerages, as well as in the enormous benefits broad-based financial planning brings to individual investment decisions. NAPFA continues to provide leadership in the profession, recently requiring, for example, that its CFPs take counseling classes in order to maintain NAPFA membership.

Ultimately, the issue is not financial planner versus broker or fee-only versus commission. It is clear that the financial services industry is moving inexorably away from commissions toward fees. In the meantime, the critical questions each individual looking for professional help must answer concern an advisor's integrity and his or her expertise.

I'm not sure I want a personal financial advisor. Is there some other way the consumer movement can help me?

The consumer movement in the financial services industry has three legs: financial planners, discount brokers, and mutual funds. At the movement's purest, the planners are fee-only and the mutual funds are no-load (i.e., no commission). If you don't want a financial advisor, combining discount brokers with no-load mutual funds is definitely the way to go.

A mutual fund is basically an investment company that invests your money—and the money of many other investors—generally in a diversified manner. The majority of mutual funds invest primarily in stocks, but you can choose from thousands of bond and money market funds too. A major advantage of mutual funds is the public availability of data on their performance over the years and detailed information on investment philosophy and style.

When I first came into the profession in the 1970s, most mutual funds carried an 8.5 percent load. That is, 8.5¢ of every $1 that you invested went to pay sales commissions to the mutual fund company, the brokerage house, and the broker. Slowly more and more investment companies began offering no-load funds, ones that carried no fee at all. Originally no-load funds were shunned by the full-service brokerages because they couldn't make any money from them. Then, in the 1980s, discount broker Charles Schwab—one of the visionaries of the consumer movement—got the idea of offering a long list of no-load funds, charging only a fraction of a percentage point to buy them, and reporting portfolio results to clients on one convenient statement. For the first time, an individual consumer—you or I, the typical small- to medium-size investor—could review his or her mutual funds in one report every month and monitor their performance, instead of having to juggle different reports from different investment houses at different time intervals. This ease and power made Schwab a strong market for no-load mutual funds and pulled business away from full-service brokerages. As Schwab's marketplace power grew, he talked the mutual fund companies into paying the transaction fee, taking that burden off individuals. This allowed Schwab to offer consumers a no-commission investment service under its "one-source" program, a plan that has since been copied by many other brokerage houses. Then Schwab went the next step by setting up a division that does nothing but cater to the needs of financial professionals, many of whom are fee-only advisors.

Schwab's success set off a stampede of imitators, and other discount brokerage houses entered the marketplace. The trend is so strong that even full-service companies are now offering no-load mutual funds and fee-based financial planning. It is worth your while to investigate the services of a number of these brokerage houses before settling on one. The potential for conflicts of interest, however, remains in any firm that makes substantial income from commissions and offers in-house products.

The effects of the consumer movement have been extraordinary. Market pressure has forced mutual fund loads down, so that the average fully loaded fund now charges only 5 percent instead of the old 8.5 percent. Even more important for an advisorless consumer are the thousands of no-load mutual funds now available. Middle-class Americans can hire some of the best money managers on the face of the Earth via mutual funds and profit from their expertise in the stock and bond markets. They also can buy and sell stocks directly through discount brokerage houses for transaction costs that are a fraction of what the full-service brokerage houses charge. And, with the knowledge explosion of the information age, consumers can find a wealth of excellent investment data at the public library, on the newsstand magazine rack, or through the Internet. A list of information resources is provided in the closing pages of this chapter.

What should I look for in a financial advisor?

Seek out the advisor with the Knowledge you don't have, the Understanding to listen to your deep concerns, and the Vigor to implement and stick to an investment plan.

One of the major reasons to use a financial advisor is to reduce the risk of investing. An advisor helps eliminate the emotional cycle of investor psychology that can lead us to buy and sell at exactly the wrong moments, and he or she can save us from making bad decisions during times of upheaval, stress, or change in our personal lives. Knowing that another person stays on top of financial matters and is available to turn to in moments of crisis is more than a comfort. It is good insurance that we can stay the course to achieve our financial objectives.

In selecting an advisor, personal issues of trust and compatibility, which have to do with Understanding, are as significant as professional competence, which is an issue of Knowledge. It is important to check out a candidate's educational background, certifications, and staff support. You also should determine how well his or her investment philosophy would have performed over the past several decades. It is perhaps most important, though, to select someone who inspires trust, who gives you the sense that you are listened to, whose integrity is obvious and unquestionable, who is excited by what he or she is doing, and who communicates with you clearly and understandably.

In a way, an investment advisor is like a family priest or minister, a rabbi or mullah, a best friend, or a counselor. He or she is someone who identifies with us, understands and empathizes with your life mission, and is willing to work with you to help you go as deep and as far as you can. Since you are working toward Money Maturity, rather than a simple acquisition of more and more, you should look for something from a financial advisor other than return on investment—the quality of honesty and the ability to connect with your deepest concern.

A good place to begin a search for a financial advisor is to call the two leading financial planning professional organizations—the Institute of Certified Financial Planners (ICFP) and NAPFA; phone numbers appear at the end of the chapter—and ask for the names of members in your area. You also can ask friends and acquaintances for the names of financial advisors they have worked with and liked—or disliked.

Go have a chat with the candidates you are considering. Sit down with them, and try to learn how and who they are. Some will charge you for this initial meeting, some won't. Remember that you are looking for a professional relationship to last a lifetime and help you on the way toward Money Maturity, not a quick fix or instant salvation at a bargain-basement price.

FURTHER SOURCES OF INFORMATION

The search for Knowledge never ends. Since practical Knowledge is by nature ephemeral and transient, there's always something new under the sun. In the following pages, I recommend a short list of important information resources that can get you started on your search.

A word of caution: I consult these resources not because their opinions are brilliant or their figures always correct, complete, and unbiased. Rather, I immerse myself in these sources of information so that over time I will know enough to form my own opinions. Reading and listening to how other experts think about the market and the economy has opened me not to "tips" on the latest "hot" stock but to different ways of thinking. Print, electronic, and online media should be used as ways of getting an education in how to think financially.

NEWSPAPERS AND MAGAZINES

Most of these are available both in print and online through the Internet.

- *Barron's* (<www.barrons.com>)—If you want to know how professionals from the world of finance and economics are thinking about the stock market, this is the periodical to read.
- *Business Week* (<www.businessweek.com>)—A comprehensive business newsweekly.
- *Forbes*—An encyclopedic biweekly review of current business and financial news and ideas. Every year the August or September issue is devoted to a review of mutual funds.
- *Fortune* (<www.pathfinder.com/@@CZmAAgcAwwNP BQ*D/ fortune>)—A business biweekly.
- *Investor's Business Daily* (<www.investors.com>)—Business news and comprehensive data on stocks and mutual funds.
- *Journal of the American Association of Individual Investors*— Published by American Association of Individual Investors (AAII), an independent nonprofit corporation. Thoughtful, consumer-oriented monthly dealing with investing and financial planning issues.
- *The Economist* (<www.economist.com>)—The best-written and most in-depth weekly covering international business and political news.
- *The Wall Street Journal* (<www.dowjones.com>)—This daily bible of the financial industry provides a wealth of business and

political news and analysis. The Friday edition offers enhanced mutual funds reporting.

- *Worth* (<www.worth.com>)—Monthly articles on business, finance, and economics. Owned by Fidelity Investments.

TELEVISION

Three TV networks report news on the stock market and financial developments throughout the day: CNNfn, CNBC, and Bloomberg Television.

INTERNET

The Internet offers a richness of financial information, chat rooms with other people interested in financial issues, investment data, even the ability to buy and sell stocks, bonds, and mutual funds electronically. A good place to begin financial web surfing is the personal finance channel on Infoseek (<www.infoseek.com>), an easy-to-use World Wide Web search engine. There you will find links leading to sites dealing with investing, mutual funds, news and publications, taxes, and insurance.

A few other notable sites:

- *FinanCenter, Inc.* (<www.financenter.com>)—This site offers a host of calculators for financial tasks, such as figuring out your retirement savings rate, personal budgeting, the comparative advantages of renting or owning a house, and returns on various investment vehicles. There's also helpful consumer information including explanations of confusing credit card terms.
- *Morningstar Mutual Funds* (<www.morningstar.net>)—This highly useful encyclopedia offers excellent information on thousands of mutual funds, including historical returns, investment objectives, costs, portfolio components, and risk measurements.
- *Securities and Exchange Commission* (<www.sec.gov>)—The SEC is the organization that regulates the investment industry. You can use this site to check out complaints on a financial firm you're considering or look up securities laws and regulations.

- *Value Line* (<www.valueline.com>)—Much like Morningstar, a source of information that can help in evaluating mutual funds. Value Line offers a similar service on stocks.

FINANCIAL PLANNER ORGANIZATIONS AND REFERRALS

The National Association of Personal Financial Advisors (NAPFA) is the largest organization of fee-only financial planners. The organization's national headquarters can refer you to NAPFA members who practice in your area:

National Association of Personal Financial Advisors
1130 Lake Cook Road, Suite 105
Buffalo Grove, IL 60089
(888) 333-6659

Another important financial planning organization is the Institute of Certified Financial Planners (ICFP), which represents both commissioned and fee-based financial planners. Like NAPFA, ICFP's national office is happy to help consumers locate members who practice in your area.

Institute of Certified Financial Planners
3801 East Florida Avenue, Suite 708
Denver, CO 80210
(800) 322-4237 / (303) 759-4900
Fax: (303) 759-0749
E-mail: icfp@icfp.org

COMPUTER APPLICATIONS

A personal computer can be a great help in handling many of the Knowledge aspects of money—from setting up a monthly budget to balancing your checkbook and tracking mutual funds. Two basic kinds of applications are available.

If you want to custom-design your own financial tools, a spreadsheet is the application of choice. A number of well-known spread-sheets are on the market, and any one of them will serve the task well.

If you're looking for a more tailored application, try a personal finance program. The core of these programs is a checkbook-type register that handles checking, savings, and credit card accounts. Data entered in the register can then be used for tasks like tax planning, net worth calculations, and budgeting. Some of the programs feature Internet connections to banks or brokerage houses that allow you to computerize your banking and investment tasks. In some cases you even can write and send checks electronically for a monthly fee. The most popular of these programs (and the companies that produce them, along with their Web addresses) are

- Kiplinger's Simply Money (CD Titles, <www.cdtitles.com)
- Money 98 Financial Suite (Microsoft, <www.microsoft.com/money>)
- Quicken (Intuit, <www.intuit.com>)
- WealthBuilder (Reality Online, <www.moneynet.com>)

GOING FURTHER
WITH THE
SEVEN STAGES
OF
MONEY MATURITY

For further information on

- Two- and three-day workshops for individuals and organizations on the Seven Stages of Money Maturity given by George Kinder and other trained professionals
- Corporate consulting on The Seven Stages of Money Maturity
- Support groups
- Teacher training and certification
- Supporting publications, videotapes, audiotapes and tools

Consult Money Maturity's Web site—www.sevenstages.com—
or call toll-free 1-877-7STAGES.

INDEX